BARRON'S
FOREIGN LANGUAGE GUIDES

W9-BVW-907

GERMAN
Idioms

SECOND EDITION

Henry Strutz, M.A.
Former Associate Professor of Languages
SUNY Technical College at Alfred, N.Y.

BARRON'S

ISBN-13: 978-0-7641-4383-0
ISBN-10: 0-7641-4383-2

Library of Congress Control Number 2009940228

Printed in China

Contents

Vorwort iv

Preface vi

Deutsche Redewendungen 1

Abkürzungen—Deutsch-Englisch 242

Abbreviations—English-German 251

Maße und Gewichte 263

Weights and Measures 265

Common English Idioms 267

Index 289

Vorwort

Dieser Band enthält mehr als 2000 deutsche Redewendungen, die in alphabetischer Reihenfolge nach ihren Schlüsselwörtern angeordnet sind, mit Anwendungsbeispielen und englischen Übersetzungen. Mit Ausnahme derjenigen, die gerade am Anfang ihres Sprachlernens stehen, wird das Buch allen Benutzern nützlich sein. Selbst die, die sich nur kurze Zeit mit der Sprache befasst haben, werden viele Konstruktionen erkennen, die in beiden Sprachen ähnlich sind, aber voneinander geringfügig abweichen. Gerade diese Abweichungen machen sie zur Idiomatik. Schwer zu lernen ist es nicht, dass *warten, hoffen* und *denken* "to wait," "to hope," und "to think" heißen. Der Haken liegt bei den ihnen nachfolgenden Verhältniswörtern (manchmal die ,,Teufelchen" des Sprachstudiums genannt). Daher werden "to wait for" und "to hope for" nicht mit *für*, sondern mit *auf* übersetzt.

Bei vielen Beispielsätzen handelt es sich nicht nur um die Redewendung allein, sondern auch um zusätzlich Idiomatistches, das der Eigenheit, der Besonderheit des Deutschen an sich zuzuschreiben ist. Im Deutschen sowie im Englischen muss nicht jeder Satz mit dem Subjekt anfangen. Gegenüber dem Englischen ist es aber im Deutschen weit gebräuchlicher, Sätze mit anderen Satzteilen zu beginnen. Normaler-und idiomatischerweise werden Sätze wie *Mir hat er nichts davon gesagt* oder *Das hätte ich nicht getan* ins Englische mit dem Subjekt am Anfang übersetzt: "He said nothing about it to me" und "I wouldn't have done that." Im Deutschen wird auch das Präsens zur Bezeichnung der Zukunft weitaus häufiger als im Englischen gebraucht. Das deutsche *nicht* ist weit beweglicher als das englische "not," wenn es darum geht, spezifische Teile eines Satzes zu verneinen. Im Deutschen wird auch reichlich Gebrauch von *doch*, *ja*, *noch* usw. gemacht, was den Sinn oft erheblich ändert. Diese und andere Besonderheiten des Deutschen tragen dazu bei, viele der Beispielsätze in mehr als einer Hinsicht ,,idiomatisch" zu gestalten.

Wort-für-Wort Übersetzungen der Anwendungsbeispiele kommen nur selten vor. Umschreibungen sind oft nötig oder wünschenswert. Zum Beispiel: *Quark* ist eine Art Weißkäse (white soft-curd cheese). Doch schien die Übersetzung "jelly-fish" (*Qualle*) geeigneter für den Goethe-Spruch: *Getretener Quark wird breit, nicht stark.* Dieses, sowie andere Goethe-Zitate wie *Die Kirche hat einen guten Magen* und *In der Beschränkung zeigt sich der Meister* werden oft von Deutschen gebraucht, obwohl sie nicht immer wissen, dass sie von Goethe stammen. Ähnlich ergeht es vielen, die Schuberts Vertonung von Wilhelm Müllers *Am Brunnen vor dem Tore* für ein Volks-lied halten. Auch im Englischen stammen viele Sprüche, die man für Sprichwörter hält, oft von Shakespeare, Pope, Bacon usw.

Einzelne Sprachen drücken oft dieselbe Idee aus, aber in unterschiedlichen Bildern. Daher haben Englischsprachige mit einer dunklen Vergangenheit "a skeleton in the closet" (*ein Skelett im Schrank*). Deutschsprachige haben *eine Leiche im Keller.* "A millstone around the neck" eines Englischsprachigen ist bei einem Deutschsprachigen *ein Klotz am Bein.* Und nach-dem sie leibliche Hüllen, Mühlensteine, Klötze und dergleichen abgestreift haben, behaupten Englischsprachige, die Toten "push up daisies" (*schieben die Gänseblümchen hoch*), während deutsche Verstorbene *sich die Radieschen von unten ansehen.* Auf ihren Vorteil bedachte Schranzen "butter up" (*schmieren Butter um*) ihre Opfer, während sie im Deutschen ihnen *Honig um den Mund schmieren.* Wenn die Katze aus dem Haus ist, leben sich Mäuse in deutschsprachigen Ländern aus, indem sie „auf dem Tisch tanzen", während es weniger spezifisch auf englisch heißt: "When the cat's away, the mice will play." *Eine alte Jacke* auf deutsch ist "old hat" auf englisch. Das englische Äquivalent für *Wem die Jacke passt, der zieht sie an* ist "If the shoe fits, wear it." (*Wenn dir der Schuh passt, zieh ihn an.*)

In Ihrer Muttersprache werden Ihnen viele Redewendungen wie eine alte Jacke vorkommen. Sich mit ihren Äquivalenten in einer Fremdsprache vertraut zu machen, wird Ihnen ein interes-santes und belohnendes Unternehmen sein, denn niemand beherrscht eigentlich eine Sprache, ohne ihre Redewendungen gut zu kennen. Zu diesem Ziel wird Ihnen dieses Buch ver-helfen.

Preface

This volume contains over 2,000 German idioms arranged under their key words in alphabetical order, with sentences illustrating their use, and accompanied by their translations into English. Except for students who are just beginning to learn German, the book will be useful at any level of expertise. Even those who have studied the language for less than a year will recognize many constructions in the two languages that are similar, yet slightly different. It is precisely such differences that make them idioms. It is not hard to learn that *warten* means "to wait," that *hoffen* means "to hope," that *denken* is "to think." The difficulty comes with the prepositions (sometimes called the "little devils" of language study) used after them. The German idiom for "to wait for" is *warten auf*, not *für*. The same is true of *hoffen auf* (to hope for). German also idiomatically distinguishes between *denken an*, and *denken von*, whereas English uses only "to think of."

The sentences accompanying the idioms illustrate their use in a context. Aside from using the idiom itself, the sentences often are additionally idiomatic due to basic structural patterns in German. In English and German a sentence does not have to start with a subject, whereas in German it is much more common to begin a sentence with a dative, accusative, or genitive object, or with a prepositional phrase or adverb, rather than the subject. Simple sentences such as *Mir hat er nichts davon gesagt* or *Das hätte ich nicht getan* would normally be idiomatically translated into English as "He said nothing about it to me" and "I wouldn't have done that." Further, the present tense is used with a future implication in both languages, but more frequently in German. To negate a particular sentence element, the German *nicht* can be moved around much more than the English "not." German also makes very liberal use of "flavoring particles" like *doch, ja,* etc. These and many other features of German (e.g., time expressions coming before place) contribute to making many of the accompanying sentences "idiomatic" on several levels.

Word-for-word translations of the sentences in this book are extremely rare. Often, paraphrases are necessary or preferable.

For instance *Quark* means "soft cheese." But in the saying *Getretener Quark wird breit, nicht stark*, "jellyfish" was a more appropriate rendering. The saying is from Goethe—as are a few others in the book, e.g., *Die Kirche hat einen guten Magen* and *In der Beschränkung zeigt sich erst der Meister*. Such sayings are commonly used, although not all Germans who say them are aware that they are by Goethe, just as many who sing Wilhelm Müller's words to Franz Schubert's *Am Brunnen vor dem Tore* think it is a folk song. In English too, many sayings believed to be folk-based are sometimes drawn from Shakespeare, Pope, Bacon, etc.

Different languages often express the same idea, but in diverse images. Thus, Anglophones with a nefarious past have "a skeleton in the closet," while German speakers have "a corpse in the cellar" (*eine Leiche im Keller*). "The millstone around the neck" of an English speaker is "a log on the leg" (*Klotz am Bein*) of a German speaker. And once they've shuffled off mortal coils, millstones, logs, and such, the departed are said to be "pushing up daisies" in English, but Germans declare that the deceased are "looking at the radishes from below" (*Sie sehen sich die Radieschen von unten an*). Advantage-seeking sycophants "butter up" their victims in English, whereas in German they "smear honey about the mouth" (*Honig um den Mund schmieren*) of their mark. German mice live it up even more than those in English lands, for they "dance on the table when the cat's away" (*Wenn die Katze aus dem Haus ist, tanzen die Mäuse auf dem Tisch*). A German "old jacket" (*eine alte Jacke*) is an English "old hat" and "if the shoe fits, wear it" is *Wem die Jacke passt, der zieht sie an*.

In your native language many idioms will seem "old hat" to you. Familiarizing yourself with their counterparts in a foreign language will be interesting and rewarding, for no one can be said to be really proficient in a language until he or she possesses an "idiomatic" command of it. This book will help you to achieve that goal.

DEUTSCHE REDEWENDUNGEN
(German Idioms)

A — *das A*

Wer A sagt, muss auch B sagen. *Once you've started something you've got to follow through.*

das A und O sein — *to be essential, indispensable.*

Beim Studium der vergleichenden Religionswissenschaft ist Toleranz das A und O. *Tolerance is indispensable when studying comparative religion.*

---

aasen — *to be wasteful*

mit dem Geld aasen — *to throw money around.*

Eine Zeitlang aaste er mit dem Geld jede Nacht in der Kneipe. *For a time he threw money around every night in the tavern.*

mit seiner Gesundheit aasen — *to burn the candle at both ends.*

Weil er an nichts außer sich glaubt, aast er mit seiner Gesundheit. *Because he believes in nothing outside himself, he burns the candle at both ends.*

---

die Abbitte — *pardon*

Abbitte leisten — *to ask for pardon; to make amends.*

Mit den Blumen wollte er ihr Abbitte leisten. *He wanted to make amends to her with the flowers.*

---

abbrechen — *to break off*

sich keinen abbrechen — *not to strain o.s.*

Er hat mir ein bisschen geholfen; aber dabei hat er sich keinen abgebrochen. *He helped me a little, but he didn't strain himself.*

---

der Abbruch — *demolition*
  Abbruch tun — *to do damage*.
  Durch ihre Schriften und Reden hat sie der Bewegung viel Abbruch getan.
  By her writings and speeches she's done much damage to the
  movement.

der Abend — *evening*
  Es ist noch nicht aller Tage Abend. — *Nothing is definite yet.*
  Sie haben keine Kinder, aber es ist noch nicht aller Tage Abend. *They*
  don't have children, but it's not over yet.

aber — *but; really*
  Die Chefin duldet kein Aber. *The boss won't put up with any objections.*
  Das war aber schön! *That was really nice!*

abermals — *once again; once more*
  Sieben Jahre waren abermals verstrichen, und der Holländer trat wieder
  ans Land. *Seven years had passed once more, and the Dutchman came*
  on shore again.

abessen — *to eat up; clear plates*
  abgegessen haben — *to have worn out one's welcome*.
  Dein Onkel hat bei uns abgegessen. *Your uncle has worn out his welcome*
  with us.

abfahren — *to depart*
  Der letzte Zug nach Marienbad ist abgefahren. *The last train for*
  Marienbad has left.
  Dein Freund bekommt den Posten nicht — für ihn ist dieser Zug
  abgefahren. *Your friend won't get the position — he's missed the boat.*

die Abfuhr — *removal; rebuff*
  sich eine Abfuhr holen — *to be rejected*.
  Mit seinen Vorschlägen für die Giftmüllabfuhr holte er sich eine Abfuhr.
  His proposals for toxic waste removal were rejected.

abhören — *to eavesdrop; to tap (telephone, etc.)*
Nachdem die Gespräche des Gangsters abgehört wurden, verhaftete man ihn. *After the gangster's conversations were tapped, he was arrested.*

---

ablaufen — *to flow away (out); empty*
ablaufen lassen — *to send packing.*
Er versuchte wieder freundlich zu sein, aber sie ließ ihn ablaufen. *He tried to be friendly again, but she sent him packing.*

---

abmalen — *to paint a picture*
Da möchte ich nicht abgemalt sein! *I wouldn't be caught dead there!*

---

abnehmen — *to take off; to take from*
abnehmen — *to buy.*
Eine solche Geschichte nehm ich euch nicht ab. *I'm not buying your story.*

abnehmen — *to review.*
Die Königin nahm die Parade ab. *The queen reviewed the parade.*

abnehmen — *to lose weight.*
Sie hat viel abgenommen. *She's lost a lot of weight.*

die Beichte abnehmen — *to hear confession.*
Anglikanische Priesterinnen können auch die Beichte abnehmen. *Anglican priestesses can also hear confessions.*

abnehmend — *waning.*
Bei abnehmendem Mond will die Isispriesterin nichts unternehmen. *When the moon is waning the priestess of Isis won't undertake anything.*

---

abreißen — *to tear down; tear off*
nicht abreißen — *to continue unabated.*
Der Streit um das Bauvorhaben reißt nicht ab. *The dispute concerning the building project continues unabated.*

---

der Absatz — *heel*
auf dem Absatz kehrtmachen — *to turn on one's heels.*
Zutiefst beleidigt, machte die Diva auf dem Absatz kehrt und verließ die Bühne. *Deeply insulted, the diva turned on her heels and left the stage.*

der Abschluss — *conclusion*
  einen Abschluss haben — *to graduate; have a degree.*
  Er hat keinen Universitätsabschluss. *He has no university degree.*

  zum Abschluss bringen — *to conclude.*
  Wir hoffen, das Geschäft bald zum Abschluss zu bringen. *We hope to conclude the deal soon.*

---

abschminken — *to remove makeup; get something out of one's head*
  Sie hat sich die Augen abgeschminkt. *She removed her eye makeup.*
  Ich soll die Verantwortung dafür übernehmen? Das kannst du dir abschminken. *Me take responsibility for that? You can put that out of your mind.*

---

abschnallen — *to unfasten; unbuckle; be flabbergasted*
  Was uns die Arbeit an Mühe gekostet hat, da schnallst du ab. *You'd be flabbergasted at how much trouble the job caused us.*

---

absehen — *to foresee; predict*
  In absehbarer Zeit lässt sich das nicht machen. *In the foreseeable future it won't be possible to do that.*

  es abgesehen haben — *to be out for.*
  Der Geizhals erklärte, alle hätten es auf sein Geld abgesehen. *The miser declared that everyone was after his money.*

  es abgesehen haben — *to have it in for.*
  Der Gefreite glaubte, dass der Feldwebel es auf ihn abgesehen hatte. *The private thought the sergeant had it in for him.*

---

die Absicht — *intention*
  sich mit der Absicht tragen — *to be thinking about.*
  Seit Jahren trägt er sich mit der Absicht, sein Geschäft auszubauen. *For years he's been thinking about expanding his business.*

---

absitzen — *to serve out a prison sentence*
  Nachdem er seine Strafe abgesessen hat, will er nie wieder auf die schiefe Bahn. *After serving his sentence, he never wants to stray from the straight and narrow again.*

---

abspielen — *to play*

   vom Blatt abspielen —*to play at sight.*

   Die Pianistin spielte die Beethoven-Sonate vom Blatt ab. *The pianist played the Beethoven Sonata at sight.*

   sich abspielen — *to happen; be set.*

   Das alles soll sich gestern abgespielt haben? *All that is supposed to have happened yesterday?*

   Wo spielt sich die Szene ab? *Where is the scene set?*

---

der Abstand — *distance*

   Abstand nehmen — *to refrain from; give up (on).*

   Die Senatorin hat von ihrem Plan Abstand genommen. *The senator gave up on her plan.*

   auf Abstand gehen — *to back out.*

   Sie erklärten sich zum Kauf bereit aber jetzt gehen sie auf Abstand. *They declared they were ready to buy, but now they're backing out.*

   mit Abstand — *by far.*

   Sie ist mit Abstand die beste Kandidatin. *She is by far the best candidate.*

---

absteigen — *to get off; come down*

   Die Gräfin stieg von ihrem Pferd ab. *The countess got off her horse.*

   gesellschaftlich absteigen — *to decline in social status; to come down in the world.*

   Wegen vieler Skandale ist sie gesellschaftlich abgestiegen. *Because of many scandals her social status has declined.*

   absteigen — *to stay at an inn/hotel.*

   Trotzdem steigt sie nur noch in Nobelhotels ab. *But she still stays only at ritzy hotels.*

---

abtun — *to dismiss*

   Der Roman wurde von einigen Kritikern als Schund abgetan. *The novel was dismissed as trash by some critics.*

   abgetan sein — *to be finished, over.*

   Für sie war die Sache damit abgetan. *For them that was the end of the matter.*

---

abwarten — *to wait and see*

Sie wollen die Entwicklung der Dinge abwarten. *They want to wait and see how things develop.*

abwarten und Tee trinken — *to wait patiently and see what happens.*
Wir können nur abwarten und Tee trinken. *We can only wait patiently and see what happens.*

die Abwesenheit — *absence*

durch Abwesenheit glänzen — *to be conspicuous by one's absence.*
Bei der Sitzung glänzte er durch Abwesenheit. *At the meeting he was conspicuous by his absence.*

abwinken — *to wave aside; flag down*

bis zum Abwinken — *in great profusion; galore.*
Auf dem Fest gab es Champagner bis zum Abwinken. *At the feast there was champagne galore.*

ach — *oh (dear)*

mit Ach und Krach — *by the skin of one's teeth.*
Mit Ach und Krach hat die Partei die Wahl gewonnen. *The party won the election by the skin of its teeth.*

mit Ach und Weh — *moaning and groaning.*
Mit vielem Ach und Weh gab er endlich nach. *With much moaning and groaning he finally gave in.*

die Achse — *axis; axle*

auf (der) Achse sein — *to be on the move/go.*
Ich bin den ganzen Tag auf Achse gewesen und möchte mich jetzt ausruhen. *I've been on the go all day and want to rest now.*

die Achsel — *shoulder*

die Achsel zucken — *to shrug one's shoulders.*
Er hat nur die Achsel gezuckt. *He just shrugged his shoulders.*

auf die leichte Achsel nehmen — *to underestimate; minimize.*
Ihr seelisches Leiden sollten Sie nicht auf die leichte Achsel nehmen. *You shouldn't minimize her psychic suffering.*

über die Achsel ansehen — *to look down on*.
Jetzt ist sie reich und sieht die alten Schulfreunde über die Achsel an. *Now she's rich and looks down on her old school friends*.

die Achterbahn — *roller coaster*
Achterbahn fahren — *to ride the roller coaster; be unstable*.
Der Aktienmarkt fährt noch Achterbahn. *The stock market is still unstable*.

die Achtung — *respect; attention*
Alle Achtung! — *Well done!*
Keiner glaubte, dass unsere Kandidatin so viele Stimmen erhalten würde. Alle Achtung! *Nobody thought our candidate would get so many votes. Well done!*

der Acker — *field*
sich vom Acker machen — *to scram, clear off*.
Die Polizei kam und er machte sich schnell vom Acker. *The police came and he cleared off fast*.

die Adresse — *address*
Diese Warnung/der Vorwurf geht an Ihre eigene Adresse. *This warning/reproach is directed to you personally*.

an der richtigen/falschen Adresse sein — *to have come to the right/wrong place*.
Wenn Sie Geld von uns erwarten, dann sind Sie an der falschen Adresse. *If you expect money from us, you've come to the wrong place*.

der Affe — *monkey*
einen Affen gefressen haben — *to be nuts about*.
Er hat an seiner neuen Freundin einen Affen gefressen. *He's nuts about his new girlfriend*.

seinem Affen Zucker geben — *to indulge in one's hobby; to talk to please oneself*.
Ich hörte nicht mehr zu, denn jeder wollte nur seinem Affen Zucker geben. *I stopped listening because all were talking just to please themselves*.

7

sich einen Affen kaufen — *to get drunk.*
Gestern abend hat er sich wieder einen Affen gekauft. *He got drunk again last night.*

vom wilden Affen gebissen sein — *to be off one's rocker.*
Wenn du das glaubst, bist du vom wilden Affen gebissen. *If you believe that, you're off your rocker.*

---

zum Affen halten — *to make a monkey out of*
Er versuchte, mich zum Affen zu halten. *He tried to make a monkey out of me.*

---

die Affenschande — *a crying shame*
Es wäre eine Affenschande, ihre Dichtungen zu vernachlässigen. *It would be a crying shame to neglect her literary works.*

---

der Affenzahn — *monkey tooth*
mit einem Affenzahn — *extremely fast.*
Mit der Magnetschwebebahn fährt man mit einem Affenzahn. *With the magnetic levitation train one travels extremely fast.*

---

die Aktie — *stock*
Seine Aktien steigen. *His prospects are improving.*
Wie stehen die Aktien? *How are things?*

---

der Akzent — *accent*
Akzente setzen — *to set a course; to indicate directions.*
Gleich nach Amtsantritt wollte die Präsidentin Akzente setzen. *Right after taking office the president wanted to set a course.*

---

der Alarm — *alarm*
Alarm schlagen — *to raise (sound) an alarm.*
Zum Glück hatten Umweltschützer rechtzeitig Alarm geschlagen. *Fortunately, environmentalists had sounded the alarm in time.*

---

das Alibi — *alibi*
eine Alibifunktion haben — *to serve as an excuse, be token.*

Die paar Frauen unter den Konferenzteilnehmern hätten nur eine
Alibifunktion, behauptete sie. *The few women attending the conference
were only tokens, she claimed.*

---

das All — *the universe; space*
Isolde hoffte, Tristan im All wiederzufinden. *Isolde hoped to find Tristan
again in the universe.*

---

der/die Alleinerziehende — *single parent*
Es gibt immer mehr Alleinerziehende. *There are more and more single
parents.*

---

der Alleingang — *independent initiative*
etwas im Alleingang tun — *to do something on one's own.*
Wenn ich jünger wäre, würde ich's im Alleingang tun. *If I were younger
I'd do it on my own.*

---

die Alleinherrschaft — *dictatorship*
Obwohl das Land eine Alleinherrschaft ist, gibt's auch ein Parlament.
Although the country is a dictatorship, there is also a Parliament.

---

der/die Alleinstehende — *person living on his/her own*
Für viele ältere Alleinstehende ist das Fernsehen ein Trost. *For many
elderly people who live alone, television is a consolation.*

---

all — *every; all*
alle zwei Tage — *every other day.*
Sie besucht uns alle zwei Tage. *She visits us every other day.*

---

allemal — *any time; every time*
Alles, was er kann, das kann doch Annie allemal. *Anything he can do,
Annie can do too.*

---

allenfalls — *at most; at the outside*
Es waren allenfalls fünfzig Leute im Konzertsaal. *There were at most 50
people in the concert hall.*

allenfalls — *if necessary; if need be.*
Allenfalls könnten wir's im Alleingang machen. *If necessary, we could do it on our own.*

---

alt — *old*
   beim Alten bleiben — *to stay the same.*
   Seine Versprechen klangen nach Fortschritt, aber es blieb alles beim Alten. *His promises sounded like progress, but everything stayed the same.*

   es/alles beim Alten lassen — *to leave things as they were.*
   Es wäre besser, wenn Sie alles beim Alten gelassen hätten. *It would have been better if you'd left everything alone.*

   alt — *used.*
   Altöl und Altpapier können wieder verwertet werden. *Used oil and (waste) paper can be recycled.*

---

der Alltag — *everyday life; a typical day*
   Ich will Ihnen sagen, wie mein Alltag aussieht. *I'll tell you what a typical day in my life is like.*

---

alltäglich — *commonplace; ordinary*
   Alltägliches interessiert uns nicht. *The commonplace doesn't interest us.*

---

das Amt — *office; official agency*
   von Amts wegen — *in an official capacity.*
   "Ich bin von Amts wegen hier," erklärte der Polizeibeamte. *"I'm here in an official capacity," declared the policeman.*

---

der Amtsschimmel — *bureaucracy; red tape*
   den Amtsschimmel reiten — *to be a stickler for red tape; to do everything by the book.*
   Wir mussten warten, weil die Beamten den Amtsschimmel reiten wollten. *We had to wait because the officials wanted to do everything by the book.*

   Der Amtsschimmel wiehert — *bureaucracy reigns.*
   In seiner Abteilung wiehert laut der Amtsschimmel. *In his department bureaucracy reigns supreme.*

---

an — *at; on; to*

an (und für) sich — *basically*.

An und für sich habe ich nichts dagegen. *Basically I have nothing against it.*

an sich — *in itself/themselves*.

Einige von Kants Ideen sind an sich nicht schlecht. *Some of Kant's ideas aren't bad in themselves.*

---

anbeißen — *to bite into; to take a bite of*

Schneewittchen biss den Apfel an. *Snow White bit into the apple.*

zum Anbeißen sein — *to look good enough to eat*.

Die Zwerge fanden sie zum Anbeißen schön. *The dwarves thought she looked good enough to eat.*

---

anbinden — *to tie up*

kurz angebunden — *curt, abrupt(ly)*.

Er antwortete kurz angebunden auf alle Fragen. *He answered all questions abruptly.*

anbinden — *to pick a quarrel*.

Der Matrose war betrunken und wollte mit allen anbinden. *The sailor was drunk and wanted to pick a quarrel with everyone.*

---

anbringen — *to put up*

In der Wohnung brachten wir viele Plakate von Toulouse-Lautrec an. *We put up many Toulouse-Lautrec posters in the apartment.*

---

der Anfang — *beginning*

den Anfang machen — *to be the first to begin*.

Keiner wagte, den Anfang zu machen. *No one dared to be the first to begin.*

den Anfang nehmen — *to begin; have its beginning*.

Ihrer Theorie nach nahm die Sprache ihren Anfang in der Musik. *According to her theory language began in music.*

---

anfangen — *to begin*

anfangen mit — *to do with; to make of*.

Was sollen wir damit anfangen? *What are we supposed to do with that?*

---

die Angel — *hinge; fishing rod and line*

jmdm. an die Angel gehen — *to swallow bait/fall for s.o.'s line.*

Viele sind dem Schwindler an die Angel gegangen. *Many fell for the con man's line.*

aus den Angeln gehen — *to fall apart at the seams.*

Das Wirtschaftssystem ist aus den Angeln gegangen. *The economic system fell apart at the seams.*

aus den Angeln heben — *to turn upside down.*

Durch den Krieg wurde ihr Leben aus den Angeln gehoben. *Their life was turned upside down by the war.*

aus den Angeln sein — *to be out of joint.*

Hamlet fand, dass die Welt aus den Angeln war. *Hamlet thought the world was out of joint.*

---

die Angst — *fear*

Angst haben — *to be afraid.*

Zuerst hatte das Mädchen große Angst vor dem Tod. *At first the girl was very afraid of death.*

Angst und Bange haben — *to be very afraid.*

Er hatte Angst und Bange vor der Wurzelbehandlung, aber es war nicht so schlimm. *He was terrified of the root canal, but it wasn't so bad.*

die Angstmacherei — *scare tactics*

Die Senatorin bezeichnete die Argumente ihres Gegners als Angstmacherei. *The senator called her opponent's arguments scare tactics.*

---

anhaben — *to have on*

Nur der Junge wagte zu sagen, dass der Kaiser nichts anhatte. *Only the boy dared to say that the emperor had nothing on.*

anhaben — *to harm.*

Sie glaubten, dass in der Kirche niemand ihnen etwas anhaben könnte. *They thought that no one could harm them in the church.*

---

der Anhieb — *thrust*
  auf Anhieb — *right away; at first go.*
  Auf Anhieb verstand ich nicht, was sie wollten. *I didn't understand right away what they wanted.*

---

der Anker — *anchor*
  vor Anker gehen — *to drop anchor; get married; settle down.*
  Der alte Frauenheld will endlich vor Anker gehen. *That old womanizer finally wants to settle down.*

---

ankommen — *to arrive*
  ankommen — *to find acceptance; to be popular.*
  Ihre Gemälde kommen beim Publikum gut an. *Her paintings are popular with the public.*

  ankommen — *to get somewhere.*
  Ohne Beziehungen wäre er nicht angekommen. *Without connections he wouldn't have gotten anywhere.*

  auf etwas ankommen — *to depend on.*
  Es kommt darauf an, ob wir genug Zeit haben. *It depends on whether we have enough time.*

  auf etwas ankommen — *to matter, count.*
  Beim Sport kommt es auf jede Sekunde an. *In sports every second counts.*

  es auf etwas ankommen lassen — *to take a chance on s.t.*
  Obwohl er an Popularität verloren hat, will der Präsident es auf neue Wahlen ankommen lassen. *Although his popularity has declined, the president is willing to risk new elections.*

  gegen etwas nicht ankommen — *to fight a losing battle against s.t.*
  Seit den Umbauarbeiten kommen wir gegen den Schmutz nicht mehr an. *Ever since the renovation work began, we've been fighting a losing battle against the dirt.*

---

anlegen — *to invest*
  sich etwas angelegen sein lassen — *to make it one's business; to see to it that.*
  Ich werde es mir angelegen sein lassen, ihrem Freund behilflich zu sein. *I'll make it my business to help your friend.*

---

anmachen — *to turn on*

Es wird schon dunkel; mach's Licht an! *It's getting dark already; turn the light on.*

Diese Rockgruppe macht viele Jugendliche ungeheuer an. *This rock group really turns on many young people.*

anmachen — *to dress a salad.*

Hast du den Salat schon angemacht? *Have you dressed the salad yet?*

---

der Anmarsch — *marching up; advance*

im Anmarsch sein — *to be on the way.*

Durchgreifende Veränderungen sind im Anmarsch. *Drastic changes are on the way.*

---

anschreiben — *to write up; to write to; give credit*

Der Wirt wollte ihm nichts mehr anschreiben. *The innkeeper didn't want to give him any more credit.*

gut/schlecht angeschrieben sein — *to be in someone's good/bad books.*

Sie ist bei ihren Vorgesetzten gut angeschrieben. *She is in her superior's good books.*

---

der Anschluss — *connection*

im Anschluss an — *immediately following.*

Im Anschluss an die Pressekonferenz fand eine Diskussion statt. *Immediately following the press conference a discussion took place.*

---

der Anspruch — *claim*

Anspruch erheben — *to make a claim.*

Zuerst wollte sie keinen Anspruch auf das Geld erheben. *At first she didn't want to make a claim on the money.*

Ansprüche stellen — *to make demands; be demanding.*

In dieser Schule werden die höchsten Ansprüche an Studenten und Lehrer gestellt. *In that school the greatest demands are made of teachers and students.*

in Anspruch genommen sein — *to be too busy.*

Besprechen Sie das mit meinen Kollegen — ich bin zu sehr in Anspruch genommen. *Discuss that with my colleagues — my time is all taken up.*

die Anstalt — *institution*
   Anstalten treffen — *to make a move to do*.
   Trotz der späten Stunde machte er keine Anstalten nach Hause zu gehen.
     Despite the late hour he made no move to go home.

der Anstand — *decency; objection*
   Anstand nehmen — *to object; to take offense*.
   Die Senatorin nahm an der Gesetzesvorlage keinen Anstand. *The senator*
     didn't object to the proposed bill.
   Oma nahm an den Kraftausdrücken im Stück keinen Anstand. *Grannie*
     took no offense at the strong language in the play.

der Anteil — *share*
   Anteil nehmen — *to be interested in*.
   Sie hat stets großen Anteil am Theater gehabt. *She's always been very*
     interested in the theater.

der Antrieb — *drive (vehicle)*
   neuen Antrieb geben — *to give fresh impetus*.
   Ihre Gegenwart hat uns neuen Antrieb gegeben. *Her presence has given*
     us fresh impetus.

   aus eigenem Antrieb — *of one's own accord*.
   Er hat es aus eigenem Antrieb getan. *He did it of his own accord.*

antun — *to do to*
   es angetan haben — *to be captivated; taken with*.
   Die Schauspielerin hat es ihm sehr angetan. *He is entirely taken with the*
     actress.

die Antwort — *answer*
   keine Antwort schuldig bleiben — *to be quick to reply*.
   Die Senatorin blieb ihren Gegnern keine Antwort schuldig. *The senator*
     was quick to reply to her opponents.

anwurzeln — *to take root*
   wie angewurzelt stehenbleiben — *to be rooted to the spot.*
   Statt zu fliehen, blieben sie wie angewurzelt stehen, als sie das Ungeheuer
   erblickten. *Instead of fleeing, they stood rooted to the spot when they
   saw the monster.*

der Anzug — *suit*
   aus dem Anzug fallen — *to be extremely thin.*
   Der Milliardär aß kaum mehr und fiel aus dem Anzug. *The billionaire
   rarely ate any more and was extremely thin.*

   aus dem Anzug springen — *to fly off the handle.*
   Spring doch nicht gleich aus dem Anzug, wir kommen bald. *Keep your
   shirt on, we're coming soon.*

der Apfel — *apple*
   für einen Apfel und ein Ei — *for very little money.*
   Sie haben das Grundstück für einen Apfel und ein Ei gekauft. *They bought
   the land for very little money.*

   in den sauren Apfel beißen — *to bite the bullet.*
   Auch ich hab keine Lust dazu, aber einer muss doch in den sauren Apfel
   beißen. *I don't feel like it either, but someone's got to bite the bullet.*

der Apparat — *apparatus; appliance; telephone*
   am Apparat bleiben — *to hold the line.*
   Bleiben Sie bitte am Apparat! *Please hold the line.*

der April — *April*
   in den April schicken — *to play an April Fool's joke on; to send on an
   April Fool's errand.*
   Die Büroangestellten schickten ihren neuen Kollegen in den April. *The
   office workers sent their new colleague on an April Fool's errand.*

das Arbeiterdenkmal — *workers' monument*
   ein Arbeiterdenkmal machen — *to lean idly on a shovel.*
   Einer von ihnen arbeitete wie ein Pferd, während die anderen ein
   Arbeiterdenkmal machten. *One of them worked like a horse, while the
   others stood by idly.*

die Arbeitgeber — *employers; management*

    die Arbeitnehmer — *employees; labor.*

    Arbeitgeber und Arbeitnehmer waren mit dem Tarifvertrag zufrieden.
    Management and labor were satisfied with the union contract.

---

arg — *bad*

    im Argen liegen — *to be in disorder.*

    In seiner Abteilung liegt noch vieles im Argen. *There is still much that's
    not in order in his department.*

    sich ärgern — *to get angry.*

    Mensch, ärgere dich nicht so darüber — es ist nur ein Spiel! *Man, don't
    get angry about it — it's only a game.*

---

der Arm — *arm*

    der verlängerte Arm — *tool.*

    Die Reporterin behauptete, der Bürgermeister sei nur der verlängerte
    Arm der Mafia. *The reporter asserted the mayor was merely the tool of
    the Mafia.*

    einen langen Arm haben — *to be very influential.*

    In der Stadt hat die Mafia einen langen Arm. *The Mafia is very influential
    in the city.*

    jmdn. auf den Arm nehmen — *to take s.o. onto one's arm; to pull s.o.'s
    leg/put on.*

    Ich glaube, du nimmst mich wieder auf den Arm. *I think you're putting
    me on again.*

    in die Arme laufen — *to run into.*

    Beim Einkaufen bin ich gestern meinem alten Schulkameraden in die
    Arme gelaufen. *While shopping yesterday I ran into my old school
    friend.*

    unter die Arme greifen — *to come to the aid of.*

    Sie hat den Kriegsopfern unter die Arme gegriffen. *She came to the aid of
    the war victims.*

---

arm — *poor*

  arm dran sein — *to be in a bad way.*

  Menschen, die nicht lieben können, sind arm dran. *People who can't love are in a bad way.*

---

der Ärmel — *sleeve*

  aus dem Ärmel schütteln — *to come up with just like that.*

  Frank L. Wright sagte, er könnte seine vielen Bauprojekte nur so aus dem Ärmel schütteln. *Frank L. Wright said he could come up with his many building projects just like that.*

  die Ärmel aufkrempeln — *to roll up one's sleeves.*

  Die Ingenieure krempelten die Ärmel auf und planten den Tunnel unter dem Ärmelkanal. *The engineers rolled up their sleeves and planned the tunnel under the English Channel.*

  im Ärmel haben — *to have up one's sleeve.*

  Der Zocker hatte noch mehr Asse im Ärmel. *The professional gambler had still more aces up his sleeve.*

---

die Armut — *poverty*

  sich ein Armutszeugnis ausstellen — *to proclaim one's ignorance/inadequacy.*

  Durch ihre dumme Kritik hat sie sich nur ein Armutszeugnis ausgestellt. *She merely proclaimed her own ignorance with her stupid review.*

---

das As — *ace*

  ein As auf der Bassgeige sein — *to be an ace on the bass fiddle; to be a clever devil.*

  Selbst Sherlock Holmes hat er überlistet; er ist ein As auf der Bassgeige. *He outsmarted even Sherlock Holmes; he's a clever devil.*

---

aufbringen — *to summon up*

  Ich weiß nicht, wie ich den Mut dazu aufbringen werde. *I don't know how I'll summon up the courage for it.*

  aufbringen — *to infuriate.*

  Nachdem die Königin erfuhr, dass Schneewittchen noch lebte, war sie sehr aufgebracht. *After the queen heard the news that Snow White still lived, she was infuriated.*

aufbringen — *to set against.*
Er tat alles, um sie gegen einander aufzubringen. *He did everything to set them against each other.*

der Aufbruch — *departure, setting out on a journey*
die Aufbruchstimmung — *spirit of optimism/get up and go.*
Nach dem letzten Wahlsieg herrscht Aufbruchstimmung in der Partei. *After the last electoral victory, the party's optimistic.*

auffliegen — *to fly up; to expose, bust*
Die Reporterin ließ den Schwindler auffliegen. *The reporter exposed the swindler.*

aufgeben — *to give up*
eine Anzeige aufgeben — *to take an ad.*
Sie hat eine Zeitungsanzeige aufgegeben. *She took an ad in the newspaper.*

aufgehen — *to rise*
Um wieviel Uhr ist die Sonne aufgegangen? *At what time did the sun rise?*

aufgehen — *to work out.*
Minnie mogelt, wenn die Patience nicht aufgeht. *Minnie cheats when the game of patience doesn't work out.*

aufgehen — *to realize.*
Die Bedeutung dieser Ereignisse ist mir erst später aufgegangen. *Only later did I realize the meaning of these events.*

aufgehen in — *to be completely absorbed in.*
Die Botanikerin geht ganz in ihrer Arbeit auf. *The botanist is completely absorbed in her work.*

aufheben — *to pick up*
Sie hob die bunten Herbstblätter auf. *She picked up the colorful autumn leaves.*

viel Aufheben(s) machen — *to make a fuss.*
Mach doch nicht immer so viel Aufheben! *Don't always make such a fuss.*

aufheben — *to store*.

Sie hob die Blätter in einem Buch auf. *She stored the leaves in a book.*

gut aufgehoben sein — *to be in good hands*.

Bei ihnen sind Sie gut aufgehoben. *You're in good hands with them.*

aufheben — *to cancel; supersede*.

Die neuen Vorschriften heben die alten auf. *The new regulations supersede the old ones.*

---

aufreißen — *to tear open*

Der schüchterne Junge versuchte, bei der Party aufzureißen. *The shy boy tried to open up to people at the party.*

---

aufschieben — *to postpone*

Aufgeschoben ist nicht aufgehoben. *Deferred doesn't mean defunct. (There'll always be another opportunity.)*

---

auftreiben — *to get together*

Wir haben endlich das dafür nötige Geld aufgetrieben. *We finally got together the money necessary for it.*

auftreiben — *to stir up*.

Der Wind hat die Blätter aufgetrieben. *The wind stirred up the leaves.*

---

das Auge — *eye*

In meinen Augen ist das ein böses Zeichen. *To my mind that's a bad sign.*

sehenden Auges — *with full awareness*.

Sehenden Auges hat die Firma die Folgen wahrgenommen, aber nichts dagegen getan. *The company was completely aware of the consequences, but did nothing about it.*

aufs Auge drücken — *to compel*.

Der Präsidentin wurde die Steuerreform aufs Auge gedrückt. *The tax reform was forced on the president.*

ins Auge fallen — *to catch someone's eye*.

Im Schaufenster ist ihr ein Kollier besonders ins Auge gefallen. *In the shop window a necklace caught her eye.*

mit einem blauen Auge davonkommen — *to get off easy.*

Der gedopte Sportler kam mit einem blauen Auge davon; ihm wurde nur der Titel aberkannt. *The drug-taking athlete got off lightly; they just took away his title.*

mit einem lachenden und einem weinenden Auge — *with mixed emotions.*

Mit einem lachenden und einem weinenden Auge legte er sein Amt nieder. *He had mixed feelings about resigning from his office.*

unter vier Augen — *privately.*

Das müssen wir unter vier Augen besprechen. *We'll have to discuss that privately.*

Aus den Augen aus dem Sinn. *Out of sight out of mind.*

das Augenmaß — *sense of proportion.*

Augenmaß haben — *to be able to size up/gauge situations.*

Wir müssen die Lage mit viel Augenmaß betrachten. *We'll have to take a long and careful look at the situation.*

---

ausbaden — *to take the rap for/carry the can for (Brit.)*

Was du getan hast, muss ich jetzt ausbaden. *Now I've got to take the rap for what you did.*

---

das Ausbleiben — *absence*

Ich konnte mir sein Ausbleiben nicht erklären. *I couldn't understand his absence.*

ausbleiben — *to fail to materialize; not happen.*

Der erhoffte Sieg blieb aus. *The hoped for victory didn't happen.*

---

ausgehen — *to go out*

von etwas ausgehen — *to think; act on the assumption.*

Ich gehe davon aus, dass er die Wahrheit gesagt hat. *I'm acting on the assumption that he told the truth.*

---

auskommen — *to get by on*

Mit einem so niedrigen Gehalt kommt er kaum aus. *He scarcely gets by on such a low salary.*

auskommen — *to get on with.*
Es ist nicht leicht, mit ihm auszukommen. *It's not easy to get on with him.*

das Ausland — *foreign countries; abroad*
Sie lebten lange im Ausland. *They lived abroad for a long time.*

auslasten — *to load fully; to operate/use at full capacity*
Die Fabrik ist nur zur Hälfte ausgelastet. *The factory is operating only at half capacity.*

auslernen — *to finish one's apprenticeship*
Man lernt nie aus. *One is never done learning.*

auslöffeln — *to spoon out*
die Suppe/etwas auslöffeln. *To take the consequences.*
Du hast alles verkehrt gemacht und musst jetzt die Suppe auslöffeln. *You messed up everything and have to take the consequences now.*

ausrutschen — *to slip and fall*
Der Eiskunstläufer rutschte auf dem Glatteis aus. *The figure skater slipped and fell on the ice.*

ausrutschen — *to put one's foot into it.*
Beim Empfang auf der Botschaft rutschte sie wieder aus. *At the embassy reception she put her foot in it again.*

ausschildern — *to put up signs*
ausgeschildert sein — *to have signs; be marked.*
Die Straße ist gut ausgeschildert. *The road is well marked.*

der Bach — *brook*
den Bach heruntergehen — *to go down the drain.*
Wir wollen nicht, dass das Errungene den Bach heruntergeht. *We don't want everything we've achieved to go down the drain.*

die Bahn — *road*

  auf die schiefe Bahn geraten — *to go wrong.*

  Sein Sohn ist auf die schiefe Bahn geraten. *His son went wrong.*

  freie Bahn — *a clear track.*

  Alle Schwierigkeiten sind beseitigt, und wir haben jetzt freie Bahn. *All difficulties are resolved and we now have a clear track.*

  Bahn frei! — *Get out of the way! Make way! Coming through!*

  die (Eisen)Bahn — *railroad.*

  Wir sind mit der Bahn gefahren. *We went by train.*

  sich Bahn brechen — *to become established; to open up.*

  Neue Verfahren in der Mikrotechnik brechen sich Bahn. *New procedures in microtechnology are opening up.*

  sich in neuen Bahnen bewegen — *to break new ground.*

  Mit seiner Erfindung gelang es Roebling, im Brückenbau neue Bahnen zu bewegen. *Roebling's invention broke new ground in bridge building.*

der Bahnhof — *railroad station*

  Bahnhof verstehen — *to be "all Greek" or "double Dutch."*

  Ich verstand nur Bahnhof. *It was all Greek to me.*

  einen großen Bahnhof bereiten — *to roll out the red carpet.*

  Man bereitete der Mannschaft einen großen Bahnhof. *They rolled out the red carpet for the team.*

der Balken — *beam*

  dass sich die Balken biegen — *like crazy, like all get out.*

  Im Haushalt wird so viel gestrichen, dass sich die Balken biegen. *They're making budget cuts like crazy.*

der Ball — *ball*

  am Ball bleiben — *to keep at it.*

  Die Reporterin blieb für ihre Zeitung am Ball. *The reporter kept at it for her newspaper.*

  am Ball sein — *to be on the ball.*

  Sie ist immer am Ball. *She's always on the ball.*

den Ball wieder rund machen — *to sort things out.*

Bei den Verhandlungen versuchen wir den Ball wieder rund zu machen. *We're trying to sort things out during the negotiations.*

die Bandage — *bandage*

mit harten Bandagen kämpfen — *to pull no punches.*

Du musst lernen, mit harten Bandagen zu kämpfen. *You must learn to pull no punches.*

die Bank — *bench*

auf die lange Bank schieben — *to put off.*

Schieben Sie das nicht auf die lange Bank! *Don't put that off.*

durch die Bank — *every single one; the whole lot.*

Sie stimmten durch die Bank gegen seine Bestätigung. *Every single one of them voted against his confirmation.*

vor leeren Bänken spielen — *to play to an empty house.*

Wegen Angst vor Terroristen mussten wir gestern Abend vor leeren Bänken spielen. *Because of fear of terrorists we had to play to an empty house last night.*

der Bär — *bear*

jemandem einen Bären aufbinden — *to pull someone's leg.*

Willst du mir damit einen Bären aufbinden? *Are you trying to pull my leg?*

einen Bärendienst erweisen — *to do a disservice.*

Er wollte helfen, aber er hat uns einen Bärendienst erwiesen. *He wanted to help, but he did us a disservice.*

auf der Bärenhaut liegen — *to laze, lounge about.*

Den ganzen Tag liegt er auf der Bärenhaut, trotzdem hat er immer einen Bärenhunger. *He lazes about all day, yet he's always ravenous.*

eine Bärenruhe haben — *to be completely unflappable.*

Trotz aller Krisen hat er immer eine Bärenruhe. *Despite all crises he remains completely unflappable.*

bärbeißig — *grouchy.*

Sind Sie immer so bärbeißig? *Are you always so grouchy?*

zwischen Baum und Borke sitzen — *to be on the horns of a dilemma*.
Die Präsidentin sitzt zwischen Baum und Borke. *The president is on the horns of a dilemma*.
Bäume wachsen nicht in den Himmel — in der Beschränkung zeigt sich der Meister. — *There are limits to everything. It's limitations that test a master's mettle*.

---

baumeln — *to dangle; to swing (hang)*
Der Scheriff schwor, dass er den Räuber baumeln lassen würde. *The sheriff swore he'd see the bandit hang*.

---

bedienen — *to wait on*
vorn und hinten bedienen — *to wait on hand and foot*.
Der braucht jemand, der ihn vorn und hinten bedient. *He needs someone who'll wait on him hand and foot*.

bedienen — *to serve*.
Wer bedient in diesem Restaurant? *Who is serving in this restaurant?*

sich bedienen — *to help oneself*.
Hier gibt's keine Bedienung; Sie müssen sich selbst bedienen. *There's no service here; you have to help yourself*.

---

der Begriff — *concept*
Für meine Begriffe ist das eine veraltete Methode. *To my way of thinking, that's an outmoded method*.

ein Begriff sein — *to be well known*.
Diese Marke ist ein Begriff für Qualität. *This brand is well known for quality*.

schwer von Begriff sein — *to be slow on the uptake*.
Sag's ihm wieder; er ist schwer von Begriff. *Tell him again; he's slow on the uptake*.

im Begriff sein etwas zu tun — *to be about to do something*.
Die Gräfin war im Begriff auszugehen, als das Telefon klingelte. *The countess was about to go out when the phone rang*.

---

der Bart — *beard*

um des Kaisers Bart streiten — *to quarrel about trifles.*

Statt um des Kaisers Bart zu streiten, solltet ihr euch mit den wirklichen Streitfragen beschäftigen. *Instead of squabbling about petty details, you should deal with the real issues.*

---

der Bauch — *belly*

aus dem hohlen Bauch — *instinctively, with a gut feeling.*

Aus dem hohlen Bauch scheint mir der Plan fragwürdig. *My gut feeling is that the plan is questionable.*

den Bauch voll schlagen — *to overeat, stuff oneself.*

Jeden Tag kommt sein Onkel und schlägt sich bei uns dem Bauch voll. *Every day his uncle comes and stuffs his belly (face) at our place.*

die Beine in den Bauch stehen — *to be on one's feet for a long time.*

Stühle gab's nicht; wir mussten uns die Beine in dem Bauch stehen. *There were no chairs and we had to stand for a long time.*

mit etwas auf den Bauch fallen — *to fall flat on one's face.*

Mit den neuen Plan sind wir auf den Bauch gefallen. *We fell flat on our face with that new plan.*

sich vor Lachen den Bauch halten — *to split one's sides laughing.*

Die Komikerin war hinwerfend; wir hielten uns den Bauch. *The comic was a scream. We split our sides laughing.*

---

bauen — *to build*

bauen auf — *to build on; to count on.*

Als Optimist baut er trotzdem auf bessere Zeiten. *As an optimist, he's counting on better times.*

---

der Bauklotz — *building brick*

Bauklötze staunen — *to be staggered, flabbergasted.*

Die Chemikerin staunte Bauklötze, als sie die Mutation beobachtete. *T... chemist was flabbergasted when she saw the mutation.*

---

der Baum — *tree*

Bäume ausreißen können — *to feel ready to take on anything.*

Zuerst glaubte er, Bäume ausreißen zu können. *At first he felt ready ... take on anything.*

bei — *near; at; with; in*
  bei — *care of.*
  Schreiben Sie ihm bei Müller & Sohn! *Write him c/o Müller & Son.*

  bei — *at someone's home.*
  Gestern waren wir bei ihnen. *We were at their place yesterday.*

  bei — *in the work of.*
  Sie schrieb über das Persische bei Goethe. *She wrote on Persian elements in Goethe's work.*

  bei — *over.*
  Bei einer Tasse Kaffee sprachen wir über Goethe. *We talked about Goethe over a cup of coffee.*

  bei — *in case of.*
  Bei Feuer Scheibe einschlagen. *In case of fire, break glass.*

beilegen — *to enclose with*
  Meinem Brief lege ich einen Zeitungsartikel bei. *With my letter I enclose a newspaper article.*

  beilegen — *to attach.*
  Legen Sie der Sache viel Bedeutung bei? *Do you attach much importance to the matter?*

das Bein — *leg*
  auf den Beinen sein — *to be on one's feet.*
  Ich bin seit sieben Uhr auf den Beinen. *I've been on my feet since seven o'clock.*

  auf die Beine bringen — *to launch.*
  Es ist schwer, ein solches Unternehmen auf die Beine zu bringen. *It's difficult to launch an enterprise like that.*

  ein Bein stellen — *to trip (up).*
  Er hat sich selbst ein Bein gestellt. *He tripped himself up.*

  jmdm./etwas Beine machen — *to make s.o./s.t. get going/get a move on.*
  Die Präsidentin will der flauen Wirtschaft Beine machen. *The president wants to get the sluggish economy moving.*

sich die Beine in die Hand nehmen — *to take off fast*.
Der Junge warf den Schneeball und nahm dann die Beine in die Hand.
  The boy threw the snowball and then took off fast.

wieder auf die Beine kommen — *to get back on one's feet*.
Wir hoffen, dass Adeles Tante bald wieder auf die Beine kommt. *We hope*
  Adele's aunt gets back on her feet soon.

wieder auf den Beinen sein — *to be back on one's feet*.
Sie ist wieder auf den Beinen. *She's back on her feet again.*

---

bekommen — *to receive*
  es über sich bekommen — *to bring oneself to do something*.
  Ich konnte es nicht über mich bekommen, ihnen sofort die ganze Wahrheit
    zu sagen. *I couldn't bring myself to tell them the whole truth right away.*

  bekommen — *to agree with*.
  Die makrobiotische Kochkunst bekam uns nicht ganz. *Macrobiotic*
    cooking didn't entirely agree with us.

  Wohl bekomm's! *To your good health! (Enjoy!)*

---

bereiten — *to prepare*
  Freude bereiten — *to give pleasure*.
  Mit eurem Geschenk habt ihr mir viel Freude bereitet. *With your gift*
    you've given me much pleasure.

---

der Berg — *mountain; hill*
  goldene Berge versprechen — *to promise the moon*.
  Er versprach ihr goldene Berge. *He promised her the moon.*

  nicht hinter dem Berg halten — *to be unhesitating*.
  Mit Kritik hielt die Opposition nicht hinter dem Berg. *The opposition did*
    not hesitate to criticize.

  über alle Berge sein — *to be miles away*.
  Der Dieb war schon über alle Berge. *The thief was already miles away.*

  über den Berg sein — *to be out of the woods*.
  Es geht ihr besser, aber sie ist noch nicht über den Berg. *She's feeling*
    better, but she's not yet out of the woods.

---

bergab — *downhill*

"Es geht bergab mit uns," behauptete der Pessimist. *"Things are going downhill for us," asserted the pessimist.*

bergauf — *uphill*

"Es geht bergauf mit uns," erklärte der Optimist. *"Things are looking up for us," declared the optimist.*

der Beruf — *occupation, profession*

den Beruf verfehlt haben — *to have missed one's calling.*

Er glaubt, seinen Beruf verfehlt zu haben. *He thinks he's missed his calling.*

von Beruf sein — *to do, exercise a profession.*

Ich bin Bauarbeiter von Beruf. Was sind Sie von Beruf? *I'm a construction worker. What do you do?*

der Bescheid — *information*

Bescheid geben/sagen — *to inform; tell.*

Sagen Sie ihr Bescheid, dass wir spät kommen. *Tell her that we'll be late.*

Bescheid stoßen — *to tell off.*

Wenn er wieder versucht, mir 'was vorzumachen, stoß ich ihm gehörig Bescheid. *If he tries to fool me again, I'll tell him off.*

Bescheid wissen — *to be informed; to know one's way around or with.*

Entschuldigung, wissen Sie hier Bescheid? *Pardon me, do you know your way around here?*

der Bescheid — *decision.*

Wir erhielten einen abschlägigen Bescheid. *We received a refusal (negative decision).*

der Besen — *broom*

einen Besen fressen — *to eat one's hat.*

Wenn dem wirklich so ist, fress ich einen Besen. *If that's really the case, I'll eat my hat.*

Neue Besen kehren gut. *A new broom sweeps clean.*

die Besserung — *improvement*
  Gute Besserung! *Get well soon!*
  auf dem Wege der Besserung sein — *to be on the road to recovery.*
  Sie war schwer krank, jetzt ist sie aber auf dem Wege der Besserung. *She was very sick, but now she's getting better.*

---

best — *best*
  Am besten nehmen wir die Autobahn. *We'd best take the freeway.*
  Besten Dank für das Paket! *Many thanks for the package.*
  in den besten Jahren sein — *to be in one's prime.*
  Fräulein Brodie war in den besten Jahren. *Miss Brodie was in her prime.*
  zum Besten haben/halten — *to put one over on.*
  Er versuchte, uns zum Besten zu haben. *He tried to put one over on us.*

---

der Betreuer — *social worker*
  Der Betreuer macht zweimal die Woche die Hausarbeiten für sie. *The social worker does the housework for them twice a week.*

---

die Betreuung — *looking after*
  Wir haben eine Krankenpflegerin zur Betreuung der Großeltern eingestellt. *We hired a nurse to look after our grandparents.*

---

der Betrieb — *business*
  außer Betrieb sein — *to be out of order.*
  Die Rolltreppe im Kaufhaus war außer Betrieb. *The escalator in the department store was out of order.*

  Betrieb herrschen — *to be busy.*
  Nachmittags bei uns im Laden herrscht viel Betrieb. *Afternoons it's always very busy in our store.*

  den ganzen Betrieb aufhalten — *to hold everyone up.*
  Vielleicht hast du recht, aber du brauchst nicht den ganzen Betrieb aufzuhalten. *Maybe you're right but you don't have to hold everyone up.*

  in Betrieb nehmen — *to put into service, operation.*
  Wann wird die neue Bahnlinie in Betrieb genommen? *When will the new rail line be put into service?*

---

betucht — *well-heeled, well off*

Nur (gut) betuchte Leute gehören diesem Verein an. *Only well-heeled people belong to this club.*

---

sich bewahrheiten — *to come true; turn out to be true*

Einige ihrer Prophezeiungen haben sich schon bewahrheitet. *Some of her prophecies have already come true.*

---

der Beweis — *proof*

unter Beweis stellen — *to give proof of.*

Sie hat ihre Kochkünste unter Beweis gestellt. *She has given proof of her culinary skills.*

---

die Biege — *bend*

eine Biege fahren — *to go for a spin.*

Er wollte eine Biege fahren, aber wegen der Umweltverschmutzung sagten wir nein. *He wanted to go for a spin, but we said no because of environmental pollution.*

---

biegen — *to bend*

auf Biegen oder Brechen — *by hook or by crook, one way or another.*

Auf Biegen oder Brechen werden wir's schon schaffen. *One way or another we'll manage it.*

---

das Bier — *beer*

jemands Bier sein — *to be someone's business.*

Das ist weder mein noch dein Bier. *That's not your business or mine.*

bierernst — *deadly serious.*

Nimm's nicht so bierernst! *Don't take it with such deadly seriousness.*

---

das Bild — *picture*

sich ein Bild machen — *to form an impression.*

Durch archäologische Funde können wir uns ein Bild von der Kultur der alten Mayas machen. *Through archaeological finds we can form an impression of ancient Mayan culture.*

---

die Bildung — *education*
  die Leute von Besitz und Bildung — *the propertied and educated classes.*
  Die Partei versuchte, die Leute von Besitz und Bildung anzusprechen. *The party tried to appeal to the propertied and educated classes.*

  Einbildung ist auch eine Bildung! — *Such (your) conceit knows no bounds.*
  Du wärst für den Posten geeigneter gewesen? Na, Einbildung ist auch eine Bildung! *You would have been more suited for the post? Your conceit knows no bounds.*

  der Bildungsroman — *novel of character formation/development.*
  Wir haben Bildungsromane von Goethe, Keller und Hesse gelesen. *We read novels of character formation by Goethe, Keller, and Hesse.*

die Binse — *reed; marsh grass*
  in die Binsen gehen — *to go down the drain; fall apart.*
  Er tröstete sich mit Binsenwahrheiten, nachdem seine Ehe in die Binsen gegangen war. *He consoled himself with truisms after his marriage fell apart.*

  die Binsenwahrheit — *truism.*
  Er sammelt Binsenwahrheiten für sein Buch. *He's collecting truisms for his book.*

die Birne — *pear; head; light bulb*
  eine weiche Birne haben — *to be dim-witted, soft in the head.*
  Der hat ein gutes Herz aber 'ne weiche Birne. *He's got a good heart but he's a bit dim-witted.*

blasen — *to blow*
  jemandem den Marsch blasen — *to give someone a bawling out.*
  Wenn's der Chef erfährt, wird er dir den Marsch blasen. *If the boss finds out he'll give you a bawling out.*

  Trübsal blasen — *to lament, sing the blues.*
  Man vermeidet ihn, weil er immer nur Trübsal bläst. *People avoid him because he's always singing the blues.*

das Blatt — *leaf*

Das Blatt hat sich endlich gewendet — *Things have finally taken a different turn.*

ein unbeschriebenes Blatt sein — *to be an unknown quantity.*
Diese Kandidatin ist noch ein unbeschriebenes Blatt. *This candidate is still an unknown quantity.*

---

blau — *blue*

blau machen — *to skip school, work (call in sick without being sick).*
Er macht oft blau, weil er auch schwarzarbeitet. *He often calls in sick because he's got another undeclared job.*

blau sein — *to be drunk, plastered.*
Er war wieder völlig blau. *He was completely plastered again.*

blauer Dunst — *rubbish.*
Alles, was er sagte, war nur blauer Dunst. *Everything he said was just rubbish.*

sein blaues Wunder erleben — *to get a nasty surprise.*
Wenn sich das doch bewahrheitet, werden Sie ihr blaues Wunder erleben. *But if that turns out to be true, you'll get a nasty surprise.*

---

das Blaue — *the blue*

das Blaue vom Himmel herunterlügen — *to lie through one's teeth.*
Um Geschäfte zu machen, lügt er das Blaue vom Himmel herunter. *To make business deals, he lies through his teeth.*

ins Blaue hineinreden — *to engage in idle chatter, talk aimlessly.*
Glaub ihm nicht; er redet nur ins Blaue hinein. *Don't believe him; he's just talking so he can hear himself talk.*

ins Blaue schießen — *to fire a shot in the dark, fire at random.*
Der Detektiv hatte ins Blaue geschossen und ins Schwarze getroffen. *The detective fired a shot in the dark and hit the mark (bullseye).*

blauäugig — *blue-eyed; naïve, starry-eyed.*
Blauäugiger Optimismus nützt uns jetzt nichts. *Naïve optimism is of no use to us now.*

---

das Blech — *sheet metal*
  Blech reden — *to talk nonsense.*
  Red kein Blech. *Don't talk rubbish.*

bleiben — *to remain; be*
  Wir warten schon lange. Wo bleibt das Essen? *We've been waiting for some time. Where's the food?*

  außen vor bleiben — *to be excluded, ignored.*
  Solche radikalen Begriffe bleiben noch in der großen Gesellschaft außen vor. *Such radical concepts are still ignored in society at large.*

  dabei bleiben — *to stick to.*
  Ich hab's versprochen und ich bleibe dabei. *I promised it and I'm sticking to it.*

  vom Leibe bleiben — *to keep away.*
  Bleib mir vom Leibe mit solch skandalösen Geschichten! *Keep away from me with such scandalous stories.*

blind — *blind*
  blinden Alarm schlagen — *to turn in a false alarm; to cry wolf.*
  Der Junge hat wieder blinden Alarm geschlagen. *The boy turned in a false alarm again.*

  blinder Passagier — *stowaway.*
  Sie versuchten als blinde Passagiere, das Land zu verlassen. *They tried to leave the country as stowaways.*

das Blümchen — *little flower*
  der Blümchenkaffee — *weak coffee; coffee substitute.*
  Heimlich goss er Rum in seinen Blümchenkaffee. *Furtively, he poured rum into his weak coffee.*

  die Blume — *flower.*
  durch die Blume sagen — *to say in a roundabout way.*
  Sie hat es nicht direkt sondern durch die Blume gesagt. *She didn't say so directly but in a roundabout way.*

der Bock — *billy goat; buck; fun, inclination*
Ihn stößt wieder der Bock. *He's being ornery/contrary again.*

einen Bock schießen. *To make a blunder/blooper/howler.*
Er hat wieder einen großen Bock geschossen. *He made another whale of a blunder.*

Bock/Lust haben auf — *to feel like.*
Sie sagt, sie hätte es nur aus Bock getan; das ist aber keine Entschuldigung. *She says she did it just because she felt like it; but that's no excuse.*

der Boden — *ground; soil*
am Boden liegen — *to be in a sorry state.*
In der Gegend liegt die Stahlindustrie total am Boden. *In that area the steel industry is in a very sorry state.*

den Boden unter den Füßen wegziehen — *to pull the rug out from under.*
Sie entzogen ihre Hilfe, und damit zogen sie mir den Boden unter den Füßen weg. *They withdrew their aid and thus pulled the rug out from under me.*

der Bogen — *arc; curve; detour*
den Bogen heraushaben — *to have gotten the hang of it.*
Endlich hab ich den Bogen heraus! *I've finally gotten the hang of it!*

den Bogen überspannen — *to overstep the mark, go too far.*
Schau zu, dass du den Bogen nicht wieder überspannst! *Be careful you don't go too far again.*

einen großen Bogen machen — *to go out of one's way to avoid.*
Viele machen einen großen Bogen um die Zahl 13. *Many go out of their way to avoid the number 13.*

die Bohne — *bean*
Bohnen in den Ohren haben — *to play deaf.*
Der Kellner hat mich gehört und gesehen, kommt aber nicht. Hat wohl Bohnen in den Ohren. *The waiter saw and heard me, but he doesn't come. He must be playing deaf.*

Jede Bohn' hat ihren Ton or **Jedes Böhnchen hat sein Tönchen/Jedes Böhnchen gibt sein Tönchen.** *Beans produce flatulence.*

Iss nicht zu viele Bohnen; du weißt ja, jede Bohn' hat ihren Ton. *Don't eat too many beans; you know each bean has its own tone.*

nicht die Bohne — *not a scrap/whit/bit.*

Die Kritiker haben nicht die Bohne von ihrem Roman verstanden. *The critics didn't understand her novel at all.*

---

bombensicher — *absolutely safe*

Der Finanzberater meint, es sei eine bombensichere Sache und werde einen Bombenerfolg haben. *The financial advisor says it's absolutely safe and will be a smash hit.*

---

das Boot — *boat*

jmdn. mit ins Boot holen — *to make s.o. part of a group, firm etc.*

Statt sie anzufeinden, sollten wir sie vielleicht lieber ins Boot holen. *Instead of making enemies of them, maybe we should get them to come on board.*

im selben Boot/in einem Boot sitzen — *to be in the same boat.*

Schließlich sitzen wir alle in einem Boot. *After all, we're all in the same boat.*

---

der Braten — *roast*

den Braten riechen — *to smell a rat.*

Der Gangster hatte den Braten gerochen und ging nicht in die Falle. *The gangster smelled a rat and didn't fall into the trap.*

---

braun — *brown; Nazi*

Schnell verdrängte er seine braune Vergangenheit, schloss sich eifrig den Roten an, und paktierte auch mit den Schwarzen und Grünen.

He quickly supressed his Nazi past, enthusiastically joined the Reds, and dealt with the Blacks (conservatives, clerics) and Greens (ecologists) too.

braungebrannt — *suntanned.*

Nick kam braungebrannt aus Afrika zurück. *Nick came back from Africa with a suntan.*

---

der Brei — *porridge*

  um den heißen Brei herumreden — *to beat about the bush.*
  Hör doch auf, um den heißen Brei herumzureden, und sag mir alles
    sofort! *Stop beating about the bush and tell me everything right away.*

  zu Brei schlagen — *to beat to a pulp.*
  Die Hooligans haben ihn zu Brei geschlagen. *The hooligans beat him to
    a pulp.*

---

breit — *wide*

  sich breit machen — *to spread.*
  Unruhe macht sich in vielen Schichten der Bevölkerung breit. *Unrest is
    spreading in many groups in the population.*

  in die Breite gehen — *to get fat.*
  Iss nicht so viele Torten oder du gehst in die Breite. *Don't eat so many
    tarts or you'll get fat.*

  in die Breite wirken — *to reach a large audience.*
  Mit ihrem neuen Buch will die Professorin mehr in die Breite wirken.
    With her new book the professor wants to reach a larger audience.

---

brennen — *to burn*

  Gebranntes Kind scheut das Feuer. *Once bitten, twice shy.*

  darauf brennen, etwas zu tun — *to be dying (longing) to do something.*
  Wir brennen darauf, die ganze Geschichte zu hören. *We're dying to hear
    the whole story.*

---

die Bresche — *breech, gap*

  sich in die Bresche schlagen für — *to go to bat for, stand up for.*
  Seine Frau hat sich für ihn in die Bresche geschlagen. *His wife stood up
    for him.*

---

das Brett — *board*

  das Brett/Holz bohren, wo es am dünnsten ist — *to look for a too-
    simple solution.*
  Dieser Faulpelz will immer das Holz bohren, wo es am dünnsten ist.
    That lazybones is always looking for an easy way out.

ein dickes Brett bohren — *to cope with a difficult problem.*

Die Verhandlungen laufen — es gibt noch viele dicke Bretter zu bohren. *Negotiations are continuing — there are still many thorny problems to deal with.*

ein Brett vor dem Kopf haben — *to be slow on the uptake; have a mental block.*

Heute habe ich ein Brett vor dem Kopf. *My head isn't on straight today.*

---

der Brief — *letter*

blauer Brief — *warning letter; pink slip.*

Es heißt, fast die Hälfte der Belegschaft soll einen blauen Brief bekommen. *They're saying half the workforce is going to get pink slips.*

---

bringen — *to bring*

es auf etwas bringen — *to get as far as.*

Die Splitterpartei brachte es nur auf fünftausend Stimmen. *The splinter party only got (as far as) 5,000 votes.*

es weit bringen — *to amount to much.*

Sie glaubten, Hans würde es nie weit bringen. *They thought Hans would never amount to much.*

---

das Brot — *bread*

Das ist eine brotlose Kunst. *There's no money in that.*

brotlos machen — *to put out of work.*

Die Arbeiter hatten Angst, dass die Roboter sie brotlos machen würden. *The workers were afraid the robots would put them out of work.*

die Brotzeit — *coffee/lunch break.*

Während der Dreharbeiten in München freuten wir uns auf die Brotzeit. *While making a movie in Munich we looked forward to the lunch break.*

---

das Brötchen — *roll*

kleine Brötchen backen — *to operate on a small scale.*

Wir backen noch kleine Brötchen aber wir haben große Pläne. *We're still small potatoes but we have great plans.*

kleinere Brötchen backen — *to limit operations, downsize.*
Wegen der Kürzungen müssen wir leider noch kleinere Brötchen backen.
Because of cutbacks we'll have to downsize even more.

der Bruch — *fracture*
Deutschsprachigen Schauspielern sagt man: "Hals- und Beinbruch!" *One
says "break a leg and your neck" to German-speaking actors.*

in die Brüche gehen — *to collapse.*
Ihre Ehe droht, in die Brüche zu gehen. *Their marriage is in danger of
collapsing.*

bruchlanden — *to crash-land.*
Die Pilotin musste bruchlanden. *The pilot had to crash-land.*

die Brücke — *bridge*
alle Brücken hinter sich abbrechen — *to burn one's bridges behind one.*
Jetzt bereuen wir's, alle Brücken hinter uns abgebrochen zu haben. *Now
we're sorry we burned all our bridges behind us.*

Brücken schlagen — *to build bridges; establish ties.*
Die ehemaligen Feinde versuchen jetzt, Brücken zu einander zu schlagen.
The former enemies are now trying to build bridges to each other.

eine goldene Brücke bauen — *to smooth the way for.*
Er meinte, sein Onkel würde ihm im Geschäft eine goldene Brücke bauen.
He thought his uncle would smooth the way for him in the business.

bügeln — *to iron*
geschniegelt und gebügelt — *all spruced up.*
Für den Staatsbesuch war die Stadt geschniegelt und gebügelt. *The city
was all spruced up for the state visit.*

der Buhmann — *whipping boy; bogeyman*
Nach den Enthüllungen in der Zeitung wurde er zum Buhmann der
Nation. *After the revelations in the newspaper, he became the nation's
scapegoat.*

die Bühne — *stage*
  reibungslos über die Bühne gehen — *to go off without a hitch.*
  Es ist alles reibungslos über die Bühne gegangen. *Everything went off
    without a hitch.*

bunt — *multicolored*
  Ein bunt gemischtes Publikum verkehrt in dem Lokal. *A very mixed
    clientele patronizes that place.*

  bunter Abend — *evening of music and entertainment.*
  Nächste Woche veranstaltet das Hotel einen bunten Abend. *Next week the
    hotel is arranging for an evening of music and entertainment.*

  es zu bunt treiben — *to go too far.*
  Diesmal hat er es zu bunt getrieben. *This time he went too far.*

  zu bunt werden — *to get to be too much for.*
  Es wurde mir zu bunt, und ich ging nach Hause. *Things got to be too
    much for me and I went home.*

der Busch — *bush*
  auf den Busch klopfen — *to sound out.*
  Er klopfte bei mir auf den Busch, ob ich ihn unterstützen würde. *He
    sounded me out as to whether I'd support him.*

  im Busch sein — *to be brewing.*
  Ich weiß nicht genau, was sie vorhaben, aber etwas ist im Busch. *I don't
    know for sure what they're planning, but something's brewing.*

  sich in die Büsche schlagen — *to slip away; to go underground.*
  Kafkas Affe dachte daran, seinem Käfig zu entkommen, und sich in die
    Büsche zu schlagen. *Kafka's monkey thought of escaping its cage and
    slipping away.*
  Man gab ihm eine neue Identität und er schlug sich in die Büsche. *They
    gave him a new identity and he went underground.*

die Butter — *butter*
  in (bester) Butter sein — *to be going smoothly.*
  Sie hatten einige Schwierigkeiten, aber jetzt ist alles in bester Butter. *They
    had some difficulties, but everything is going smoothly now.*

der Chaot — *anarchist; violent demonstrator*
  ein Chaot sein — *to be terribly disorganized*.
  Jetzt ist er sehr scharf auf Ordnung, aber in jungen Jahren war er ein
    furchtbarer Chaot. *Now he's keen on order, but when he was young he
    was terribly disorganized.*

das Dach — *roof*
  unter Dach und Fach bringen — *to complete successfully; wrap up*.
  Sie hat jetzt ihre Dissertation unter Dach und Fach. *She's now successfully
    completed her dissertation.*

der Damm — *levee; embankment; roadway*
  wieder auf dem Damm sein — *to be feeling fit again*.
  Onkel Otto war krank, aber jetzt ist er wieder auf dem Damm. *Uncle Otto
    was sick, but now he's feeling fit again.*

der Dampfer — *steam ship*
  auf dem falschen Dampfer sitzen — *to be barking up the wrong tree*.
  Der Detektiv saß wieder auf dem falschen Dampfer. *The detective was
    barking up the wrong tree again.*

der Dämpfer — *mute; damper*
  einen Dämpfer aufsetzen — *to dampen enthusiasm*.
  Er versuchte, mir einen Dämpfer aufzusetzen, aber ich ließ mich nicht
    kleinkriegen. *He tried to dampen my enthusiasm, but I wouldn't be
    intimidated.*

41

dauern — *to last*
   der Dauerbrenner — *slow-burning oven; long-lasting success.*
   Einige ihrer Lieder sind zu Dauerbrennern geworden. *Some of her songs have become long-lasting successes.*

---

der Daumen/das Däumchen — *thumb*
   den Daumen aufs Auge halten — *to pressure; put the screws on.*
   Du brauchst mir nicht den Daumen aufs Auge zu halten, ich beuge mich dem allgemeinen Willen. *You don't have to pressure me; I yield to the general will.*

   den (die) Daumen drücken — *to keep one's fingers crossed for.*
   Ich werde dir den Daumen drücken, dass alles gut klappt. *I'll keep my fingers crossed for you that everything goes right.*

   die Daumen drehen/Däumchen drehen — *to twiddle one's thumbs.*
   Jetzt musst du handeln, statt nur die Daumen zu drehen. *You've got to take action now instead of just twiddling your thumbs.*

   über den Daumen peilen — *to make a rough estimate.*
   Über den Daumen gepeilt, dürfte die Oase nicht mehr weit weg sein. *At a rough estimate, the oasis shouldn't be too far off now.*

---

die Decke — *cover, blanket; ceiling, roof*
   Mir fällt die Decke auf den Kopf; ich brauche Tapetenwechsel. *I'm going stir-crazy; I need a change of scenery.*

   an die Decke gehen — *to hit the ceiling.*
   Geh nicht gleich an die Decke! *Don't fly off the handle right away.*

   sich nach der Decke strecken — *to make do with what's available, cut one's coat according to one's cloth.*
   Dein Vater ist arbeitslos und wir müssen uns jetzt nach der Decke strecken. *Your father's unemployed and we have to make do with less now.*

---

denken — *to think*
   Das hätte ich mir denken können! *I might have known!*
   Denken ist Glückssache — *thinking is a matter of chance, and you weren't lucky.*

Gedacht, getan! *No sooner said than done.*

zu denken geben — *to make suspicious.*
Sein Verhalten gab mir zu denken. *His behavior made me suspicious.*

denken an — *to think of.*
Goethe dachte an das Röslein und später an die Urpflanze. *Goethe thought of the little rose and later of the primordial plant.*

nicht im Traum an etwas denken — *to not dream of, have no intention of.*
Ich denke nicht im Traum daran, ihn einzuladen. *I wouldn't dream of inviting him.*

denken über — *to think about.*
Sie weiß nicht, wie sie über seinen Brief denken soll. *She doesn't know what to think about his letter.*

---

deutsch — *German*
   der deutsche Michel — *simple, honest, provincial German.*
Sie war den Wählern zu dynamisch, die eher einen deutschen Michel, eine Zipfelmütze, wollten.
She was too dynamic for the voters, who preferred a simple, colorless gal from Dullsville.

---

die Diät — *diet*
   Diät machen — *to be on a diet.*
Er macht wieder Diät. *He's on a diet again.*

diät essen/kochen/leben — *to eat/cook/live according to a diet.*
Er isst diät, und seine Frau kocht diät für ihn. *He eats according to a diet, and his wife prepares diet meals for him.*

---

dicht — *thick; sealed*
   nicht ganz dicht sein — *to be a little cracked/crazy.*
Franz ist nett aber nicht ganz dicht. *Franz is nice but a little cracked.*

dichtmachen — *to close; to shut up shop.*
Wir haben heute den Laden etwas früher dichtgemacht. *We closed the store a little earlier today.*

---

dichten — *to write poetry*

In seiner Jugend dichtete er Tag und Nacht. *In his youth he wrote poetry day and night.*

sein Dichten und Trachten — *all one's thoughts.*

Jetzt ist sein Dichten und Trachten nur auf Geld gerichtet. *Now all he thinks about is money.*

---

dick — *thick; fat*

dick machen — *to make pregnant.*

Er hat seine Freundin dick gemacht. *He got his girlfriend pregnant.*

dick werden — *to get fat.*

Sie isst viel Schlagsahne, wird aber nicht dick. *She eats lots of whipped cream, but she doesn't get fat.*

durch dick und dünn gehen — *to go through thick and thin.*

Wir sind mit einander durch dick und dünn gegangen. *We've been through thick and thin together.*

es dick haben — *to be well off.*

Er ließ uns zahlen, obwohl wir es gar nicht so dick haben. *He let us pay even though we're not well off at all.*

dicke Luft — *pessimistic atmosphere.*

Wegen des Übernahmeversuchs herrscht dicke Luft auf der Chefetage. *The atmosphere on the executive floor is pretty bleak because of the takeover attempt.*

sich dicke tun — *to show off.*

Auf dem Rummelplatz tat er sich mit seiner Kraft dicke. *At the fair he showed off his strength.*

---

dienen — *to serve*

ausgedient haben — *to be history, be passé.*

In den diesjährigen Modekollektionen haben Extreme ausgedient. *In this year's fashion collections, extremes are passé.*

---

der Dienst — *service*

Dienst ist Dienst, und Schnaps ist Schnaps. *Work is one thing and pleasure is another/you shouldn't mix business and pleasure.*

vom Dienst — *on (official) duty; stock, constant.*

Die Rolle hab ich abgelehnt; ich bin es satt, immer den Bösewicht vom Dienst zu spielen. *I turned down the role; I'm fed up with always playing the stock villain.*

---

das Ding — *thing*

Es geht nicht mit rechten Dingen zu. *There's something crooked going on.*

Gut Ding will Weile haben. *It takes time to do things right.*

vor allen Dingen — *above all.*

Vor allen Dingen müssen die Kriegsopfer betreut werden. *Above all, the victims of the war need to be looked after.*

Aller guten Dinge sind drei! — *All good things come in threes!/The third try will be lucky.*

"Aller guten Dinge sind drei," sagten das Ehepaar und ihr Hausfreund. *"All good things come in threes," said the married couple and their friend.*

dingfest machen — *to arrest; apprehend.*

Bislang hat ihn die Polizei nicht dingfest machen können. *Up to now the police haven't been able to apprehend him.*

---

donnern — *to thunder*

Es donnerte. *There was thunder.*

eine donnern — *to give a good whack.*

Es riss ihm die Geduld, und er donnerte dem Jungen eine. *His patience ran out and he gave the boy a good whack.*

---

doppelt — *double*

doppelt gemoppelt — *to repeat unnecessarily.*

Das ist wieder doppelt gemoppelt. *That's more unnecessary repetition.*

doppelter Boden — *false bottom.*

Der Dieb versteckte den Schmuck in einer Kiste mit doppeltem Boden. *The thief hid the jewels in a box with a false bottom.*

---

das Dornröschen — *Sleeping Beauty*
   aus seinem Dornröschenschlaf erwachen — *to become active after a period of torpor.*
   Mir wär's lieber, wenn unser einst so beschauliches Dörfchen nicht aus seinem Dornröschenschlaf erwacht wäre. *I'd rather our once picturesque little village had stayed a sleepy hamlet.*

---

der Draht — *wire*
   auf Draht bringen — *to get into shape; bring up to scratch/speed.*
   Die neue Chefin versucht das Unternehmen auf Draht zu bringen. *The new boss is trying to get the company into shape.*

   auf Draht sein — *to be a live wire; be on the ball.*
   Sie wird Erfolg haben, denn sie ist immer auf Draht. *She will be successful for she's always on the ball.*

   einen Draht haben — *to be well in with, have a connection with/line to.*
   Er glaubt einen Draht zum Herrgott zu haben. *He thinks he has a direct line to God Almighty.*
   Unsere Partei hat einen besseren Draht zu den Wählern. *Our party is more in touch with the voters.*

---

der Drahtesel — *bicycle*
   In Münster sieht man viele Drahtesel. *One sees many bikes in Münster.*

---

der Dreck — *dirt*
   den Karren aus dem Dreck ziehen — *to get out of/clean up a mess.*
   Wir stecken noch im Dreck aber vielleicht wird der neue Präsident den Karren aus dem Dreck ziehen. *We're still in the muck, but maybe the new president will clean up the mess.*

   Dreck am Stecken haben — *to have a shady past/skeletons in the closet.*
   Es hat sich herausgestellt, dass der große Moralapostel selber Dreck am Stecken hat. *It turned out that the great moral crusader had skeletons in his closet.*

---

drehen — *to turn*
   es drehen und wenden, wie man will — *to examine from every possible angle.*

Du kannst es drehen und wenden, wie die willst, es läuft alles auf dasselbe hinaus. *You can examine it from every possible angle, it still amounts to the same thing.*

Filme drehen — *to make movies.*
Sie träumt davon, Filme zu drehen. *She's dreaming of making movies.*

---

dreizehn — *thirteen*
Jetzt schlägt's (aber) dreizehn! — *That's too much!*
Sie verlangen wieder Geld? Jetzt schlägt's aber dreizehn! *They're asking for money again? That's going too far!*

---

dreschen — *to thresh*
mit der Faust auf den Tisch dreschen — *to pound the table with one's fist.*
Um seinen Worten Nachdruck zu verleihen, drischt er oft mit der Faust auf den Tisch. *To lend emphasis to his words, he often pounds the table with his fist.*

Phrasen dreschen — *to mouth trite phrases.*
In seiner Rede hat er aber nur Phrasen gedroschen. *But all he did in his speech was mouth trite phrases.*

---

drücken — *to press; push*
Die drückende Hitze drückte auf die Stimmung. *The oppressive heat dampened the mood.*

die Oppositionsbank drücken — *to be in the opposition.*
Früher bildeten sie die Regierung; jetzt drücken sie die Oppositionsbank. *Formerly they formed the government; now they're in the opposition.*

die Schulbank drücken — *to go to school.*
Er war schon 15 Jahre alt und wollte nicht mehr die Schulbank drücken. *He was already 15 years old and didn't want to go to school any more.*

ans Herz drücken — *to hug close.*
Nach der langen Trennung drückte er sie ans Herz. *After the long separation, he hugged her close.*

sich drücken — *to shirk; avoid.*
Er drückte sich vor jeder Arbeit. *He avoided any kind of work.*

---

drum — *around*
  mit allem Drum und Dran — *with all the trimmings*.
  Wenn Ulla heiratet, muss es mit allem Drum und Dran sein. *When Ulla gets married, it'll have to be with all the trimmings*.

drunter — *underneath*
  drunter und drüber — *topsy-turvy*.
  Es ist jetzt alles drunter und drüber. *Everything is topsy-turvy now*.

du — *you*
  auf du und du sein — *to be very familiar with*.
  "Die Bürger unserer Stadt leben mit der Kunst auf du und du," sagte stolz die Bürgermeisterin. *"The citizens of our town are very familiar with the arts," said the mayor proudly*.

dumm — *stupid*
  Das ist mir einfach zu dumm! *I've had enough of that!*
  Mir ist ganz dumm im Kopf. *My head is swimming*.
  Man nennt sie eine dumme Gans, aber sie ist eigentlich sehr gescheit. *They call her a silly goose, but she's really very astute*.

  für dumm verkaufen — *to put one over on*.
  Er versuchte, mich für dumm zu verkaufen. *He tried to put one over on me*.

  aus Dummsdorf sein — *to be born yesterday*.
  Er glaubt, wir sind aus Dummsdorf. *He thinks we were born yesterday*.

das Dunkel — *darkness; mystery*
  Das Dunkel um den Schatz des Priamos hat sich gelichtet. *The mystery surrounding Priam's treasure has been cleared up*.

  im Dunkeln liegen — *to be unknown*.
  Das Motiv der Täter liegt noch im Dunkeln. *The perpetrators' motives are still unknown*.

der Dünkel — *arrogance, conceit*
  einen ungeheuren Dünkel haben — *to be very conceited*.

Ohne jede Berechtigung dazu, hat er einen ungeheuren Dünkel. *Without any justification at all for it, he is immensely conceited.*

In einigen Kreisen gibt es noch Standesdünkel. *In some circles there is still class snobbery.*

der Dunkelmann — *shady character*

Auch im Zeitalter der Aufklärung hat es Dunkelmänner gegeben. *In the Age of Enlightenment too, there were shady characters.*

die Dunkelziffer — *unreported number*

Tausende erkranten am neuen Medikament und die Dunkelziffer dürfte noch größer sein. *The new drug made thousands sick, and the number of unreported cases is probably even greater.*

---

durch — *through*

durchbeißen — *to bite through.*

Ohne sein Gebiss konnte er das Brot nicht durchbeißen. *Without his false teeth he couldn't bite through the bread.*

sich durchbeißen — *to get out of a tight spot.*

Am Ende konnten sich Max und Moritz nicht mehr durchbeißen. *At the end Max and Moritz couldn't get out of a tight spot anymore.*

durchdrehen — *to grind, chop; to crack up.*

Auf der Tropeninsel war es so heiß, dass der Missionar durchdrehte. *It was so hot on the tropical island that the missionary cracked up.*

durchgehen — *to walk through; to run off and leave.*

Gauguin ist seiner Familie durchgegangen. *Gauguin ran off and left his family.*

durchgreifen — *to take drastic measures.*

Die Senatorin versprach, gegen die Kriminalität hart durchzugreifen. *The senator promised to take drastic measures against crime.*

durchnehmen — *to go through (a text); gossip about.*

In der Schule haben wir alle Dramen Grillparzers durchgenommen. *In school we went through all of Grillparzer's plays.*

Sie nehmen noch die neue Nachbarin durch. *They're still gossiping about the new neighbor.*

---

sich durchschlagen — *to fight (make) one's way through.*
Trotz aller Hindernisse schlug sie sich erfolgreich durch. *Despite all obstacles, she fought her way through successfully.*

durchschneiden — *to cut through.*
Einst glaubte man, dass der Mars von Kanälen durchschnitten war. *Once it was believed that Mars was crisscrossed by canals.*

---

der Durst — *thirst*
Durst haben — *to be thirsty.*
Er hat immer Durst. *He's always thirsty.*

Durst haben auf — *to be thirsty for.*
Er hatte großen Durst auf ein Bier. *He was very thirsty for a beer.*

einen über den Durst trinken — *to have a drink beyond one's limit.*
Das ist nicht das erste Mal, das er einen über den Durst trinkt. *This is not the first time that he drinks beyond his limit.*

---

die Ebbe — *low tide*
Ebbe in der Kasse/im Geldbeutel/im Portemonnaie — *short on funds.*
Nach der Renovierung ist nun Ebbe in der Kasse. *We're low on funds now, after the renovation work.*

---

die Ecke — *corner*
an allen Ecken und Enden — *all over the place; everywhere.*
An allen Ecken und Enden gab es Unzufriedenheit. *There was dissatisfaction everywhere.*

Ecken und Kanten haben — *to have rough edges; be idiosyncratic, difficult to get along with.*
Er hat seine Ecken und Kanten aber ich mag ihn doch gern. *He's not easy to get along with but I'm still quite fond of him.*

eine Ecke sein — *to be at some distance.*
Bis dahin ist es noch eine ganze Ecke. *That's still quite a way off.*

um die Ecke bringen — *to bump off, rub out, kill.*
Der Mafiachef ließ seinen Rivalen umbringen. *The Mafia boss had his rival rubbed out.*

um sieben Ecken verwandt sein — *to be distantly related.*
Sie ist mit meiner Frau um sieben Ecken verwandt sein. *She's distantly related to my wife.*

---

edel — *noble; fine*
Die Winzer kosteten den edlen Wein und sprachen von der Edelfäule. *The vintners tasted the fine wine and spoke of noble rot.*

die Edelschnulze — *pretentious schmaltz.*
Elsa liebte den Roman, obwohl die Professorin ihn als Edelschnulze abgetan hatte. *Elsa loved the novel even though the professor had dismissed it as pretentious schmaltz.*

der Edelstahl — *stainless steel.*
Einige Winzer sprachen von den Vorteilen des Edelstahls. *Some vintners spoke of the advantages of stainless steel.*

der Edelstein — *precious stone; gem.*
Der ästhetische Edelmann sammelte Edelsteine aller Farben. *The aesthetic nobleman collected gems in all colors.*

Effeff (aus dem Effeff verstehen) — *to know thoroughly*
Sie versteht ihr Fach aus dem Effeff. *She knows her subject thoroughly.*

---

die Ehe — *marriage*
in wilder Ehe leben — *to live together without benefit of clergy, without being officially married.*
Vor der Trauung hatten sie schon lange Jahre in wilder Ehe gelebt. *Before the marriage ceremony they had already lived together for a long time.*

---

die Ehre — *honor*
der Wahrheit die Ehre geben — *to tell the truth.*
Um der Wahrheit die Ehre zu geben, möchte ich lieber nichts damit zu tun haben. *To tell the truth, I'd prefer to have nothing to do with it.*

sich die Ehre geben — *to have the honor of inviting*.

Wir geben uns die Ehre, Sie zu unserem Julfest einzuladen. *We have the honor of inviting you to our Yuletide celebration*.

ehrenamtlich — *honorary; voluntary*.

Viele ehrenamtliche Mitarbeiter helfen uns, die Armen zu ernähren. *Many volunteer co-workers help us to feed the poor*.

---

das Ei — *egg*

das Ei des Kolumbus — *simple, obvious solution*.

Zuerst lehnten sie seine Erfindung ab, aber später sahen sie ein, dass sie das Ei des Kolumbus war. *At first they rejected his invention, but later they realized that it was the obvious solution*.

sich gleichen wie ein Ei dem anderen — *to be as alike as two peas in a pod*.

Sie gleichen sich wie ein Ei dem anderen. *They are as alike as two peas in a pod*.

sich um ungelegte Eier kümmern — *to worry in advance*.

Kümmere dich nicht um ungelegte Eier. *Don't cross that bridge before you come to it*.

wie aus dem Ei gepellt — *neat as a pin, spick and span, dressed to the nines*.

Warum läuft er heute herum wie aus dem Ei gepellt? *Why's he walking around dressed to the nines today?*

---

die Eile — *haste*

Eile haben — *to be urgent*.

Die Sache hat Eile. *The matter is urgent*.

---

eilen — *to hasten*

Eile mit Weile. *Make haste slowly*.

es eilig haben — *to be in a hurry*.

Sie haben's immer eilig. *They're always in a hurry*.

---

der Eimer — *pail, bucket*

im Eimer sein — *to be down the drain*.

Alles wofür wir jahrelang gearbeitet haben, ist jetzt im Eimer. *Everything we worked for for years is now down the drain.*

---

ein — *one*

ein für allemal — *once and for all.*

Ein für allemal sag ich dir, ich will nichts damit zu tun haben. *Once and for all I'm telling you I want nothing to do with it.*

---

einfallen — *to occur to; think*

Es fiel ihm nichts Neues ein. *He couldn't think of anything new.*

Lass dir so etwas ja nicht einfallen! *Don't even think of doing anything like that!*

---

der Eingang — *entrance*

Eingang finden — *to become established.*

Sie hat im Fernsehen Eingang gefunden. *She's become established in television.*

eingängig — *easily accessible; catchy.*

Sie schrieb die eingängige Musik zu dieser Fernsehwerbung. *She wrote the catchy music to this TV ad.*

eingängig erklären — *to explain simply and clearly.*

Könnten Sie mir das vielleicht eingängiger erklären? *Could you explain that to me more simply and clearly?*

---

eingehen — *to enter*

Elisabeth hoffte, dass Tannhäuser mit ihr in das ewige Reich eingehen würde. *Elisabeth hoped that Tannhäuser would enter the Kingdom of Heaven with her.*

das Risiko eingehen — *to take/run the risk.*

Trotzt genetischer Belastung will sie das Risiko eingehen und das Kind austragen. *Despite genetic defects she wants to take the risk and carry the baby to term.*

---

eingehen — *to arrive*

Der Brief ist bei uns noch nicht eingegangen. *We haven't received the letter yet.*

in die Geschichte eingehen — *to go down in history.*
Der General hoffte, in die Geschichte einzugehen. *The general hoped to go down in history.*

Kompromisse eingehen — *to make compromises.*
Er erklärte sich bereit, Kompromisse einzugehen. *He declared that he was ready to make compromises.*

---

einhaken — *to hook in*
eingehakt — *arm in arm.*
Eingehakt betraten sie den Ballsaal. *Arm in arm they entered the ballroom.*

---

einhergehen — *to walk around; be accompanied by*
Alter geht nicht immer mit Krankheit einher. *Old age isn't always accompanied by illness.*

---

einmal — *once*
auf einmal — *suddenly; at once.*
Auf einmal stand er auf und ging weg. *He suddenly stood up and went away.*

einmal ist keinmal — *trying something once doesn't count.*
Du hast's nur einmal versucht? Einmal ist keinmal. Versuch's doch noch einmal! *You tried it only once? Once isn't enough. Try it again.*

nicht einmal — *not even.*
Er hat nicht geschrieben, nicht einmal angerufen. *He didn't write, didn't even telephone.*

Versuch nicht, alles auf einmal zu tun. *Don't try to do everything at once.*

---

einschlagen — *to bash in*
Und willst du nicht mein Bruder sein, so schlag ich dir den Schädel ein. *If you won't be my buddy I'll bash your head in.*

einen Weg einschlagen — *to take a path.*
Sie dachte an das Gedicht von Frost über den nicht eingeschlagenen Weg. *She thought of the poem by Frost about the road not taken.*

---

einsetzen — *to put in; appoint*

Wir setzten Karpfen in den Teich ein. *We put carp into the pond.*

Sie hat ihn als Testamentsvollstrecker eingesetzt. *She appointed him executor of the will.*

sich einsetzen — *to work for.*

Seit Jahren setzt sie sich für die soziale Gerechtigkeit ein. *For years she's worked for social justice.*

---

einsitzen — *to serve a prison sentence*

Er sitzt für vier Jahre ein. *He's serving a four-year prison sentence.*

---

einstecken — *to put in; plug in*

eine Niederlage einstecken — *to swallow (endure) a defeat.*

Sie hat gesiegt, aber ihre Partei hat eine Niederlage einstecken müssen. *She won, but her party had to swallow a defeat.*

---

das Eisen — *iron*

ein heißes Eisen — *a controversial issue; a hot potato.*

Ein so heißes Eisen will kein Politiker jetzt anfassen. *No politician wants to touch a hot potato like that now.*

Man muss das Eisen schmieden, solange es heiß ist. *You've got to strike while the iron is hot.*

zum alten Eisen zählen — *to write off as too old.*

Er fühlte sich noch stark, und wollte sich nicht zum alten Eisen zählen lassen. *He still felt strong and didn't want to be written off as too old.*

---

die Eisenbahn — *railroad*

(die) höchste Eisenbahn sein — *to be high time.*

Es ist die höchste Eisenbahn, dass wir nach Hause fahren. *It's high time for us to go home.*

---

der Elefant — *elephant*

sich wie ein Elefant im Porzellanladen benehmen — *to behave like a bull in a china shop.*

Ich weiß, er ist noch jung, aber er braucht sich nicht wie ein Elefant im Porzellanladen zu benehmen. *I know he's still young, but he doesn't have to behave like a bull in a china shop.*

der Ellbogen — *elbow*

seine Ellbogen gebrauchen — *to elbow one's way; to be pushy.*

Richard weiß, seine Ellbogen zu gebrauchen. *Richard knows how to be pushy.*

keine Ellbogen haben — *to lack drive.*

Robert ist intelligenter, aber er hat keine Ellbogen. *Robert is more intelligent, but he lacks drive.*

---

die Eltern — *parents*

nicht von schlechten Eltern sein — *to be not bad at all.*

Obwohl sie nicht gewonnen hat, war ihr Sprung nicht von schlechten Eltern. *Although she didn't win, her jump wasn't bad at all.*

---

der Empfang — *receipt; reception*

in Empfang nehmen — *to accept.*

Voll Freude nahm sie den Preis in Empfang. *Full of joy, she accepted the prize.*

---

das Ende — *end*

am Ende — *at the end; after all's said and done.*

Am Ende musste er's doch machen. *After all was said and done he had to do it anyway.*

am Ende sein — *to be exhausted.*

Nach dem Rennen war ich am Ende. *After the race I was exhausted.*

am falschen/richtigen Ende anfassen — *to go about in the wrong/right way.*

Er hat die Sache am falschen Ende angefasst. *He went about the matter in the wrong way.*

das bessere Ende haben — *to win, come out ahead.*

Unsere Mannschaft hat endlich das bessere Ende gehabt. *Our team finally won.*

das dicke Ende — *The worst is yet to come; the time when the piper will have to be paid.*

Später kommt das dicke Ende noch. *Later the piper will have to be paid.*

das Ende vom Lied — *the (unpleasant) end of the story.*

Das Ende vom Lied war dann, dass sie ihn sitzen ließ. *The end of the story was that she then jilted him.*

ein Ende machen — *to put an end to; stop.*

Mit ihrem Zeit- und Geldverschwenden muss ein Ende gemacht werden. *Their waste of time and money must be stopped.*

Ende gut, alles gut. *All's well that ends well.*

kein Ende nehmen — *to not come to an end.*

Der Film schien kein Ende nehmen zu wollen. *It seemed the movie would never (come to an) end.*

letzten Endes — *finally; after all.*

Letzten Endes ist er doch auch ein Mensch. *After all, he's a human being too.*

zu Ende führen — *to complete.*

Hat sie das Projekt zu Ende geführt? *Did she complete the project?*

---

die Entwicklung — *development*

in der Entwicklung sein — *to be an adolescent.*

Er ist noch in der Entwicklung. *He's still an adolescent.*

das Entwicklungsland — *developing country.*

Die Regierung plant, mehr Entwicklungshelfer in die Entwicklungsländer zu schicken. *The government plans to send more volunteer workers to the developing countries.*

---

der Erfolg — *success*

Erfolg haben — *to be successful.*

T. Williams letzte Stücke hatten keinen Erfolg. *T. Williams's last plays weren't successful.*

der Erfolg hat viele Väter. *Nothing succeeds like success.*

Viele wollten das Telefon, das Auto, die Glühbirne erfunden haben. Der Erfolg hat viele Väter. *Many claimed to have invented the telephone, the automobile, the light bulb. Nothing succeeds like success.*

---

sich erfreuen — *to enjoy oneself*
  sich großer Beliebtheit erfreuen — *to be popular.*
  Die Schauspielerin erfreut sich noch großer Beliebtheit. *The actress is still very popular.*

---

ernähren — *to feed*
  Wird das Kind mit der Flasche ernährt? *Is the child being bottlefed?*

  seinen Mann ernähren — *to make a good living.*
  Ihr Geschäft geht gut und ernährt seinen Mann. *Their business is doing well and making them a good living.*

  sich ernähren — *to live on; to eat.*
  Sie ernährt sich nur von Biokost. *She eats only organically grown foods.*

---

der Ernst — *seriousness*
  Ist das Ihr Ernst? *Do you really mean that?*

  der Ernst des Lebens — *the serious side of life.*
  Für die Kinder beginnt bald genug der Ernst des Lebens. *The serious side of life will begin soon enough for the children.*

  tierischer Ernst — *deadly seriousness.*
  Von seinem tierischen Ernst habe ich genug. *I've had enough of his deadly seriousness.*

---

erst — *first*
  fürs Erste — *for the present.*
  Die neue Chefin sagte, sie wolle fürs Erste nichts ändern. *The new boss said she didn't want to change anything for the present.*

  zum Ersten, zum Zweiten, zum Dritten. *Going once, going twice, sold!* (auction).
  Ich wollte mehr für das Gemälde bieten, aber der Versteigerer hatte schon "Zum ersten, zum Zweiten, zum Dritten" ausgerufen. *I wanted to bid more for the painting, but the auctioneer had already announced, "Going once, going twice, sold!"*

---

das Erstaunen — *amazement*
  in Erstaunen setzen — *to amaze.*

Das plötzliche Erscheinen des Engels setzte uns in Erstaunen. *The angel's sudden appearance amazed us.*

der Esel — *donkey*

Wenn man den Esel nennt, kommt er gerennt. *Speak of the devil and there he is.*

den Sack schlagen, und den Esel meinen — *to accuse an (innocent) subordinate because one is afraid to go after the boss.*
Sie beschuldigten den Sekretär, nicht den Präsidenten—man schlägt den Sack, meint aber den Esel. *They accused the secretary not the president—it's the little fellow who always gets it.*

die Eselei — *a stupid, foolish thing.*
Das war aber eine Eselei! *That was a stupid thing to do!*

die Eselsbrücke — *mnemonic device.*
Trotz der Eselsbrücken vergaß er alles. *Despite the mnemonic devices, he forgot everything.*

der Eskimo — *eskimo*

Das haut den stärksten Eskimo vom Schlitten! *That's too much for anybody!*

essen — *to eat*

zu Abend essen/Abendbrot essen — *to have dinner/supper.*
Ich möchte mit dir zu Abend essen. *I'd like to have dinner with you.*

zu Mittag essen — *to eat lunch.*
Wo sollen wir zu Mittag essen? *Where shall we have lunch?*

die Eule — *owl*

Eulen nach Athen tragen — *to carry coals to Newcastle.*
Da sein Onkel Winzer ist, hieße es Eulen nach Athen tragen, ihm eine Flasche Wein zu schenken. *Since his uncle's a vintner, it would be like carrying coals to Newcastle to give him a bottle of wine.*

die Eulenspiegelei — *practical joke; tomfoolery.*
Seine Eulenspiegeleien waren nicht immer harmlos. *His practical jokes weren't always harmless.*

F

das Fach — *subject; trade*

vom Fach sein — *to be a professional, an expert.*

Wir sind nicht vom Fach aber wir wissen, was wir wollen. *We're not experts, but we know what we want.*

das Fachchinesisch — *technical jargon; mumbo-jumbo, gobbledygook.*

Hast du was vom Fachchinesisch der Rechtsanwälte verstanden? *Do you catch any of the lawyers' legalese?*

fachsimpeln — *to talk shop.*

Wenn ihr weiter so fachsimpelt, hau ich ab. *If you persist in talking shop, I'm taking off.*

in der Fachwelt — *among experts.*

In der Fachwelt wird sie sehr hochgeschätzt. *She's very highly thought of among experts.*

---

der Faden — *thread*

alle Fäden fest in der Hand halten — *to keep a tight rein on.*

Die Chefin hält alle Fäden fest in der Hand. *The boss keeps a tight rein on everything.*

Fäden spinnen — *to weave a web of intrigue.*

Iago wurde nie müde, seine Fäden zu spinnen. *Iago never tired of weaving his web of intrigues.*

keinen trockenen Faden mehr am Leib haben — *to be soaked to the skin.*

Es goss in Strömen und ich hatte keinen trockenen Faden mehr am Leibe. *It was pouring rain and I was soaked to the skin.*

---

die Fahne — *flag*

eine Fahne haben — *to reek of alcohol.*

Obwohl er eine Fahne hatte, beteuerte er, nicht betrunken zu sein. *Although he reeked of alcohol, he insisted that he wasn't drunk.*

sich auf die Fahnen schreiben — *to espouse; to make part of one's platform, program.*

Nach der Niederlage muss sich die Partei jetzt neue Ideale auf die Fahnen schreiben. *After the defeat, the party must now espouse new ideals.*

fahnenflüchtig werden — *to desert*
Die Soldaten wurden fahnenflüchtig. *The soldiers deserted.*

fahren — *to travel; drive*
Was ist in dich gefahren? Fahr zum Teufel! *What's gotten into you? The devil take you!*

aus der Haut fahren — *to blow one's top.*
Du brauchst nicht gleich aus der Haut zu fahren. *You needn't blow your top right away.*

über den Mund fahren — *interrupt; cut off.*
Die Journalisten fuhren einander dauernd über den Mund. *The journalists kept interrupting each other.*

fallen — *to fall*
Ihre beiden Söhne sind im Krieg gefallen. *Her two sons died in the war.*
Kein einziges Wort ist über unsere Ansprüche gefallen. *Not a single word was said about our claims.*
Manchmal fällt sie in ihren scharmanten Dialekt. *Sometimes she lapses into her charming dialect.*

falsch — *false*
ein falscher Fünfziger (Fuffziger) sein — *to be dishonest; be phony as a three-dollar bill.*
Sie hielt ihre Anwältin für einen falschen Fünfziger. *She thought her lawyer was dishonest.*

Farbe — *color*
Farbe bekennen — *to show one's colors, take a stand.*
Wenn ein Schwarz-Weiß-Denker Farbe bekennen muss, sieht er meistens Rot. *When those who think in black and white are forced to show their true colors, they usually see red.*

das Fass — *barrel*

das Fass zum überlaufen bringen — *to be the last straw.*

Diese Beleidigung brachte das Fass zum überlaufen. *That insult was the last straw.*

dem Fass den Boden ausschlagen — *to take the cake.*

Das schlug dem Fass den Boden aus. *That took the cake.*

ein Fass ohne Boden — *a bottomless pit.*

Noch mehr Geld for das Bauprojekt? Das ist ein Fass ohne Boden. *Still more money for the building project? That's a bottomless pit.*

vom Fass — *from the barrel.*

Er trinkt gerne Bier vom Fass. *He likes draft beer.*

---

die Faust — *fist*

auf eigene Faust — *on one's own initiative.*

Haben Sie es auf eigene Faust unternommen? *Did you undertake it on your own initiative?*

sich ins Fäustchen lachen — *to laugh up one's sleeve.*

Der Schwindler lachte sich ins Fäustchen. *The swindler laughed up his sleeve.*

faustdick — *fist thick.*

Das war eine faustdicke Lüge. *That was a barefaced lie.*

es faustdick hinter den Ohren haben — *to be crafty, sly.*

Sie spielt gern die Unschuld vom Lande, doch hat sie es faustdick hinter den Ohren. *She likes to play the innocent country girl, but she's sly.*

---

die Feder — *feather*

sich mit fremden Federn schmücken — *to take credit for another's work.*

Dieser Dümmling machte einen lächerlichen Versuch, sich mit fremden Federn zu schmücken. *That dummy made a ridiculous attempt to pass that off as his own.*

---

fein — *fine*

das Feinste vom Feinen — *the best of the best.*

Sie ist Feinschmeckerin und isst nur das Feinste vom Feinen. *She is a gourmet and eats only the best of the best.*

sich zu fein sein — *to feel above, think o.s. too good for.*
Der Chef war sich nicht zu fein, mit anzupacken. *The boss didn't feel above lending us a helping hand.*

klein aber fein — *small but good.*
Unser Laden ist klein aber fein. *Our store is small but good.*

vom Feinsten sein — *to exemplify the best.*
Dieser Tempel ist buddhistische Architektur vom Feinsten. *This temple is one of the finest examples of Buddhist architecture.*

---

die Feier — *party; celebration*
Keine Feier ohne Meier. *He never misses a party.*
Man muss die Feste feiern, wie sie fallen. *You've got to make hay while the sun shines.*
Machen wir noch 'ne Flasche auf. Man muss die Feste feiern, wie sie fallen. *Let's open another bottle. There's always a reason to party.*

der Feierabend — *evening time after work; retirement.*

Feierabend machen — *to knock off from work.*
Jetzt mach ich Feierabend und geh nach Hause. *I'm going to knock off from work now and go home.*

die Feierabendbeschäftigung — *leisure time activity.*
Sie widmet sich immer mehr ihren Feierabendbeschäftigungen. *She spends more and more time on leisure time activities.*

---

das Feld — *field*
aus dem Feld schlagen — *to get rid of; to beat out.*
Es ist ihrer Firma gelungen, die Konkurrenz aus dem Felde zu schlagen. *Their firm succeeded in beating out the competition.*

zu Felde ziehen — *to crusade, campaign.*
Er zog zu Felde gegen seine Feinde. *He campaigned against his enemies.*

---

ferner — *furthermore; in addition*
ferner liefen — *also ran.*
Er strengte sich an, um nicht wieder unter: "ferner liefen" eingestuft zu werden. *He made a great effort not to be classified as an also ran again.*

---

fernsehen — *to watch television*

Die Kinder wollten fernsehen. *The children wanted to watch television*.

fertig — *finished*

    fertig machen — *to finish up; to ruin*.

    Dieser Klatschreporter hat schon viele Prominente fertig gemacht. *This gossip columnist has already ruined many prominent people*.

    fertig werden — *to cope/deal with*.

    Verschiedene Religionen halfen ihm, mit seinen inneren Ängsten fertig zu werden. *Various religions helped him to deal with his inner anxieties*.

    völlig fertig sein — *to be thoroughly exhausted*.

    Nach der langen Reise waren wir völlig fertig. *After the long trip, we were thoroughly exhausted*.

fest — *solid; firm*

    fest befreundet sein — *to be close friends; to go steady*.

    Sie sind mit einander fest befreundet. *They're going steady*.

    festfahren — *to get stuck; to be bogged down, stalled*.

    Die festgefahrenen Tarifverhandlungen sollen wieder aufgenommen werden. *The stalled wage negotiations are to be resumed*.

    festsitzen — *to be stranded*.

    Wegen des Streiks sitzen viele Passagiere im Flughafen fest. *Because of the strike, many passengers are stranded at the airport*.

die Festbeleuchtung — *festive lights; all the lights blazing*

Was soll diese Festbeleuchtung? Ich hab keine Elekrizitätsaktien. *Why is this place all lit up? I haven't got any stocks in the electric company*.

das Fett — *fat*

    das Fett abschöpfen — *to skim off the cream*.

    Das Fett hat der Senator für sich abgeschöpft. *The senator skimmed off the cream for himself*.

    sein Fett kriegen — *to get it*.

    Wenn Mutti dich erwischt, wirst du dein Fett kriegen. *If mother catches you, you're going to get it*.

ins Fettnäpfchen treten — *to put one's foot in it/put one's foot in one's mouth*.

Da bist du wieder ins Fettnäpfchen getreten. *There you've gone and put your foot in it again*.

die fetten Jahre — *the good times*.

In den fetten Jahren lebten sie auf großem Fuß. *In the good times they lived in great style*.

fettgedruckt — *in boldface type*.

Er hat nur die fettgedruckten Stellen gelesen. *He just read the passages in boldface*.

---

der Fetzen — *rag, scrap, tatter, shred*

dass die Fetzen fliegen — *like all get out*.

Wir wollen feiern, dass die Fetzen fliegen. *We want to celebrate like mad*.

in Fetzen gehen — *to fall to pieces, to tatter*.

Beim Rave hab ich so viel getanzt, dass mein Kleid fast in Fetzen ging. *I danced so much at the rave that my dress almost fell to pieces*.

---

das Feuer — *fire*

Feuer geben/haben — *to give/have a light*.

Können Sie mir bitte Feuer geben? *Can you give me a light, please?*

Feuer haben — *to be spirited*.

Die Weine und die Pferde der ungarischen Gräfin haben Feuer. *The Hungarian countess' wines and horses are spirited*.

das Feuer vom Himmel holen — *to be very bright*.

Er hat das Feuer vom Himmel nicht geholt. *He's not very bright*.

Feuer und Flamme sein — *to be full of enthusiasm*.

Zuerst war er ganz Feuer und Flamme für die Ideale der Revolution. *At first he was full of enthusiasm for the ideals of the revolution*.

zwischen zwei Feuer geraten — *to get caught in the crossfire of opposing camps*.

Indem sie versuchte, beiden Seiten gerecht zu werden, geriet sie zwischen zwei Feuer. *By trying to be fair to both sides she got caught in the crossfire*.

die Feuerprobe — *acid test.*

Ihre Liebe hat die Feuerprobe der Trennung bestanden. *Their love has passed the acid test of separation.*

---

finden — *to find*

Niemand weiß, was sie an ihm findet. *No one knows what she sees in him.*

sich finden — *to work out all right.*

Später wird sich schon alles finden. *Everything will work out all right later.*

---

der Finger — *finger*

die Finger lassen — *to keep hands off; stay away from.*

Lass die Finger von einer solchen Person! *Stay away from a person like that!*

lange Finger machen — *to steal; to have sticky fingers.*

Jemand unter ihnen hat lange Finger gemacht. *One among them did some stealing.*

Wenn man ihm den kleinen Finger reicht, nimmt er gleich die ganze Hand. *Give him an inch and he'll take a mile.*

fingerfertig — *nimble fingered.*

Nimm dich in acht vor fingerfertigen Taschendieben. *Watch out for nimble-fingered pickpockets.*

---

die Fingersprache — *sign language*

Jane sprach und benutzte gleichzeitig die Fingersprache. *Jane spoke and simultaneously used sign language.*

das Fingerspitzengefühl — *a special feeling for; tact.*

Dafür muss man Fingerspitzengefühl haben. *You have to have a special feeling for that.*

---

der Fisch — *fish*

Kennen Sie den Zungenbrecher: "Fischers Fritz fischt frische Fische, frische Fische fischt Fischers Fritz." *Do you know the tongue-twister: "Fischer's Fritz fishes fresh fish, fresh fish fishes Fischer's Fritz."*

ein dicker/großer Fisch — *crime boss, kingpin, big fish.*
Der Polizei ging ein dicker Fisch ins Netz. *The police caught a big fish in their net.*

faule Fische — *lame excuses.*
Das sind alles nur faule Fische und die nehm ich dir nicht ab. *All that is just lame excuses and I'm not buying them.*

weder Fisch noch Fleisch/weder Fisch noch Vogel. *Neither fish nor fowl.*
Das ist so ein Zwitterding. Weder Fisch noch Fleisch. *That's a kind of hybrid, a crossbreed. Neither fish nor fowl.*

Der Gast ist wie der Fisch, er bleibt nicht lange frisch. *Guests and fish stink after three days.*

---

der Flachs — *flax; kidding*
Ich glaube, er hat nur Flachs gemacht, aber bei ihm weiß man nie. *I think he was just kidding, but you never know with him.*

---

die Flagge — *flag*
Flagge zeigen — *to show one's true colors, take a stand.*
Du musst jetzt Flagge zeigen, Farbe bekennen. *You've got to take a stand now, show your true colors.*

---

die Flasche — *bottle*
die Einwegflasche — *nondeposit (disposable) bottle.*
die Mehrwegflasche — *deposit (returnable, recyclable) bottle.*
Sind diese Ein- oder Mehrwegflaschen? *Are these disposable or returnable bottles?*

---

das Fleisch — *flesh; meat*
sich ins eigene Fleisch schneiden — *to cut off one's nose to spite one's face.*
Er wusste, dass er sich dabei ins eigene Fleisch schnitt, aber er tat es trotzdem. *He knew that he was cutting off his nose to spite his face, but he did it anyway.*

---

der Fleiß — *diligence*

  Ohne Fleiß, keinen Preis. *If you want rewards, you've got to work for them.*

---

die Fliege — *fly*

  Ihn stört die Fliege an der Wand. *Every little thing upsets him.*

  die Fliege/'ne Fliege machen — *to scram, buzz off.*

  Du gehst mir auf den Keks; mach jetzt 'ne Fliege! *You're getting on my nerves; buzz off!*

  zwei Fliegen mit einer Klappe schlagen — *to kill two birds with one stone.*

  Es gelang ihr, zwei Fliegen mit einer Klappe zu schlagen. *She succeeded in killing two birds with one stone.*

  fliegen — *to fly; be fired.*

  "Du musst einlenken oder du fliegst," drohte der Chef. *"You must compromise or you'll be fired," threatened the boss.*

---

die Flinte — *shotgun*

  die Flinte ins Korn werfen — *to throw in the towel.*

  Jetzt ist nicht die Zeit, die Flinte ins Korn zu werfen. *Now is not the time to throw in the towel.*

  vor die Flinte kommen — *to get into one's gun sights; to get one's hands on.*

  Der soll mir nur vor die Flinte kommen! *Just let me get my hands on him!*

---

der Floh — *flea*

  die Flöhe husten (niesen) hören — *to know it all before it happens.*

  Dein Onkel meint immer, die Flöhe husten zu hören. *Your uncle always thinks he knows everything before it happens.*

  jmdm. einen Floh ins Ohr setzen — *to put a bee in someone's bonnet.*

  Ich will aber gar nicht nach Australien auswandern. Wer hat dir diesen Floh ins Ohr gesetzt? *I have no intention of emigrating to Australia. Who put that bee in your bonnet?*

  Angenehmes Flohbeißen! *Good night. Sleep tight. Don't let the bedbugs bite!*

---

flöten — *to flute*
  flöten gehen — *to go down the drain; be wasted*.
  Unsere Pläne gingen flöten. *Our plans went down the drain*.

  Flötentöne beibringen — *to teach a thing or two*.
  Diesem Besserwisser werde ich schon die Flötentöne beibringen. *I'll teach that smart aleck a thing or two*.

---

die Flucht — *flight*
  die Flucht noch vorne greifen/antreten — *to make offense the best defense, make counter-charges; to take the bull by the horns*.
  Der Senator beantwortete keine Frage der Reporter, griff aber die Flucht nach vorne. *The senator answered none of the reporters' questions but made countercharges instead*.

---

der Fluss — *river*
  in Fluss bringen — *to get going*.
  Sie brachte das Gespräch wieder in Fluss. *She got the conversation going again*.

  im Fluss sein — *to be in a state of flux; to be in progress*.
  Die Verhandlungen sind noch im Fluss. *The negotiations are still in progress*.

---

die Folge — *consequence*
  Folge leisten — *to accept*.
  Gerne leiste ich Ihrer Einladung Folge. *I gladly accept your invitation*.

---

der Fön/Föhn — *Alpine wind; electric hair dryer*
  Der Fön ist kaputt. *The hair dryer is broken*.

  fönen — *to blow-dry*.
  Der Umwelt zuliebe fönt sie ihre Haare nicht mehr. *For the sake of the environment she doesn't blow-dry her hair any more*.

---

die Frage — *question*
  außer Frage stehen — *to be certain*.
  Natürlich steht meine Unterstützung außer Frage. *Of course my support is certain*.

in Frage kommen — *to be a possibility.*

Wie kann ein solcher Mensch für einen so hohen Posten in Frage
  kommen? *How can someone like that be a possibility for such a high
  position?*

nicht in Frage kommen — *to be out of the question.*

Keine Bange, seine Ernennung kommt gar nicht in Frage. *Don't worry, his
  appointment is out of the question.*

in Frage stellen — *to cast doubt on.*

Die Journalistin stellte die Glaubwürdigkeit des Senators in Frage. *The
  journalist cast doubt on the senator's credibility.*

eine Frage stellen — *to put (ask) a question.*

Die Priester stellten ihm drei Fragen. *The priests asked him three
  questions.*

gefragt sein — *to be in demand.*

Karten für dieses Stück sind sehr gefragt. *Tickets for this play are much in
  demand.*

überfragt sein — *to be asked too much; to not know the answer.*

Als man mich bat, die Relativitätstheorie zu erklären, da war ich
  überfragt. *They asked too much of me when they asked me to explain
  the theory of relativity.*

sich fragen — *to wonder.*

Ich frage mich, ob er es wirklich so machen sollte. *I wonder if he should
  really do it that way.*

---

frei — *free*

Ist hier noch frei? *Is this seat taken?*

ein Zimmer frei haben — *to have a room available.*

Haben Sie noch ein Doppelzimmer frei? *Do you still have a double room
  available?*

die Freiberufler — *freelance professionals.*

Viele Freiberufler können zu Hause arbeiten. *Many freelance
  professionals can work at home.*

---

das Fressen — *food for animals; grub*
  ein gefundenes Fressen — *a real gift/feeding frenzy.*
  Der letzte Skandal über den Senator war für die Medien ein gefundenes
    Fressen. *The last scandal concerning the senator was a real gift to the
    media.*

  fressen — *to eat (animals); to eat ravenously.*
  Friss, Vogel, oder stirb! *Take it or leave it!/Root hog or die!/Do or die!*
  Wir mussten die schlechten Bedingungen annehmen, friss, Vogel, oder
    stirb! *We had to accept the poor terms, we had no choice.*

Friedrich Wilhelm — *John Hancock (signature)*
  Setz deinen Friedrich Wilhelm hier unten, dann ist alles in Ordnung. *Put
    your John Hancock here and everything will be in order.*

frisch — *fresh*
  auf frischer Tat ertappen — *to catch red-handed.*
  Die Panzerknacker wurden auf frischer Tat ertappt. *The safe crackers
    were caught red-handed.*

---

der Fuchs — *fox*
  wohnen, wo sich die Füchse gute Nacht sagen — *to live in a remote
    area, "the sticks."*
  Wir würden gerne wohnen, wo sich die Füchse gute Nacht sagen. *We'd
    like to live in a remote area.*

---

führen — *to lead*
  ein Gespräch führen — *to carry on a conversation.*
  Sie hatte keine Zeit, ein langes Gespräch mit ihnen zu führen. *She had no
    time to carry on a long conversation with them.*

---

der Führerschein — *driver's license*
  den Führerschein machen — *to learn to drive; take the driving test.*
  Sie hat den Führerschein noch nicht gemacht. *She hasn't learned how to
    drive yet.*

---

fünf — *five*

fünf gerade sein lassen — *to turn a blind eye; bend the rules a little.*

Die Lehrerin ist sehr streng, aber manchmal lässt sie fünf gerade sein. *The teacher is very strict but sometimes she bends the rules a little.*

fünf Minuten vor zwölf — *the eleventh hour; the last minute.*

Es ist fünf Minuten vor zwölf; wir müssen handeln! *It is the eleventh hour; we must act!*

---

funkeln — *to sparkle*

funkelnagelneu — *brand new.*

Das Dorfmuseum ist funkelnagelneu. *The village museum is brand new.*

---

das Fürchten — *fear*

jmdn. das Fürchten lehren — *to put the fear of God into s.o.*

das Fürchten lernen — *to find out what fear really is.*

Wenn die Fusion klappt wird die Konkurrenz das Fürchten lernen. *If the merger comes off, the competition will learn the meaning of fear.*

---

für sich — *alone*

Greta wollte für sich sein. *Greta wanted to be alone.*

---

der Fuß — *foot*

auf freien Fuß setzten — *to set free; release.*

Die Gefangenen wurden auf freien Fuß gesetzt. *The prisoners were released.*

auf großem Fuß leben — *to live in grand style.*

Trotz, oder vielmehr dank ihrer Schulden, leben sie noch auf großem Fuß. *Despite, or rather thanks to their debts, they still live in great style.*

auf Kriegsfuß stehen — *to be on a hostile footing.*

Der Senator steht jetzt mit seinen ehemaligen Freunden auf Kriegsfuß. *The senator is now on a hostile footing with his former friends.*

Fuß fassen — *to gain a foothold; become established; take root.*

In dem Land hat die Demokratie nie richtig Fuß gefasst. *Democracy never really took root in that country.*

---

der Gang — *movement; course; walk*

der Fleischergang/Metzgergang/Schneidergang — *fool's errand.*
Hoffentlich lohnt es sich diesmal; ich will wieder keinen Metzgergang
machen. *I hope it'll be worthwhile this time; I don't want to go on
another fool's errand.*

einen Gang nach Kanossa machen/einen Kanossagang machen — *to
eat humble pie, apologize profusely.*
Ich hatte eigentlich recht, musste aber einen Kanossagang machen.
I really was right; nevertheless I had to eat humble pie.

einen Gang zurückschalten — *to take things easier.*
Der Arzt riet ihm, einen Gang zurückzuschalten. *The doctor advised him
to take things easier.*

Gänge machen — *to do errands.*
Wir haben noch einige Gänge zu machen. *We still have some errands to
do.*

im Gang sein — *to be going on.*
Die Verhandlungen sind noch im Gang. *The negotiations are still going
on.*

in Gang bringen — *to get going; start up.*
Er brachte die Maschine in Gang. *He got the machine going.*

gang und gäbe sein — *to be usual, customary.*
In anderen Ländern sind solche Prüfungen gang und gäbe. *In other
countries such exams are customary.*

---

ganz — *whole(ly)*

ganz und gar — *totally, absolutely.*
Das ist ganz und gar unmöglich. *That's absolutely impossible.*

im Ganzen/im großen Ganzen/im Großen und Ganzen — *on the
whole/by and large/in general.*

Im Großen und Ganzen sind wir damit einverstanden. *In general, we agree*.

Im Ganzen hat sie's gut gemacht. *On the whole she did well*.

---

das Garn — *yarn*
  ein Garn spinnen — *to spin a yarn, tell tales*.
  Abends in der Kneipe spinnt der alte Seemann sein Garn. *Evenings in the tavern the old sailor tells his tales*.

  ins Garn gehen — *to fall into a trap*.
  Die Schwerverbrecher gingen der Polizei ins Garn. *The dangerous criminals fell into the police's trap*.

---

die Gasse — *lane; alley*
  mit dem Hund Gassi gehen — *to take the dog for a walk*.
  Mit dem Hund geh ich gern Gassi. *I like to take the dog for a walk*.

---

der Gaul — *horse, nag*
  Einem geschenkten Gaul schaut man nicht ins Maul. *You don't look a gift horse in the mouth*.

  Auch der beste Gaul strauchelt einmal. *Even the best horse can stumble./We all have our off days*.

---

geben — *to give*
  Einstand geben — *to play one's first match; to celebrate starting a new job*.
  Gestern hat sie Einstand gegeben. *Yesterday she played her first match*.

  es gibt — *there is, there are*.
  Da gibt's nichts, du musst dich wehren. *There is nothing else to do about it; you must defend yourself*.

  sich geben — *to declare*.
  Die Senatorin gab sich mit dem Ergebnis zufrieden. *The senator declared she was satisfied with the result*.

  sich geben — *behave*.
  In diesem Stadtviertel kann sich jeder geben, wie er will. *In this section of the city all can behave as they please*.

von sich geben — *to utter.*

Sie gab einen Seufzer von sich, und vergab ihm wieder. *She uttered a sigh and forgave him again.*

---

das Gebet — *prayer*

sein Gebet verrichten — *to say prayers.*

Mehrmals täglich verrichtete der Brahmane sein Gebet. *Several times a day the Brahmin said his prayers.*

ins Gebet nehmen — *to give a good talking to.*

Er hatte die Absicht, seinen Sohn ins Gebet zu nehmen. *He had the intention of giving his son a good talking to.*

---

der Geburtstag — *birthday*

Geburtstag haben — *to be one's birthday.*

Marlene war bei Johnny, als er Geburtstag hatte; sie wünschte ihm mehrmals alles Gute zum Geburtstag. *Marlene was with Johnny on his birthday; she repeatedly wished him all the best for his birthday.*

---

die Geduld — *patience*

die Geduld reißen — *to run out of patience.*

Ihr riss die Geduld und sie ging nach Hause. *She ran out of patience and went home.*

Geduld bringt Rosen. *Patience brings success.*

Mit Geduld und Spucke fängt man eine Mucke. *With a little patience and ingenuity, you'll (we'll) make it.*

---

das Gefallen — *pleasure*

Gefallen finden — *to find acceptance; to be appreciated.*

Zuerst fand sie nirgends Gefallen mit ihren Gemälden und Skulpturen. *At first her paintings and sculptures weren't appreciated anywhere.*

Gefallen finden an — *to take pleasure in.*

Jetzt finden alle Gefallen an ihren Werken. *Now all take pleasure in her works.*

gefallen — *to be pleasing; like.*

Die ganze Sache gefällt uns nicht. *We don't like the whole affair.*

sich etwas gefallen lassen — *to put up with*.
Seine Überheblichkeit lassen wir uns nicht länger gefallen. *We won't put up with his arrogance any more.*

---

geheim — *secret*
   im Geheimen — *in secret; privately*.
   Im Geheimen freute sie sich darüber. *Privately she was pleased about it.*

   streng geheim — *top secret*.
   Die Sache ist streng geheim. *The matter is top secret.*

   der Geheimtipp — *insider's secret*.
   Dieses Strandhotel ist nicht mehr ein Geheimtipp; jetzt ist es von
      Touristen überrannt. *That seashore hotel isn't an insider's secret
      anymore; it's overrun with tourists now.*

---

gehen — *to go*
   auf ein Konto gehen — *to be credited to an account; to be responsible for*.
   Die Polizei glaubt, auch andere Verbrechen gehen auf sein Konto. *The
      police think he is responsible for other crimes too.*

   nach Kanossa gehen — *to capitulate, give in*.
   "Nach Kanossa gehen wir nicht," sagte der antiklerikale Bismarck. *"We
      won't go to Canossa (give in)," said anticlerical Bismarck.*

   vor die Tür gehen — *to set foot out of the house*.
   Bei dieser Kälte gehen wir nicht vor die Tür. *In this cold we're not setting
      foot out of the house.*

   gehen — *to do*.
   Das geht nicht! *That won't do!*
   Persönlich geht es uns gut, aber finanziell geht es uns schlecht. *Things are
      going well for us personally, but we're doing badly financially.*

   gehen — *to be possible*.
   Ohne ihre Erlaubnis geht's nicht. *It's not possible without her permission.*

   gehen — *to feel*.
   Gestern ging es ihm schlecht; heute geht es ihm besser. *He wasn't feeling
      well yesterday; today he's feeling better.*

   gehen — *to face*.
   Unsere Fenster gehen auf den Hof. *Our windows face the courtyard.*

gehen um — *to be a matter of.*

Es geht um Leben und Tod. *It's a matter of life and death.*

gehen um — *to be at issue, at stake; to be about.*

In den meisten Kriegen geht es mehr um Macht und Ausdehnungslust als um Gerechtigkeit. *Most wars are more about power and expansionism than justice.*

---

die Geige — *violin*

die erste/große Geige spielen — *to play first violin; to call the tune, be the star.*

Bei der Konferenz will der Chef die große Geige spielen. *The boss wants to be the star of the conference.*

Der Himmel hängt voller Geigen — *to be ecstatically happy.*

Sie verliebten sich auf den ersten Blick, und der Himmel hing ihnen voller Geigen. *They fell in love at first sight and were ecstatically happy.*

nach jemands Geige tanzen — *to dance to someone's tune.*

Er will, dass alle nach seiner Geige tanzen. *He wants everyone to dance to his tune.*

---

der Geist — *spirit*

auf den Geist gehen — *to get on one's nerves.*

Mit seinen ewigen Nörgeleien geht er mir auf den Geist. *He gets on my nerves with his constant grumbling.*

von allen guten Geistern verlassen — *to have taken leave of one's senses.*

Die Schauspielerin schien, von allen guten Geistern verlassen zu sein. *The actress seemed to have taken leave of her senses.*

der Geisterfahrer — *s.o. driving in the wrong lane.*

Die Verkehrspolizei verhaftete den Geisterfahrer. *The traffic cops arrested the delinquent driver.*

wie von/durch Geisterhand — *as if by magic/an invisible hand.*

Wie von Geisterhand öffnete sich die Tür. *The door opened as if by magic.*

geistern — *to wander like a ghost, haunt.*

Im Schloss soll's geistern. *They say the castle's haunted.*

---

das Geld — *money*

> **Geld regiert die Welt.** *Money makes the world go round.*
>
> **Geld stinkt nicht.** *Money has no smell.*
>
> **ins Geld gehen** — *to prove costly; to get expensive.*
> Seine Sammelwut geht ins Geld. *His collecting mania is getting expensive.*
>
> **nach Geld stinken** — *to be filthy rich.*
> Offenkundig stinkt er nach Geld. *He's obviously filthy rich.*

die Gelegenheit — *opportunity, possibility*

> **Gelegenheit macht Diebe.** *Opportunity makes the thief. (People will break the law if they think they can get away with it.)*
> Der Senator sagte er sei Opfer der Polizei, die ihn in eine Falle gelockt hätte. Ja, Gelegenheit macht Diebe. *The senator said he was a victim of police entrapment. Even saints aren't strangers to temptation.*

gelingen — *to succeed*

> Es ist ihnen gelungen, die Überlebenden zu bergen. *They succeeded in rescuing the survivors.*
> Mit diesem Roman gelang ihr der große Durchbruch. *This novel was her big breakthrough.*
>
> **nicht gelingen wollen** — *not to work out.*
> Das wollte ihm nicht gelingen. *That just didn't work out for him.*

gelten — *to be essential*

> Es gilt, rasch zu handeln. *It is essential to act quickly.*
>
> **gelten** — *to be meant for.*
> Die Kugel galt dem Gangster, aber sie traf seine Frau. *The bullet was meant for the gangster, but it hit his wife.*
>
> **geltend machen** — *to assert influence/rights.*
> Der Senator versuchte, seinen Einfluss geltend zu machen. *The senator tried to assert his influence.*

genießbar — *edible; potable; bearable*

Nach zwei Wochen in der Wüste waren Essen und Trinken nicht mehr genießbar. *After two weeks in the desert, our food and drink were no longer fit for consumption.*

Der alte Herr ist heute ungenießbar. *The old gentleman is unbearable today.*

nicht zu genießen sein — *to be unbearable.*

Herr Weintraub ist Genussmensch, aber gestern war er gar nicht zu genießen. *Mr. Weintraub is a hedonist, but yesterday he was quite unbearable.*

---

gerade — *straight*

    gerade dabei sein — *to be about to.*

    Ich war gerade dabei, zu Abend zu essen, als das Telefon klingelte. *I was just about to eat dinner when the telephone rang.*

    gerade recht kommen — *to be opportune.*

    Das gefundene Geld kam mir gerade recht. *The money I found was just what I needed.*

    geradeaus — *straight ahead.*

    Immer geradeaus fahren, dann an der dritten Ampel links abbiegen. *Keep on driving straight ahead then turn left at the third traffic light.*

---

geraten — *to get into*

Sie sind in ein Unwetter geraten. *They got caught in a storm.*

    ins Stocken geraten — *to get bogged down.*

    Die Verhandlungen sind ins Stocken geraten. *The negotiations have bogged down.*

    geraten — *to turn out.*

    Ihnen sind die Kinder schlecht geraten. *Their children turned out badly.*

---

das Gerede — *gossip*

    ins Gerede kommen — *to get a bad reputation.*

    Sein Benehmen und sein Unternehmen sind ins Gerede gekommen. *His behavior and his business have gotten a bad reputation.*

---

das Gericht — *court*

das Jüngste Gericht — *the Last Judgment*.

Die Theologen sprachen über den Begriff eines Jüngsten Gerichtes bei verschiedenen Religionen. *The theologians spoke of the concept of a Last Judgment in various religions.*

ins Gericht gehen — *to rebuke; to take to task*.

Die Senatorin ging mit ihren Gegnern besonders scharf ins Gericht. *The senator severely rebuked her opponents.*

vor Gericht stellen — *to put on trial*.

Die Verbrecher sollten vor Gericht gestellt werden. *The criminals were to be put on trial.*

---

gern — *gladly*

Danke für Ihre Hilfe. — Gern geschehen. *Thank you for your help. — You're welcome.*

gern haben — *to be fond of; like*.

Wir haben den Alten trotzdem gern. — *We're fond of the old man anyway.*

Ulla singt gern. — Ja, sie spielt, tanzt, und feiert auch gern. — *Ulla likes to sing. — Yes, she likes to play, dance, and celebrate too.*

---

das Gesicht — *face*

das Gesicht wahren — *to save face*.

Der Senator bemühte sich trotz allem, das Gesicht zu wahren. *The senator tried to save face despite everything.*

ein anderes Gesicht bekommen — *to take on a new character*.

Mit den letzten Enthüllungen hat die Sache ein neues Gesicht bekommen. *With the latest revelations the matter has taken on a new character.*

sein wahres Gesicht zeigen — *to show one's true colors*.

Er geriet unter Druck und zeigte sein wahres Gesicht. *He came under pressure and showed his true colors.*

---

das Gespräch — *conversation*

im Gespräch sein — *to be under discussion, consideration*.

Sie ist als mögliche Kandidatin im Gespräch. *She is under discussion as a possible candidate.*

---

gesund — *healthy*
    gesund und munter — *hale and hearty, alive and kicking.*
    Die ganze Familie ist gesund und munter. *The whole family's in good*
      health and good spirits.

    gesundbeten — *to heal by faith.*
    Der Gesundbeter versucht ihn jetzt gesundzubeten. *Now the faith healer's*
      trying to cure him.

---

die Gewalt — *power; force*
    höhere Gewalt — *an act of God.*
    Gibt es eine höhere Gewalt Klausel in dem Vertrag? *Is there an act of*
      God clause in the contract?

---

gewinnen — *to win*
    "Wie gewonnen, so zerronnen," war die Devise des Fachspielers. *"Easy*
      come, easy go" was the professional gambler's motto.

---

gießen — *to pour*
    in Strömen gießen — *to pour (rain).*
    Heute gießt es wieder in Strömen. *It's pouring again today.*

    sich einen hinter die Binde gießen — *to belt one down.*
    Er stand an der Theke und goss sich einen nach dem anderen hinter die
      Binde. *He stood at the bar and belted down one after another.*

---

das Gift — *poison*
    auf etwas Gift nehmen können — *to be able to bet one's life on.*
    Sie ist unschuldig, darauf kannst du Gift nehmen. *She's innocent; you can*
      bet your life on that.

    Gift und Galle spucken — *to spew venom; to be boiling mad.*
    Er spuckte Gift und Galle, als er die Wahrheit erfuhr. *He was boiling mad*
      when he found out the truth.

---

das Glas — *glass*
    zu tief ins Glas schauen — *to have a few too many.*
    Gestern Abend hat er wieder zu tief ins Glas geschaut. *He had a few too*
      many again last night.

das Glashaus — *glass house; greenhouse.*

Wer im Glashaus sitzt, soll nicht mit Steinen werfen. *People who live in glass houses shouldn't throw stones.*

---

die Glocke — *bell*

etwas an die große Glocke hängen — *to tell the whole world; broadcast.*

Ja, er ist vorbestraft; das brauchst du aber nicht an die große Glocke zu hängen. *Yes, he has a criminal record; but you don't have to broadcast it.*

wissen, was die Glocke geschlagen hat — *to know what's in store for.*

Du weißt, was du getan hast, und was die Glocke geschlagen hat. *You know what you've done and what's in store for you.*

---

das Glück — *luck*

auf gut Glück — *trusting to luck; at random.*

Er wählte eine Farbe auf gut Glück. *He selected a color at random.*

bei den Frauen Glück haben — *to be popular with women.*

Trotz seines hohen Alters hat Herr Bellamy noch Glück bei den Frauen. *Despite his advanced age, Mr. Bellamy is still popular with women.*

ein Glück sein — *to be a lucky/good thing.*

Es war ein Glück, dass wir sie rechtzeitig warnen konnten. *It was a good thing that we could warn them in time.*

Glück haben — *to be lucky.*

In Las Vegas hat er kein Glück gehabt. *He wasn't lucky in Las Vegas.*

Jeder ist seines Glückes Schmied. *Life is what you make it.*

sein Glück machen — *to become successful; make it.*

Sie hoffte, in der Großstadt ihr Glück zu machen. *She hoped to become successful in the big city.*

zum Glück — *luckily, fortunately.*

Zum Glück konnte ich sie noch erreichen. *Fortunately I was still able to reach them.*

glücken — *to succeed.*

Es glückte ihnen, dem Gefängnis zu entfliehen. *They succeeded in escaping from prison.*

glücklich — *happy.*

Die beiden haben die ganze Nacht getanzt und gefeiert—den Glücklichen schlägt keine Stunde. *They danced and celebrated all night—time means nothing when you're happy.*

---

die Gnade — *grace*

das Gnadenbrot geben — *to treat the old charitably.*

Wir lieben unseren alten VW Käfer und geben ihm das Gnadenbrot. *We love our old VW beetle and look after it in its old age.*

der Gnadenstoß — *death blow, finishing stroke, coup de grâce.*

Die Firma kränkelt und die Konkurrenz versucht ihr den Gnadenstoß zu geben. *The firm's in a bad way and the competition is trying to finish it off.*

---

das Gold — *gold*

Es ist nicht alles Gold, was glänzt. *All that glitters is not gold.*

Gold in der Kehle haben — *to have a golden voice.*

Die neue Sopranistin hat Gold in der Kehle. *The new soprano has a golden voice.*

nicht mit Gold aufzuwiegen sein — *to be worth (more than) one's weight in gold.*

Omas Erfahrung und Hilfe sind nicht mit Gold aufzuwiegen. *Grandma's experience and help are worth (more than) their weight in gold.*

die Goldgräberstimmung — *a spirit of unbridled optimism.*

Goldgräberstimmung macht sich unter den Anlegern breit. *A spirit of unbridled optimism is spreading among investors.*

---

das Goldkind — *darling, precious child*

Sie halten ihren Lausbuben für ein Goldkind. *They think their little rascal is a darling.*

---

goldrichtig — *absolutely on the mark*

Sie suchen Erholung und Entspannung? In unserem Hotel wären Sie goldrichtig. *You're looking for rest and relaxation? Our hotel is just the place for you.*

---

die Goldwaage — *gold balance (scale)*
  auf die Goldwaage legen — *to take too literally.*
  Du brauchst nicht alles, was er sagt, auf die Goldwaage zu legen. *You*
  don't have to take everything he says too (so) literally.

---

der Gott — *God*
  Ach du lieber Gott! *Oh my goodness!*

  dem lieben Gott den Tag stehlen — *to laze away the day.*
  Er hält es für Sünde, dem lieben Gott den Tag zu stehlen. *He thinks it a*
  sin to laze away the day.

  den lieben Gott einen guten Mann sein lassen — *to take things as they*
  come; to keep one's cool.
  Während die anderen sich aufregten, ließ er den lieben Gott einen guten
  Mann sein. *While the others got upset, he kept his cool.*

  über Gott und die Welt reden — *to talk about this, that, and everything.*
  Wir redeten über Gott und die Welt. *We talked about this, that, and*
  everything.

  wie Gott in Frankreich leben — *to live in the lap of luxury; to live the*
  life of Riley.
  Vor der Revolution lebten sie, wie Gott in Frankreich. *Before the*
  revolution they lived in the lap of luxury.

---

das Gras — *grass*
  das Gras wachsen hören — *to read too much into things; to be a know-*
  it-all.
  Du hörst wieder das Gras wachsen. *You're reading too much into things*
  again.

  das Gras wachsen lassen — *to let the dust settle.*
  Darüber soll man erst das Gras wachsen lassen. *We should first let the*
  dust settle on that.

  ins Gras beißen — *to bite the dust; to die.*
  Die Soldaten hatten keine Lust, ins Gras zu beißen. *The soldiers had no*
  desire to bite the dust.

---

grau — *gray*
  alles grau in grau sehen — *to take a pessimistic view.*
  Ihr Man sieht alles grau in grau. *Her husband takes a pessimistic view of
    everything.*

---

greifen — *to grip, grasp*
  Sie griff zur Flasche, ihr Bruder zu Drogen. *She turned to the bottle, her
    brother to drugs.*
  Der General griff nach der Macht. *The general tried to seize power.*

  um sich greifen — *to spread.*
  In der Stadt griff die Panik um sich. *Panic spread in the city.*

---

die Grenze — *border, frontier; limit*
  Alles hat seine Grenzen. *Everything has its limits.*

  über die grüne Grenze gehen — *to cross a border illegally.*
  Sie versuchten, über die grüne Grenze zu gehen. *They tried to cross the
    border illegally.*

  grenzüberschreitend — *across borders.*
  Neue grenzüberschreitende Bahnstrecken wurden geöffnet. *New
    international rail lines were opened.*

---

der Griff — *grip*
  im Griff haben — *to have the hang of; to have under control.*
  Die Ärzte sagten, sie hätten die Krankheit im Griff. *The doctors said they
    had the disease under control.*

  in den Griff bekommen — *to get the hang of; to get under control.*
  Es dauerte eine Weile, bevor ich das Gerät in den Griff bekommen
    konnte. *It took a while before I could get the hang of the apparatus.*

---

der Groschen — *coin, penny*
  Bei mir ist jetzt endlich der Groschen gefallen. *I've finally caught on now.*

  der Groschen fällt pfennigweise — *not to understand readily.*
  Du darfst nicht zu viel von ihm erwarten; bei ihm fällt der Groschen nur
    pfennigweise. *You mustn't expect too much from him; he's slow on the
    uptake.*

nicht (ganz) bei Groschen sein — *to be crazy, not to have all one's marbles*.

Onkel Otto ist nicht mehr ganz bei Groschen; wir haben ihn aber doch lieb. *Uncle Otto isn't quite all there anymore, but we're fond of him anyway.*

---

groß — *big*

Groß und Klein — *young and old, children and adults, everyone.*

Ihre Erzählungen sind immer noch bei Groß und Klein beliebt. *Her stories are still universally popular.*

Was ist das schon groß? *Big deal!/So what?*

"Unser Sohn hat wieder einen Preis gewonnen."—"Was ist das schon groß? Er bleibt ein Idiot." *"Our son won a prize again."—"So what? He's still an idiot."*

---

grün — *green*

im grünen Bereich sein — *to be normal, under control; in the safety zone.*

Es ist alles noch im grünen Bereich. *Everything is still normal.*

nicht grün sein — *to dislike.*

Die Nachbarn sind sich nicht grün. *The neighbors dislike each other.*

dasselbe in Grün sein — *to make no real difference.*

Stell den Tisch da oder da drüben, das ist dasselbe in Grün. *Put the table here or there, it makes no real difference.*

---

der Grund — *ground; basis*

auf Grund — *on the basis of.*

Auf Grund der neusten Beobachtungen wurde ihre Theorie bestätigt. *On the basis of the latest observations, her theory was confirmed.*

den Grund legen — *to lay the groundwork.*

Ich sag's ihm schon, aber zuerst muss ich den Grund dazu legen. *I'll tell him, but first I have to lay the groundwork for it.*

einer Sache auf den Grund gehen — *to investigate thoroughly; to get to the bottom of.*

Wir sind der Sache auf den Grund gegangen. *We investigated the matter thoroughly.*

in Grund und Boden — *utterly; totally; thoroughly.*
Er schämte sich in Grund und Boden. *He was thoroughly ashamed.*

gut — *good*
   es gut sein lassen — *to leave it at that.*
   Damit lassen wir's gut sein. *Let's leave it at that.*

   gut sein — *to be fond of.*
   Du weißt, ich bin dir gut. *You know I'm fond of you.*

   gutachten — *to give an expert opinion.*
   Der gutachtende Arzt trat als Zeuge der Anklage auf. *The medical expert appeared as a witness for the prosecution.*

   gutheißen — *to approve of.*
   Gewalttaten können wir nicht gutheißen. *We can't approve of violence.*

H

das Haar — *hair*
   die Haare vom Kopf fressen — *to eat out of house and home.*
   Dein Bruder frisst uns die Haare vom Kopf. *Your brother is eating us out of house and home.*

   ein Haar in der Suppe finden — *to find fault; to quibble.*
   Erstaunlich, dass er diesmal kein Haar in der Suppe fand. *Amazing, he found nothing to quibble about this time.*

   Haare auf den Zähnen haben — *to be a tough customer.*
   Die neue Chefin hat Haare auf den Zähnen. *The new boss is one tough customer.*

   kein gutes Haar lassen — *to pull to pieces; to find nothing commendable in.*
   An unseren Vorschlägen ließ sie kein gutes Haar. *She pulled our suggestions to pieces.*

   kein Haar krümmen — *not to hurt a hair on someone's head.*
   Sie wird dir kein Haar krümmen. *She won't hurt a hair on your head.*

sich in den Haaren liegen — *to bicker, be at odds with.*
Sie liegen sich dauernd in den Haaren. *They're constantly bickering.*

um ein Haar — *by a hair; almost.*
Um ein Haar hätte ihn der Blitz getroffen. *He was almost struck by lightning.*

---

haben — *to have*

es in sich haben — *to be a potent drink; to be difficult, complicated.*
Dein hausgebranntes Elixir hat's in sich! *Your home-brewed elixir is potent!*

es mit etwas haben — *to have problems with.*
Jahrelang hat er geraucht; jetzt hat er es mit der Lunge. *He smoked for years; now he's having trouble with his lungs.*

für etwas zu haben sein — *to be game for; be one's sort of thing.*
Für ein Glas Bier ist er immer zu haben. *He's always game for a glass of beer.*
Für so etwas sind wir nicht zu haben. *Something like that isn't our sort of thing.*

noch zu haben sein — *to be unattached, unmarried.*
Er wollte wissen, ob die Milliardärin noch zu haben war. *He wanted to know whether the billionairess was still unattached.*

wie gehabt — *as before; as it was.*
Sie wollte nicht mehr weitermachen wie gehabt. *She didn't want to continue as before.*

zu haben sein — *to be available.*
Seidenteppiche wie diese sind selten und nur für viel Geld zu haben. *Silk rugs like these are rare and available only for a lot of money.*

---

der Hahn — *rooster*
Danach kräht kein Hahn. *Nobody gives a hoot about that.*

der Hahn im Korb sein — *to be cock of the walk.*
Auf der Fete war der neue Millionär der Hahn im Korb. *At the party the new millionaire was cock of the walk.*

---

der Haken — *hook*

  einen Haken haben — *to have a catch, disadvantage.*

  Der technische Fortschritt hat so manchen Haken. *Technical progress has many a disadvantage.*

  Haken schlagen — *to dart sideways; be evasive.*

  Sie warf dem Präsidenten vor, Haken zu schlagen. *She accused the president of being evasive.*

  mit Haken und Ösen — *with no holds barred.*

  Die Mannschaften spielten mit Haken und Ösen. *The teams played with no holds barred.*

---

halb — *half*

  ein halbes Hemd — *a weakling, half-pint.*

  Alle hielten Kasper für ein halbes Hemd, bis er sie überraschte. *Everyone thought Kasper was a weakling, until he surprised them.*

  halbwegs — *to some extent, more or less; a bit.*

  Vorm Krieg lebten die verschiedenen Völker halbwegs friedlich zusammen. *Before the war the various ethnicities lived more or less peacefully together.*

  Jetzt geht's ihnen halbwegs besser. *They're doing a bit better now.*

---

der Halbstarke — *young hooligan*

  Er begann als Halbstarker; jetzt ist er Schwerverbrecher. *He started as a young hooligan; now he's a dangerous criminal.*

---

der Hals — *neck*

  den Hals nicht voll genug kriegen — *to be greedy.*

  Die Eroberer der Neuen Welt konnten den Hals nicht voll genug kriegen. *The conquerors of the New World were greedy.*

  einen langen Hals (lange Hälse) machen — *to crane one's (their) neck(s).*

  Alle machten lange Hälse, um die Königin zu sehen. *All craned their necks to see the queen.*

  sich auf den Hals laden — *to take on.*

  Sie wollte sich keine neuen Verpflichtungen auf den Hals laden. *She didn't want to take on any new obligations.*

sich Hals über Kopf verlieben — *to fall head over heels in love*.
König Ludwig verliebte sich Hals über Kopf in Lola. *King Ludwig fell head over heels in love with Lola*.

zum Halse heraushängen — *to be sick and tired of*.
Das Treiben der Politiker hing Lola zum Halse raus. *Lola was sick and tired of the doings of the politicians*.

---

halten — *to hold*
    eine Rede halten — *to make/deliver a speech*.
    Die Botschafterin hielt eine Rede vor der Vollversammlung der Vereinten Nationen. *The ambassador delivered a speech to the United Nations General Assembly*.

    halten auf — *to attach importance to; think highly of*.
    Dieser Kritiker hält viel auf moralisierende Stücke. *This critic thinks highly of moralizing plays*.

    halten mit — *to stick to; stay with*.
    "Halten Sie es mit den altbewährten Wahrheiten," riet er. *"Stick to the tried and true verities," he advised*.

    halten von — *to consider; think*.
    Viele hielten aber diesen Kritiker für einen Heuchler. *But many thought that critic was a hypocrite*.

    zum Narren halten — *to make a fool of*.
    Er hat uns lange genug zum Narren gehalten. *He's made a fool of us long enough*.

---

der Hammer — *hammer*
    ein dicker Hammer — *an awful blunder, mistake*.
    Die Lehrerin sammelte die in den Schulaufgaben vorgekommenen dicken Hämmer. *The teacher collected the awful mistakes in her students' homework assignments*.

    ein Hammer sein — *to be staggering (in a positive or negative way)*.
    Das ist ein Hammer! *That's terrific, fantastic! (That's totally outrageous!)*

    einen Hammer haben — *to be around the bend*.
    Dass er noch an Thor glaubt, heisst keineswegs, dass er einen Hammer hat. *The fact that he still believes in Thor doesn't mean that he's around the bend*.

die Hand — *hand*

"Hände hoch, oder wir schießen," riefen die Räuber. *"Hands up or we'll shoot," cried the robbers.*

aus einer Hand — *from one source/supplier.*

Dank den neuen Fusionen können wir jetzt alles aus einer Hand bekommen. *Thanks to the new mergers we can now get everything from one supplier.*

eine grüne Hand haben — *to have a green thumb.*

Seine Frau hat eine grüne Hand. *His wife has a green thumb.*

Hand und Fuß haben — *to make sense, be well grounded.*

Ihre Argumente haben Hand und Fuß. *Her arguments make sense.*

in der Hinterhand haben — *to have in reserve.*

Einige chemische Unternehmen haben bereits umweltfreundlichere Alternativen in der Hinterhand. *Some chemical companies already have more environmentally friendly alternatives in reserve.*

leicht von der Hand gehen — *to have a knack for.*

Das Restaurieren alter Möbel geht ihr leicht von der Hand. *She has a knack for restoring old furniture.*

mit Hand anlegen — *to pitch in.*

Alle wollten mit Hand anlegen. *Everybody wanted to pitch in.*

unter der Hand — *in secret.*

Das verbotene Buch kursierte unter der Hand. *The banned book circulated in secret.*

von der Hand weisen — *to reject out of hand.*

Nicht alle sogenannten Altweibergeschichten sind von der Hand zu weisen. *Not all so-called old wives' tales are to be rejected out of hand.*

von langer Hand vorbereiten — *to plan well in advance.*

Sie hatte die Geburtstagsfeier von langer Hand vorbereitet. *She planned the birthday party well in advance.*

zu Händen von — *to the attention of.*

Ich hab's zu Händen von Frau Meyer geschickt. *I sent it to the attention of Mrs. Meyer.*

zur Hand haben — *to have handy.*

Ich hatte kein Kleingeld zur Hand. *I had no change handy.*

der Handel — *trade, commerce*
  Handel und Wandel — *commercial and social life*.
  Durch den Krieg wurden Handel und Wandel beeinträchtigt. *Because of the war, commercial and social activities were restricted.*

---

handeln — *to trade; to do business*
  Mit ihm lässt sich nicht handeln. *There's no doing business with him.*

  handeln mit — *to deal in*.
  Diese fliegenden Händler handeln mit allem. *These peddlers deal in everything.*

  handeln über; handeln von — *to be about*.
  Worüber handelt der Roman? *What's the novel about?*
  Er handelt von betrogener Liebe. *It's about love betrayed.*

  sich handeln um — *to be a matter of, to concern*.
  Es handelt sich wieder um einen Spionagefall. *It's (a matter of) another case of espionage.*
  Es handelt sich um viel Geld. *Much money is involved.*

---

das Handgelenk — *wrist*
  aus dem Handgelenk — *offhand; off the cuff*.
  Aus dem Handgelenk konnte sie es nicht sagen. *She couldn't say offhand.*

  ein lockeres Handgelenk haben — *to be quick to slap*.
  Bleib ihm vom Leibe; er hat ein lockeres Handgelenk. *Stay away from him; he's slaphappy.*

---

der Handkuss — *kiss on the hand*
  mit Handkuss — *with the greatest pleasure*.
  Weil sie intelligent, kompetent und scharmant ist, stellte man sie mit Handkuss ein. *Because she's intelligent, competent, and charming, they were delighted to hire her.*

---

der Händler — *dealer*
  Einst war er Lebensmittelhändler; jetzt arbeitet er im Supermarkt. *Once he was a grocer; now he works in the supermarket.*

fliegender Händler — *peddler.*
In der Stadt gibt es viele fliegende Händler. *In the city there are many peddlers.*

---

im Handumdrehen — *in no time at all*
Im Handumdrehen war sie wieder da. *She returned in no time at all.*

---

das Handwerk — *craft; trade*
das Handwerk legen — *to put a stop to wrongdoing.*
Die Regierung versucht, der internationalen Müll Mafia das Handwerk zu legen. *The government is trying to put a stop to the activities of the international garbage mafia.*

Handwerk hat einen goldenen Boden. *Learning a trade assures a solid future.*

ins Handwerk pfuschen — *to try to do someone else's job; to mind someone else's business.*
Einige Polizeibeamte klagten, dass Fräulein Marple ihnen ins Handwerk pfuschte. *Some police officials complained that Miss Marple was trying to do their job.*

---

hängen — *to hang*
an etwas hängen — *to be attached to s.t.*
Die Parkwächter hängen an ihren Wäldern mit ihrem Herzblut. *The park rangers are deeply attached to their forests.*

Hans — *Johnny*
Hans im Glück sein — *to be a lucky devil.*
Sein Bruder ist ein richtiger Hans im Glück. *His brother is a real lucky devil.*

Hans Guckindieluft — *a dreamer.*
Sie nannte ihn Hans Guckindieluft und heiratete ihn nicht. *She called him a dreamer and didn't marry him.*

Hansdampf in allen Gassen sein — *to be a Jack of all trades.*
Der Schuster blieb nicht bei seinem Leisten und wurde Hansdampf in allen Gassen. *The cobbler didn't stick to his last and became a Jack of all trades.*

---

der Harnisch — *armor*
  in Harnisch bringen — *to infuriate.*
  Jeden Abend bringen ihn die Nachrichten im Fernsehen in Harnisch.
  Every evening the news on TV infuriates him.

hart — *hard*
  hart auf hart kommen/gehen — *to come down to the crunch/nitty gritty.*
  Wenn es hart auf hart kommt, wird man nicht auf ihn bauen können. *We won't be able to count on him in a tight spot.*

  hart im Nehmen sein — *to be tough, hardy.*
  Das schlechte Wetter machte ihm nichts aus; er ist hart im Nehmen. *The bad weather didn't bother him; he's tough.*

der Hase — *hare*
  ein alter Hase — *an old hand.*
  Lass dir alles von den alten Hasen erklären. *Get the old hands to explain everything to you.*
  Mein Name ist Hase. *I know nothing about the matter and want nothing to do with it. (I'm giving name, rank, and serial number and nothing more.)*

  wissen, wie der Hase läuft — *to know which way the wind is blowing.*
  Jetzt weiß er, wie der Hase läuft. *Now he knows which way the wind is blowing.*

  (nicht ganz) hasenrein sein — *to be suspect, fishy.*
  Sein Verhalten schien uns, nicht ganz hasenrein zu sein. *His behavior seemed suspect to us.*

die Haube — *bonnet*
  unter der Haube sein — *to be married.*
  Er war froh, dass die meisten seiner Töchter unter der Haube waren. *He was glad that most of his daughters were married.*

hauen — *to beat*
  aus dem Anzug hauen — *to knock for a loop.*

Der bloße Anblick hat mich aus dem Anzug gehauen. *The mere sight knocked me for a loop.*

---

der Haufen — *heap, pile*
über den Haufen werden — *to mess/screw up.*
Die letzten Ereignisse haben unsere Pläne über den Haufen geworfen. *The latest events have disrupted our plans.*

---

das Hauruck-Verfahren — *heave-ho/slam dunk approach*
Schwere Umweltprobleme wie diese lassen sich nicht im Hauruck-Verfahren lösen. *A slam-dunk approach won't solve such difficult environmental problems.*

---

das Haus — *house*
auf etwas zu Hause sein — *to be well informed.*
Auch auf diesem Gebiet ist sie zu Hause. *She's well informed in this area too.*

Haus an Haus wohnen — *to live next door.*
Wir wohnen Haus an Haus mit ihnen. *We live right next door to them.*

ins Haus stehen — *to be in store for.*
Du wirst bald erfahren, was dir ins Haus steht. *You'll soon find out what's in store for you.*

nach Hause gehen/fahren — *to go/drive home.*
Sie gingen spät nach Hause. *They went home late.*

von Haus zu Haus — *from all of us to all of you.*
Herzlichste Grüße von Haus zu Haus. *Warmest greetings from all of us to all of you.*

von Haus(e) aus — *originally, really.*
Von Hause aus ist sie Malerin. *She is really a painter.*

zu Hause — *at home.*
Er ist jetzt nicht zu Hause. *He's not home now.*
Dieser Brauch ist in Bayern zu Hause. *This custom comes from Bavaria.*

aus dem Häuschen geraten — *to go wild with excitement.*
Die Menge geriet ganz aus dem Häuschen. *The crowd went wild with excitement.*

---

haushoch — *high as a house*

  haushoch gewinnen — *to win hands down.*

  Sie hat haushoch gewonnen. *She won hands down.*

  haushoch überlegen sein — *to be vastly superior to.*

  Sie war ihren Gegnern haushoch überlegen. *She was vastly superior to her opponents.*

---

die Haut — *skin, hide*

  nicht in jemands Haut stecken mögen — *not to want to be in someone's shoes.*

  Überall sucht ihn die Polizei; ich möchte nicht in seiner Haut stecken. *The police are looking for him everywhere; I wouldn't want to be in his shoes.*

  nicht wohl in seiner Haut sein — *to be existentially ill at ease; to be discontent with one's lot.*

  Bevor sie Priesterin Gaias wurde, war ihr in ihrer Haut nicht wohl. *She was discontent before she became a priestess of Gaia.*

  hautnah — *up close.*

  In dem Tierpark kann man die Tiere hautnah erleben. *One can experience the animals up close in that zoo.*

  Sie tanzten hautnah. *They danced cheek to cheek.*

---

der Hebel — *lever*

  am längeren Hebel sitzen — *to have the upper hand; to have more leverage, clout.*

  Diesmal sitzt er leider am längeren Hebel. *This time, unfortunately, he has the upper hand.*

  alle Hebel in Bewegung setzen — *to do everything possible.*

  Die Bürgermeisterin will alle Hebel in Bewegung setzen, um den Tourismus zu fördern. *The mayor wants to do everything possible to promote tourism.*

---

heben — *to lift*

  einen heben — *to drink alcohol.*

  Dann und wann hebt sie gern einen. *Occasionally she likes to take a drink.*

---

der Heide — *pagan, heathen*

Gläubige, fromme Heiden gibt's heute überall, nicht nur auf der Heide.
There are pious, practicing heathens everywhere today, not just on the heath.

das Heidengeld — *a pile of money.*

Er hatte verteufelt viel Glück und gewann ein Heidengeld. *He was extremely lucky and won a pile.*

der Heidenrespekt — *a healthy respect.*

Sie hat einen Heidenrespekt vor Schlangen. *She has a healthy respect for snakes.*

---

der Hecht — *pike*

der Hecht im Karpfenteich sein — *to be a big fish in a small pond; to be a real live wire.*

In unserem einst friedlichen Büro ist er jetzt der Hecht im Karpfenteich. *He's a real live wire in our formerly peaceful office.*

ein toller Hecht — *an incredible fellow; a hotshot.*

Er glaubt, er sei ein toller Hecht. *He thinks he's a real hotshot.*

---

der Hehler — *receiver of stolen goods; fence*

Der Hehler ist so schlimm wie der Stehler. *The fence is as bad as the thief.*

die Hehlerei — *receiving stolen goods.*

Er machte kein(en) Hehl daraus, dass er wegen Hehlerei schon eingesessen hatte. *He made no secret of having already served a prison sentence for receiving stolen goods.*

---

das Heimchen — *cricket*

das Heimchen am Herd — *submissive little wife; homebody, hausfrau.*

Wenn du dir ein Heimchen am Herd gewünscht hast, dann hättest du eine andere heiraten sollen. *If you wanted a submissive little hausfrau then you should have married somebody else.*

---

der/die Heilige — *saint*

ein sonderbarer Heiliger — *a strange type; a queer fish.*

Der war ein sonderbarer Heiliger. *He was a strange type.*

---

der Heiligenschein — *halo*
mit einem Heiligenschein umgeben — *to be blind to faults.*
Du bist in ihn verliebt, aber du musst ihn nicht mit einem Heiligenschein
umgeben. *You're in love with him, but you mustn't be blind to his faults.*

---

heiligsprechen — *to canonize*
Jahrhunderte nach ihrer Verbrennung wurde die Jungfrau von Orleans
heiliggesprochen. *Centuries after her burning the Maid of Orleans was
canonized.*

---

das Heimspiel — *home game; a sure thing, easy victory*
Das Durchsetzen des neuen Konzepts ist keineswegs ein Heimspiel.
Implementing the new concept is anything but easy.

---

heiß — *hot*
Es wird nie so heiß gegessen wie gekocht. *Food on the plate is never as
hot as food in the pot. (There's more heat than light there. Wait till the
shouting's over.)*
Zuerst nahmen viele den Diktator nicht ernst und sagten: Es wird nie so
heiß gegessen wie gekocht. *At first many thought the dictator would
simmer down and they didn't take him seriously.*

---

der Held — *hero*
kein Held in etwas sein — *to be no great shakes at; not to be very good at.*
Er war kein Held in der Schule. *He was no star pupil.*

---

helfen — *to help*
Da hilft kein Jammer und kein Klagen. *It's no use moaning and
groaning.*
Hilf dir selbst, so hilft dir Gott. *God helps those who help themselves.*
Ihnen ist nicht mehr zu helfen. *They're beyond all help.*
Mit schönen Worten ist uns nicht geholfen. *Pretty words won't do us any
good.*

---

hell — *light*
am hellichten Tag — *in broad daylight.*

Am hellichten Tag wurde das Mordattentat verübt. *The attempted assassination was carried out in broad daylight.*

---

das Hemd — *shirt*

Das Hemd ist näher als der Rock. *Charity begins at home.*

bis aufs Hemd ausziehen — *to fleece.*
Beim Kartenspielen hatten sie ihn bis aufs Hemd ausgezogen. *They really fleeced him playing cards.*

---

der Hengst — *stallion; virile male*

der Schreibtischhengst/Verwaltungshengst — *Nasty bureaucrat (lit. "writing desk/administration stallion").*
Von diesem Schreibtischhengst am grünen Tisch lass ich mir nichts vorsagen. *I'm not going to be dictated to by that nasty bureaucrat.*

der Tastenhengst — *keyboard whiz (computer, piano).*
Kai ist echt ein Tastenhengst auf dem Tastenkasten. *Kai sure knows how to tickle the ivories.*

---

der Herr — *Mr.; master*

aus aller Herren Länder(n) — *from all over.*
"Unsere Gäste kommen aus aller Herren Länder," sagte stolz die Hotelbesitzerin. *"Our guests come from all over," said the hotel owner proudly.*

einer Sache Herr werden — *to get under control.*
Er versucht, seiner Spielleidenschaft Herr zu werden. *He's trying to get his passion for gambling under control.*

in aller Herrgottsfrühe — *at the crack of dawn.*
Wir mussten in aller Herrgottsfrühe aufstehen. *We had to get up at the crack of dawn.*

---

herrschen — *to rule; to be prevalent*
In Regierungskreisen herrscht die Ansicht, dass es zu spät ist. *The prevailing opinion in government circles is that it's too late.*

herrschen — *to be.*
Es herrschte richtiges Kaiserwetter, als wir in Rom ankamen. *The weather was really splendid when we arrived in Rome.*

---

herum — *around*

  herumlungern — *to loaf/hang around.*

  Statt herumzulungern, sollte der Junge lernen, Sport treiben, oder arbeiten. *Instead of loafing around, the boy should study, play sports, or work.*

  sich herumsprechen — *to get around by word of mouth.*

  Es hat sich unter den Studenten schnell herumgesprochen, dass die neue Professorin sehr streng ist. *Word got around fast among the students that the new professor is very strict.*

---

herunterfahren — *to drive down*

  Er möchte lieber auf seinem Motorrad herunterfahren. *He'd rather drive down on his motorcycle.*

  herunterfahren — *to play down, to deescalate.*

  Man muss versuchen, den Konflikt herunterzufahren. *One must try to deescalate the conflict.*

---

sich hervortun — *to distinguish oneself*

  Hermann Hesse hat sich auch als Maler hervorgetan. *Hermann Hesse also distinguished himself as a painter.*

---

das Herz — *heart*

  am Herzen liegen — *to really care about.*

  Jetzt ist sie ein großer Star und will nur Rollen spielen, die ihr am Herzen liegen. *Now that she's a big star, she just wants to play roles she cares about.*

  auf Herz und Nieren prüfen — *to give a good going over; to grill.*

  Er wurde vom Senatsausschuss auf Herz und Nieren geprüft. *He was grilled by the Senate committee.*

  das Herz auf dem rechten Fleck haben — *to have one's heart in the right place.*

  Er hilft uns wenig, doch hat er das Herz auf dem rechten Fleck. *He doesn't help us much, but his heart is in the right place.*

  ein Herz und eine Seele sein — *to be inseparable; to be bosom friends*

  Lange Zeit waren sie ein Herz und eine Seele. *For a long time they were inseparable.*

es nicht übers Herz bringen — *not have the heart to*.

Sie konnte es nicht übers Herz bringen, ihm alles zu sagen. *She didn't have the heart to tell him everything*.

etwas auf dem Herzen haben — *to have on one's mind*.

Hast du noch etwas auf dem Herzen, mein Sohn? *Do you still have something on your mind, my son?*

im Grunde seines Herzens — *in one's heart of hearts*.

Im Grunde ihres Herzens wusste sie, dass sie recht hatte. *In her heart of hearts she knew she was right*.

seinem Herzen Luft machen — *to give vent to one's feelings; to tell off*.

Endlich konnte sie ihrem Herzen Luft machen. *At last she could give vent to her feelings*.

Wes das Herz voll ist, des geht ihm der Mund über. *When you're excited about something, you can't help but talk about it constantly*.

---

heute — *today*

heute Morgen — *this morning*.

Heute Morgen können wir nicht. *We can't this morning*.

heute Nacht — *tonight*.

Heute Nacht will ich nicht singen. *I won't sing tonight*.

heute oder morgen — *at any time; at a moment's notice*.

Heute oder morgen kann sich alles ändern. *Everything can change at a moment's notice*.

von heute auf morgen — *very rapidly; on short notice*.

Das geht nicht von heute auf morgen. *That can't be done on such short notice*.

---

das Hickhack — *squabbling, wrangling*

Nach langem Hickhack ist das Abkommen jetzt endlich unter Dach und Fach. *After much wrangling, the agreement is finally all wrapped up*.

---

der Hieb — *blow*

hieb- und stichfest — *cast-iron, airtight*.

Die Staatsanwältin glaubt nicht an sein hieb- und stichfestes Alibi. *The district attorney doesn't believe in his cast-iron alibi*.

---

hinter — *behind*
   hinter her sein — *to pursue.*
   Lange Jahre war Javert hinter ihm her. *Javert pursued him for many years.*

hobeln — *to plane*
   Valentin sang vom Tod, der alle gleichhobelt. *Valentin sang of death,*
   which levels everyone.
   Wo gehobelt wird, da fallen Späne. *You can't make an omelette without*
   breaking eggs.

hoch, höher, höchst — *high, higher, highest*
   hoch hinaus wollen — *to have big ideas/ambitions.*
   Ich liebte sie, aber sie wollte hoch hinaus und heiratete den Millionär.
   I loved her, but she had great ambitions and married the millionaire.

   die höchste Zeit sein — *to be high time.*
   Es ist die höchste Zeit, dass wir uns auf den Weg machen. *It's high time*
   we got started.

   hoch und heilig versprechen — *to promise faithfully, solemnly.*
   Hoch und heilig versprach er ihr, keinen mehr zu heben. *He solemnly*
   promised her not to drink anymore.

   zu hoch sein — *to be beyond.*
   Die Relativitätstheorie ist uns zu hoch. *The theory of relativity is*
   beyond us.

   hohes Alter — *advanced age.*
   Trotz ihres hohen Alters hat unsere Hündin noch Freude am Essen.
   Despite her advanced age, our dog still enjoys eating.

   das Hochhaus — *high-rise.*
   In diesem Viertel gibt es viele Hochhäuser. *There are many high rises in*
   this section.

   hochnäsig — *stuck-up.*
   Das Personal in dem Nobelhotel ist sehr hochnäsig. *The staff in that ritzy*
   hotel is very stuck-up.

   die Hochrechnungen — *electoral projections.*
   Den ersten Hochrechnungen zufolge, wird die Senatorin wieder gewählt
   werden. *According to early projections the senator will be re-elected.*

der Hocker — *stool*

   locker vom Hocker — *free and easy*.

   Es gibt keinen Zwang; du kannst locker vom Hocker mit mir darüber reden. *There's no constraint; you can talk about it freely with me*.

   vom Hocker hauen — *to astound s. o.*

   Das hat uns glatt vom Hocker gehauen, dass sie sich scheiden lassen. *We were flabbergasted to hear they're getting a divorce*.

   vom Hocker locken — *to arouse interest*.

   Mit solch alten Kamellen lockt man keinen heutzutage vom Hocker. *Nobody goes for old chestnuts like that nowadays*.

---

der Hof — *court; courtyard*

   den Hof machen — *to court*.

   Jahrelang machte er ihr den Hof, aber sie heiratete einen anderen. *He courted her for years, but she married someone else*.

---

die Höhe — *height*

   auf der Höhe sein — *to feel great, fit; to be in fine form*.

   Trotz ihres hohen Alters ist Oma geistig und körperlich noch auf der Höhe. *Despite her advanced age, grandma is still in great shape mentally and physically*.

   in die Höhe gehen — *to blow one's top*.

   Der Chef geht gleich in die Höhe, wenn man das Thema berührt. *The boss blows his top when the subject is mentioned*.

   nicht ganz auf der Höhe sein — *to be a bit under the weather*.

   Onkel Otto hat wieder zu viel gefeiert und ist heute nicht ganz auf der Höhe. *Uncle Otto did a little too much celebrating again and is a bit under the weather today*.

---

das Holz — *wood*

   Holz in den Wald tragen — *to carry coals to Newcastle*.

   nicht aus Holz sein — *not to be made of stone; to have feelings*.

   Glaubst du, dass ich aus Holz bin? *Don't you think I have feelings too?*

   die Holzhammermethode — *hard-sell methods*.

   In ihrer eleganten Boutique ist die Holzhammermethode fehl am Platz. *In her elegant boutique hard sell methods are out of place*.

auf dem Holzweg sein — *to be on the wrong track*.
Die Polizei war wieder auf dem Holzweg. *The police were on the wrong
track again.*

der Honig — *honey*

Honig um den Bart (Mund) schmieren — *to flatter, to butter up*.
Alle versuchten, dem Chef Honig um den Bart zu schmieren. *They all
tried to butter up the boss (m).*
Alle versuchten, der Chefin Honig um den Mund zu schmieren. *They all
tried to butter up the boss (f).*

kein Honig(sch)lecken sein — *to be no picnic, no bed of roses*.
Eine so lange Reise mit ihm war kein Honiglecken. *A long trip like that
with him was no picnic.*

strahlen wie ein Honigkuchenpferd — *to grin like a Cheshire cat*.
Da strahlt er wieder wie ein Honigkuchenpferd. *There he is grinning like
a Cheshire cat again.*

der Hopfen — *hops*

Bei (an) ihm ist Hopfen und Malz verloren. *He's worthless, a hopeless
case.*

das Horn — *horn*

ins gleiche Horn stoßen — *to take the same line, sing the same tune*.
Sie gehören nicht derselben Partei an, doch stoßen sie oft ins gleiche
Horn. *They don't belong to the same party, but they often take the
same line.*

sich die Hörner ablaufen — *to sow one's wild oats*.
Er hat sich jetzt genug die Hörner abgelaufen! *He's sown enough wild
oats now!*

das Huhn — *chicken*

das Huhn, das goldene Eier legt, schlachten — *to kill the goose that
lays the golden eggs*.
Nimm dich in acht, das Huhn, das goldene Eier legt, nicht zu schlachten.
Be careful not to kill the goose that lays the golden eggs.

ein Hühnchen zu rupfen haben — *to have a bone to pick.*
Ich habe noch ein Hühnchen mit dir zu rupfen. *I have another bone to pick with you.*

---

das Hühnerauge — *corn (foot)*
jemandem auf die Hühneraugen treten — *to step on someone's toes.*
Pass auf, ihm nicht auf die Hühneraugen zu treten. *Be careful not to step on his toes.*

---

der Hund — *dog*
auf den Hund kommen — *to go to the dogs.*
Er ist auf den Hund gekommen. *He's gone to the dogs.*

bekannt wie ein bunter Hund — *to be a well-known figure.*
Aber einst war er bekannt wie ein bunter Hund. *But once he was a well-known figure.*

Da wird der Hund in der Pfanne verrückt! *That's mindboggling!*

ein dicker Hund — *an incredible, shocking bit of news.*
Das ist ein dicker Hund, dass sie so durchgebrannt ist! *That's incredible, her running off like that!*

mit allen Hunden gehetzt sein — *to know all the tricks.*
Ihre Anwältin ist mit allen Hunden gehetzt. *Her lawyer knows all the tricks.*

vor die Hunde gehen — *to go to the dogs; be ruined.*
Er und sein Geschäft sind vor die Hunde gegangen. *He and his business have gone to the dogs.*

wissen, wo der Hund begraben liegt — *to know the reason behind s. t., to know what's at the bottom/root of a matter.*
Ich weiß, wo der Hund begraben liegt. Seine Tante lässt ihm heimlich Geld zukommen. *I know what's behind that. His aunt's having money sent to him secretly.*

Ach, da liegt der Hund begraben! *So that's the real reason!*

---

hundert — *hundred*
vom Hundertsten ins Tausendste kommen — *to go from one subject to another.*

Nicht alle Studenten schätzen Professoren, die vom Hundertsten ins
Tausendste kommen. *Not all students appreciate professors who go
from one subject to another.*

---

der Hunger — *hunger*

Hunger ist der beste Koch. *Hunger is the best sauce.*

Hunger haben — *to be hungry.*
Habt ihr noch Hunger? *Are you still hungry?*

eine Hungerkur machen — *to go on a fasting diet.*
Er musste abspecken und eine Hungerkur machen. *He had to slim down
and go on a fasting diet.*

---

hüpfen — *to hop*

gehüpft wie gesprungen sein — *to not matter either way.*
Jetzt oder später — das ist gehüpft wie gesprungen. *Now or later, it
doesn't matter either way.*

---

der Hut — *hat*

aus dem Hut machen — *to pull out of a hat; to come up with right away.*
Sie sagte, sie könne die Sache nicht so gleich aus dem Hut machen, und
müsse darüber nachdenken. *She said she couldn't come up with
something right away and would have to think about the matter.*

Das kannst du dir an den Hut stecken! Ich will's nicht. *You can have
that! I don't want it.*

den Hut nehmen müssen — *to have to resign.*
Wegen der Korruptionsskandale mussten einige Senatoren den Hut
nehmen. *Because of corruption scandals some senators had to resign.*

eins auf den Hut kriegen — *to be rebuked; to get a chewing out.*
Er kam spät nach Hause und kriegte eins auf den Hut. *He came home late
and got a chewing out.*

Hut ab! — *Hats off!*
Hut ab vor ihrer Leistung! *Hats off to her accomplishment.*

nichts am Hut haben — *to have nothing to do with.*
Mit Fanatikern jeder Art haben wir nichts am Hut. *We have nothing to do
with fanatics of any kind.*

unter einen Hut bringen — *to reconcile.*
Es gelang der Präsidentin, verschiedene Interessen unter einen Hut zu
bringen. *The president succeeded in reconciling diverse interests.*

die Hut — *keeping, care*
  auf der Hut sein — *to be on guard; be cautious, wary.*
  Die Witwe war auf der Hut vor Schwindlern. *The widow was wary of
  swindlers.*

  in guter Hut sein — *to be in good hands.*
  In der Pension meiner Tante wärst du in guter Hut. *You'd be in good
  hands in my aunt's rooming house.*

die Idee — *idea*
  Das Kleid ist eine Idee zu eng. *The dress is just a little too tight.*

das Inland — *one's own country*
  Im In- und Ausland verkauft sich die Maschine gut. *The machine is
  selling well at home and abroad.*

der I-Punkt; das I-Tüpfelchen — *the dot over the i*
  bis auf den I-Punkt — *down to the last detail.*
  Ich bestehe darauf, dass die Rechnung bis auf den I-Punkt stimmt. *I insist
  that the bill be correct down to the last detail.*

  bis auf das letzte I-Tüpfelchen — *down to the smallest detail.*
  Nicht alle Beamten sind bis auf das I-Tüpfelchen genau. *Not all officials
  are precise down to the smallest detail.*

  der I-Tüpfel-Reiter — *stickler for detail, nitpicker.*
  Ja, aber der Beamte, mit dem wir zu tun hatten,war ein I-Tüpfel-Reiter.
  Yes, but the official we had to do with was a stickler for detail.

inwendig — *inside*
    in- und auswendig kennen — *to know inside out.*
    Ich glaubte, ihn in- und auswendig zu kennen, aber ich irrte mich.
     I thought I knew him inside out, but I was mistaken.

Ja - *yes*
    sich das Jawort/das Jawort fürs Leben geben — *to get married.*
    Sie haben sich endlich das Jawort gegeben. *They finally got married.*

die Jacke — *jacket*
    sich die Jacke anziehen — *to take something personally.*
    Du hast dir die Jacke gleich angezogen; ich sprach aber ganz im
     Allgemeinen. *You took it personally, but I was only speaking in general*
     terms.

    Wem die Jacke passt, der zieht sie an. *If the shoe fits, wear it.*

    Jacke wie Hose sein — *to make no difference.*
    Ob Sie mit Dollars oder Euros bezahlen, das ist Jacke wie Hose. *Whether*
     you pay with dollars or euros, it makes no difference.

    eine alte Jacke — *old hat.*
    Das wissen wir schon; deine Geschichte ist eine alte Jacke. *We know that*
     already; your story is old hat.

jagen — *to hunt*
    eins jagt das andere — *following in close succession.*
    Zuerst jagte ein Erfolg den anderen. Später aber jagte eine
     Pleite/Katastrophe die andere. Jetzt jagt ein Unglück das andere.
     At first, it was one success after another. But later one bankruptcy/
     catastrophe followed hard on the heels of the other. It's one misfortune
     after another now.

    ins Bockshorn jagen — *to intimidate.*
    Lassen Sie sich von ihm nicht ins Bockshorn jagen! *Don't let him*
     intimidate you.

mit etwas jagen — *to detest.*

Mit Rock-Pop Musik kann man ihn jagen. *He detests Rock-Pop music.*

das Jahr — year

in die Jahre kommen — *to get older; to get to an age.*

Wir kommen jetzt in die Jahre, wo wir lieber zu Hause bleiben. *We're now getting to an age when we prefer to stay at home.*

in jungen Jahren — *at an early age.*

Das haben wir schon in jungen Jahren gelernt. *We already learned that at an early age.*

Jahr und Tag — *many years; a year and a day.*

Wir sind seit Jahr und Tag nicht da gewesen. *We haven't been there for many years.*

Jakob — Jacob

der billige Jakob — *thrift shop; the junkman.*

Sie ist millionenschwer, aber ihre Kleider sehen aus, als ob sie vom billigen Jakob kämen. *She's worth millions, but her clothes look like they come from a thrift shop.*

der wahre Jakob — *the right and proper thing; the real McCoy, genuine article.*

Den ganzen Tag nur herumlungern, du musst doch einsehen, das ist nicht der wahre Jakob. *You must realize that loafing around all day isn't the right thing to do.*

Die vermeintliche Rolexuhr, die du vom Straßenhändler gekauft hast, ist nicht der wahre Jakob. *That supposed Rolex you bought from the street peddler isn't the genuine article.*

jobben — to work at a job

Die meisten Studenten auf dieser Uni müssen jobben. *Most students at this university have to get jobs.*

jung — young

Jung getan, alt gewohnt. *Do something early on and it'll be easier to do later.*

junge Hunde regnen — *to rain cats and dogs.*
Als wir ankamen, regnete es junge Hunde. *When we arrived it was raining cats and dogs.*

zum Junge-Hunde-Kriegen — *enough to make you flip out, give you kittens.*
In Las Vegas haben wir nur verloren. Es war zum Junge-Hunde-Kriegen! *All we did was lose in Las Vegas. It was enough to give you kittens!*

der Jux — *joke, lark*
sich einen Jux machen — *to do as a lark, spree.*
Die Jungen wollten in die Großstadt, um sich einen Jux zu machen. *The boys wanted to go to the big city to go on a spree.*

K

der Kaffee — *coffee*
kalter Kaffee — *stale, flat; old hat.*
Alles, was der Vorsitzende sagte, war nur kalter Kaffee. *Everything the chairman said was old hat.*
Kalter Kaffee macht schön. *Drink coffee cold and never look old.*

der Kaiser — *emperor*
das Kaiserwetter — *splendid weather.*
Alle Werktätigen erfreuten sich des Kaiserwetters bei der Gewerkschaftsfeier. *All the workers enjoyed the splendid weather at the union festivity.*

der Kakao — *cocoa*
durch den Kakao ziehen — *to ridicule.*
Der Senator versuchte, seinen Gegner durch den Kakao zu ziehen. *The senator tried to ridicule his opponent.*

kalt — *cold*
auf die kalte Tour; auf kaltem Wege — *with no fuss; without violence.*

Es gelang ihr, alles auf die kalte Tour zu erledigen. *She succeeded in settling everything without any fuss.*

kalt erwischen — *to catch off guard, unprepared.*
Die Hochwasserkatastrophe hat Tausende kalt erwischt. *The flood disaster caught thousands unprepared.*

kaltmachen — *to do in.*
Der Detektiv war nicht der erste, den der Gangster kaltgemacht hatte. *The detective wasn't the first one the gangster had done in.*

---

der Kamm — *comb*
  über einen Kamm scheren — *to lump together.*
Alle Bündnispartner sind nicht über einen Kamm zu scheren. *All the partners in the alliance shouldn't be lumped together.*

---

der Kanal — *canal, channel*
  den Kanal voll haben — *to be plastered; to have had as much as one can take.*
Er hat den Kanal schon voll, aber er will noch mehr. *He's already plastered, but he wants more.*
Die Wähler hatten den Kanal voll von den Versprechungen des Senators. *The voters had as much as they could take of the senator's promises.*

---

die Kandare — *curb (horses)*
  an die Kandare nehmen — *to take a strong line with.*
Der Diktator beschloss, die streikenden Arbeiter an die Kandare zu nehmen. *The dictator decided to take a strong line with the striking workers.*

---

die Kanone — *cannon*
  mit Kanonen auf Spatzen schießen — *to shoot at sparrows with cannons; to overkill.*
Das tun, hieße mit Kanonen auf Spatzen schießen. *To do that would be overkill.*

unter aller Kanone — *very bad(ly).*
Wieder hat die Mannschaft unter aller Kanone gespielt. *The team played very badly again.*

111

die Kante — *edge*
  auf die hohe Kante legen — *to put money by.*
  Du solltest jede Woche etwas auf die hohe Kante legen. *Every week you
    should put a little money by.*

kapern — *to seize a ship; to hook*
  Sie hat endlich den Milliardär gekapert. *She finally hooked the
    multimillionaire.*

  kapern — *to rope into.*
  Sie versuchten, den Geistlichen für ihren Plan zu kapern. *They tried to
    rope the clergyman into their scheme.*

das Kapitel — *chapter*
  Das ist ein anderes Kapitel. *That's another story.*
  Das is ein Kapitel für sich. *That's quite another story.*

kaputt — *broken*
  kaputtmachen — *to break; to ruin, wreck.*
  Das Kind hat ihre Puppe wieder kaputtgemacht. *The child has broken its
    doll again.*
  Die Zwangsarbeit in Sibirien machte ihn kaputt. *Forced labor in Siberia
    left him a wreck.*

  kaputtreden — *to talk to death.*
  Das Thema wurde kaputtgeredet. *The subject was talked to death.*

die Karte — *card*
  alles auf eine Karte setzen — *to stake everything on one chance; to go
    for broke.*
  Der Chef musste alles auf eine Karte setzen. *The boss had to stake
    everything on one chance.*

  auf die falsche Karte setzen — *to back the wrong horse; to choose the
    wrong means.*
  Er hat leider auf die falsche Karte gesetzt. *Unfortunately he backed the
    wrong horse.*

kartenlegen — *to read cards (tarot, etc.)*.
Carmen und die anderen Kartenlegerinnen legten Karten. *Carmen and the other fortune tellers read the cards*.

---

die Kartoffel — *potato*
Rein (rin) in die Kartoffeln, raus aus den Kartoffeln. *First it's "do this," then it's "do that."*

---

die Kasse — *cash box, cash register*
getrennte Kasse machen — *to go Dutch*.
Sie sagte ihm, dass sie nicht mehr getrennte Kasse machen wollte. *She told him she didn't want to go Dutch anymore*.

Kasse machen — *to tally up receipts*.
Die Abteilungsleiterin machte Kasse. *The department head tallied up the receipts*.

Kasse machen — *to make a lot of money*.
Einige wenige deutsche Filme konnten international Kasse machen. *Very few German movies have made a lot of money internationally*.

der Kassenschlager — *box office hit*.
Ihr letzter Film ist ein Kassenschlager. *Her latest movie is a box office hit*.

knapp bei Kasse sein — *to be short of funds*.
Wir sind wieder knapp bei Kasse und können uns das leider nicht leisten. *Unfortunately, we're short of funds again and can't afford that*.

zur Kasse bitten — *to ask to pay for*.
Nach der Katastrophe wurden die Umweltverschmutzer zur Kasse gebeten. *After the catastrophe, the environmental polluters were asked to pay for it*.

---

kassieren — *to collect; to receive money for services*
ganz schön kassieren — *to make a bundle*.
Bei dem Geschäft hat er ganz schön kassiert. *He made a bundle on the deal*.

---

der Kater — *tomcat*

　einen Kater haben — *to have a hangover.*

　Onkel Otto hat oft einen furchtbaren Kater. *Uncle Otto often has a terrible
　　hangover.*

　die Katerstimmung — *gloomy/morning after mood.*

　Nach der Wahlschlappe herrscht Katerstimmung bei uns. *After losing the
　　election we're in a gloomy mood here.*

　der Muskelkater — *sore muscles.*

　Nach den Anstrengungen von gestern hab ich heute ein bisschen
　　Muskelkater. *After yesterday's efforts my muscles are a bit sore today.*

---

die Katze — *cat*

　die Katze aus dem Sack lassen — *to let the cat out of the bag.*

　Du hast wieder die Katze aus dem Sack gelassen. *You let the cat out of the
　　bag again.*

　die Katze im Sack kaufen — *to buy a pig in a poke.*

　Wir wollen keine Katze im Sack kaufen. *We don't want to buy a pig in a
　　poke.*

　Die Katze lässt das Mausen nicht. *A leopard can't change its spots.*

　für die Katz sein — *to be wasted, for nothing.*

　Sie kamen nicht, und unsere ganze Arbeit war für die Katz. *They didn't
　　come, and all our work was for nothing.*

　Wenn die Katze aus dem Haus ist, tanzen die Mäuse auf dem Tisch.
　　When the cat's away, the mice will play.

　ein Katzensprung sein — *to be a stone's throw away.*

　Zu Fuß ist es ziemlich weit, aber mit dem Wagen ist es nur ein
　　Katzensprung. *On foot it's rather far, but with the car it's just a stone's
　　throw away.*

　Katzenwäsche machen. *to wash quickly, superficially, cat lick.*

　Statt sich zu duschen, machte er nur Katzenwäsche. *Instead of taking a
　　shower, he just washed superficially.*

---

der Kauf — *purchase*

　in Kauf nehmen — *to put up with as part of a deal.*

Die Pauschalreise war schön, doch mussten wir einige
Unannehmlichkeiten in Kauf nehmen. *The package tour was nice, but
we had to put up with some things we didn't like.*

der Kavalier — *gentleman; nobleman*
das Kavaliersdelikt — *trivial offense, peccadillo.*
Trunkenheit am Steuer ist kein Kavaliersdelikt. *Drunk driving is no trivial
offense.*

der Keks — *cookie*
auf den Keks gehen — *to get on someone's nerves, to grate.*
Die Fotografen gingen der Schauspielerin auf den Keks. *The
photographers got on the actress's nerves.*

einen weichen Keks haben — *to be soft in the head.*
Sie glauben, du hast einen weichen Keks. *They think you're soft in the
head.*

Kauf dir 'nen Keks! *Go take a walk/hike./Go jump in the lake.*

der Keller — *cellar*
im Keller sein — *to be at rock-bottom/at the bottom of the barrel.*
Die Witschaft ist im Keller und der Beliebtheitsgrad des Präsidenten ist
auch im Keller. *The economy's at rock-bottom and the president's
approval ratings are at rock-bottom too.*

in den Keller fallen/gehen — *to drop drastically.*
Computerpreise sind in den Keller gegangen. *Computer prices have
dropped dramatically.*

das Kind — *child*
das Kind beim rechten Namen nennen — *to call a spade a spade.*
Es war immer ihre Art, das Kind beim rechten Namen zu nennen. *It was
always her style to call a spade a spade.*

das Kind mit dem Bad ausschütten — *to throw out the baby with the
bathwater.*
Er hat voreilig gehandelt und das Kind mit dem Bad ausgeschüttet. *He
acted rashly and threw out the baby with the bathwater.*

das Kind schon schaukeln — *to get things sorted out*.
Trotz aller Schwierigkeiten werden wir das Kind schon schaukeln.
  Despite all difficulties, we'll get things sorted out.

mit Kind und Kegel — *with bag and baggage*.
Sie sind mit Kind und Kegel angekommen. *They have arrived with bag
  and baggage*.

sich lieb Kind machen — *to ingratiate oneself*.
Sie versuchten sofort, sich lieb Kind bei den Siegern zu machen. *They
  immediately tried to ingratiate themselves with the conquerors*.

---

der Kinderschuh — *child's shoe*
  den Kinderschuhen entwachsen sein — *not to be a child any more*.
  Du bist doch den Kinderschuhen entwachsen. *You're really not a child
    anymore*.

  die Kinderschuhe ausziehen — *to grow up*.
  Ich glaube, sie hat jetzt endlich die Kinderschuhe ausgezogen. *I think
    she's really grown up now*.

  in den Kinderschuhen stecken — *to be still in its infancy*.
  Die Mikrotechnik steckt noch in den Kinderschuhen. *Microtechnology is
    still in its infancy*.

---

von Kindesbeinen an — *from earliest childhood*
  Schon von Kindesbeinen an musste Zsupan arbeiten. *From earliest
    childhood Zsupan had to work*.

---

die Kippe — *slag heap*
  auf der Kippe stehen — *to be touch and go*.
  Mit diesem Patienten steht es auf der Kippe. *It's touch and go with this
    patient*.

---

die Kirche — *church*
  Die Kirche hat einen guten Magen. *The church has a great appetite for
    riches, whatever their source*.

  die Kirche im Dorf lassen — *to keep a sense of proportion; not to go
    overboard*.

Ja, er hätte es nicht tun sollen; aber lassen wir doch die Kirche im Dorf.
Yes, he shouldn't have done it; but let's not go overboard.

kein großes Kirchenlicht sein — *to be rather dim-witted.*
Er ist kein großes Kirchenlicht, trotzdem hat er den Posten bekommen.
He's not very bright; nevertheless he got the position.

die Kirchturmpolitik — *narrow, sectarian, local outlook.*
Uns fehlt Weitsicht; mit unserer Kirchturmpolitik erreichen wir wenig. *We
lack vision; we won't get very far with our sectarian behavior.*

---

die Kirsche — *cherry*
Mit dem/der/denen ist nicht gut Kirschen essen. *You'd better not
tangle/mess with him/her/them.*

sich wie reife Kirschen verkaufen — *to sell like hotcakes.*
Die neue Puppe verkauft sich wie reife Kirschen. *The new doll is selling
like hotcakes.*

---

der Klacks — *dollop, blob*
nur ein Klacks sein — *to be easy, a cinch.*
Für die Sportlerin war es nur ein Klacks, da hinaufzuklettern. *For the
athlete, climbing up there was a cinch.*

---

klappen — *to succeed; to go off; to work out*
Es hat alles gut geklappt. *Everything went off smoothly.*

mit etwas klappen — *to work out.*
Auch mit der dritten Ehe hat's nicht geklappt. *The third marriage didn't
work out either.*

---

der Klaps — *smack, slap*
einen Klaps haben — *to be off one's rocker.*
Ich glaube, dein Bruder hat einen Klaps. *I think your brother's off his rocker.*

---

klar — *clear*
bei klarem Verstand sein — *to be in full possession of one's faculties.*
Die Neffen wollten nicht glauben, dass ihr verstorbener Onkel bei klarem
Verstand war. *The nephews wouldn't believe that their deceased uncle
was in full possession of his faculties.*

klar wie Klärchen sein — *to be as plain as the nose on one's face*.
Es ist klar wie Klärchen, dass er in sie verliebt ist. *It's as plain as the nose on your face that he's in love with her.*

klarkommen — *to come to terms with*.
Mit seiner neuen Lage ist er noch nicht klargekommen. *He hasn't yet come to terms with his new situation.*

Klartext reden — *to talk in plain language; to be frank*.
Ich will mit Ihnen Klartext reden. *I'll be frank with you.*

klipp und klar sagen — *to say quite plainly*.
Der Senator hat es nicht klipp und klar, sondern durch die Blume gesagt. *The senator didn't come right out and say so, but he did say it in a roundabout way.*

---

die Klasse — *class*
In ihrem Garten zählt Klasse nicht Masse. *It's quality not quantity that counts in her garden.*

klasse sein — *to be first rate, classy*.
Die Vorstellung war wirklich klasse. *The performance was really first rate.*

---

klatschen — *to gossip; to slap*
Gestern war Kaffeeklatsch bei meiner Tante; dabei gestattet sie das Klatschen nur in Grenzen. *Yesterday my aunt had people over for coffee and a chat (a coffeeklatsch); but she permits gossiping only within limits.*

Beifall klatschen — *to applaud*.
Begeistert haben wir alle der Sopranistin Beifall geklatscht. *We all applauded the soprano enthusiastically.*

---

kleckern — *to make a mess; to mess with trifles*
nicht kleckern, sondern klotzen — *to forget halfway measures and go all out*.
Jetzt heißt es, nicht kleckern, sondern klotzen. *Now it's necessary to go all out and forget halfway measures.*

---

der Klee — *clover*
   über den grünen Klee loben — *to praise to the skies*.
   Er lobte die Aufführung über den grünen Klee. *He praised the performance to the skies*.

die Kleider — *dresses; clothes*
   Kleider machen Leute. *Clothes make the man (persons)*.

klein — *small*
   es kleiner haben — *to have a smaller bill*.
   Fünfhundert Euro! Haben Sie es nicht kleiner? *A five hundred euro note! Don't you have a smaller bill?*

   klein, aber fein — *small but very nice*.
   Der Computer ist klein, aber fein. *The computer is small but very nice*.

   klein, aber mein — *small but mine*.
   Die Wohnung ist klein, aber mein. *The apartment is small, but it's mine*.

   klein beigeben — *to make concessions*.
   In einigen Punkten war die Chefin bereit, klein beizugeben. *The boss was prepared to make concessions on some points*.

   von klein auf — *from childhood on*.
   Von klein auf hat sie nur Traurigkeit gekannt. *From childhood on she has known only sadness*.

   Die Kleinen hängt man; die Großen lässt man laufen. *The small fish get fried; the big ones get off scot free*.

   Wer das Kleine nicht ehrt, ist des Großen nicht wert. *Those who slight small things are not worthy of great ones*.

Kleinkleckersdorf — *any out-of-the-way hamlet*
   Kleinkleckersdorf find ich nicht auf dieser Karte. *I can't find a godforsaken hamlet on this map*.

kleinkriegen — *to intimidate*
   Opa ist nicht kleinzukriegen. *You can't keep grandpa down*.

   sich kleinkriegen lassen — *to let oneself be intimidated*.
   Er lässt sich von niemand kleinkriegen. *He won't let anyone intimidate him*.

kleinschreiben — *to write in small letters; to minimize*

Bei uns wird sein Reichtum kleingeschrieben. *His wealth counts for little with us.*

---

die Klemme — *clip (paper, hair)*

in der Klemme sitzen — *to be in a fix, bind.*

Sie haben alles auf eine Karte gesetzt, und sitzen jetzt in der Klemme. *They put all their eggs in one basket and are now in a fix.*

---

die Klinge — *blade*

die Klingen kreuzen mit — *to cross swords with.*

Der Senator und die Reporterin kreuzten wieder die Klingen. *The senator and the reporter crossed swords again.*

eine scharfe Klinge führen — *to be a formidable opponent in a discussion.*

Die Reporterin führt eine der schärfsten Klingen in der Hauptstadt. *The reporter is one of the most formidable opponents in the capital.*

über die Klinge springen lassen — *to kill; to ruin someone deliberately; to throw out of work.*

Rücksichtslos ließ der Senator seine früheren Kollegen über die Klinge springen. *Ruthlessly the senator ruined his former colleagues.*

Der neue Inhaber ließ die Hälfte der Angestellten über die Klinge springen. *The new owner threw half the employees out of work.*

---

die Klinke — *door handle*

sich die Klinke in die Hand geben — *to come and go without interruption.*

Seitdem er das Grosse Los gezogen hat, geben sich seine Verwandten die Klinke in die Hand. *Ever since he won the lottery his relatives are waiting in line to visit him.*

der Klinkenputzer — *door-to-door salesman; beggar.*

Dagwald Bumstedt kaufte dieses Gerät von einem Klinkenputzer. *Dagwood Bumpstead bought this appliance from a door-to-door salesman.*

der Kloss — *dumpling*
  einen Kloss im Hals haben — *to have a lump in one's throat.*
  Sie sah ihn an und hatte einen Kloss im Hals, als er aus dem Krieg
    zurückkam. *She looked at him and had a lump in her throat when he
    came back from the war.*

---

der Klotz — *block of wood, log*
  auf einen groben Klotz gehört ein grober Keil — *to reply to rudeness
    with (more) rudeness; to fight fire with fire.*
  Auf seine unverschämte Mitteilung werde ich bald gehörig antworten —
    auf einen groben Klotz gehört ein grober Keil. *I'll soon reply
    appropriately to his impertinent communication — you've got to fight
    fire with fire.*

  ein Klotz am Bein sein — *to be a millstone around someone's neck.*
  Sie meinte, sie wäre Filmstar geworden, wenn ihr die Kinder nicht ein
    Klotz am Bein gewesen wären. *She thinks she would have become a
    movie star if her children hadn't been a millstone around her neck.*

---

klug — *clever*
  aus etwas nicht klug werden können — *be unable to make head or tail
    of.*
  Ich hab's mehrmals gelesen, aber daraus kann ich nicht klug werden. *I've
    read it over several times, but I can't make head or tail of it.*

  Der Klügere gibt nach. *Discretion is the better part of valor.*

---

die Kneifzange — *pincers*
  mit der Kneifzange anfassen — *to touch with a ten-foot pole.*
  So etwas möchte ich nicht mit der Kneifzange anfassen. *I don't want to
    touch that with a ten-foot pole.*

---

das Knie — *knee*
  etwas übers Knie brechen — *to push/rush through.*
  Die Präsidentin sah ein, dass sie die Reformen nicht übers Knie brechen
    konnte. *The president realized that she couldn't push through the
    reforms.*

in die Knie gehen — *to cave/give in to.*

Die Regierung weigerte sich, vor den Terroristen in die Knie zu gehen.
The government refused to give in to the terrorists.

---

der Knochen — *bone*

auf die Knochen gehen — *to be backbreakingly difficult.*

Diese Arbeit geht auf die Knochen. Warum muss ich immer die
Knochenarbeit machen? *This work is backbreakingly difficult. Why do I
always have to do the menial jobs?*

bis auf die Knochen — *through and through.*

Es regnete und wir wurden bis auf die Knochen nass. *It rained and we got
wet through and through.*

in den Knochen sitzen/stecken — *to be deeply felt.*

Nach dem Terroranschlag sitzen die Angst und der Schock noch tief in
den Knochen. *After the terrorist attack people are still afraid and in a
profound state of shock.*

die Knochenarbeit — *backbreaking job.*

Für diese Knochenarbeit hab ich nur einen Hungerlohn bekommen. *All I
got for that backbreaking job was a miserable pittance.*

---

der Koch, die Köchin — *cook*

Viele Köche verderben den Brei. *Too many cooks spoil the broth.*

War die Köchin verliebt? *Was the cook in love? (i.e., Did she have her
mind on other things and neglect the food?)*

---

kochen — *to cook*

auch nur mit Wasser kochen — *to be basically the same, to put one's
pants on the same way as everyone else.*

Wir Rockstars kochen auch nur mit Wasser. *We rock stars are really just
like everybody else.*

---

der Komfort — *comfort*

mit allem Komfort und zurück — *with every imaginable luxury.*

Einer der Preise ist ein Aufenthalt in einem Hotel mit allem Komfort und zurück. *One of the prizes is a stay in a hotel with every imaginable luxury.*

---

kommen — *to come*

Wie's kommt, so kommt's. *What will be will be.*

abhanden kommen — *to misplace, lose.*

Mir ist wieder ein Handschuh abhanden gekommen. *I've lost a glove again.*

Erstens kommt es anders, und zweitens als man denkt. *First, expect the unexpected, then expect it to be different from what you thought it might be.*

Mit 30 wollte ich schon Millionär sein, aber im hohen Alter muss ich noch schuften—erstens kommt es anders, und zweitens als man denkt. *I wanted to be a millionaire at 30, but even at my advanced age I still have to slave away—things never turn out as you think.*

im Kommen sein — *to be the latest thing; be on the way up.*

Roboter sind ganz groß im Kommen. *Robots are very much on the way up.*

Der Weinhändler behauptete, australische Weine wären im Kommen. *The wine merchant declared that Australian wines were the latest thing.*

kommen zu — *occur.*

Nur selten kam es zu Aufführungen seiner Musik. *His music was performed only rarely.*

zu Geld kommen — *to get rich.*

Niemand weiß, wie er zu Geld gekommen ist. *No one knows how he got rich.*

---

können — *to be able; to know a language*

Sie kann einige Fremdsprachen. *She knows a few foreign languages.*

nichts dafür können — *not to be able to help it.*

"Ich kann ja nichts dafür, dass ich so schön und stark bin," behauptete unbescheiden der Fußballer. *"I can't help being so handsome and strong," declared the football player immodestly.*

---

das Konto — *account*
  auf jemands Konto gehen — *to be someone's fault.*
  Die Niederlage der Partei geht vor allem aufs Konto des Senators. *The*
    electoral defeat is primarily the senator's fault.

das Kontor — *office; branch office*
  ein Schlag ins Kontor — *an unpleasant surprise.*
  Der Schatzmeister verschwand mit dem Geld—war das aber ein Schlag
    ins Kontor! *The treasurer disappeared with the money—was that ever*
    a shock!

der Kopf — *head*
  Was man nicht im Kopf hat, muss man in den Füßen haben. *What your*
    head forgets means extra fetching for your feet.

  einen dicken Kopf haben — *to have a hangover.*
  Onkel Otto hat wieder einen dicken Kopf. *Uncle Otto has a hangover*
    again.

  Kopf an Kopf — *neck and neck.*
  Der Favorit erreichte das Ziel Kopf an Kopf mit unserem Pferd. *The*
    favorite finished neck and neck with our horse.

  Kopf stehen — *to be in a hubbub, go wild.*
  Nach unserem Fußballsieg stand die ganze Stadt Kopf. *After our soccer*
    win the whole town went wild.

  vor den Kopf stoßen — *to offend.*
  Der Senator will keine Sozialgruppe vor den Kopf stoßen. *The senator*
    doesn't want to offend any social group.

der Korb — *basket*
  einen Korb geben — *to turn down.*
  Grete gab Kai einen Korb und verlobte sich mit Uwe. *Grete turned down*
    Kai and got engaged to Uwe.

das Korn — *seed, grain*
  etwas aufs Korn nehmen — *to take aim at.*

Gemeinsam nahmen Goethe und Schiller die Schwächen der Zeit aufs Korn.
Together, Goethe and Schiller took aim at the weaknesses of their time.

kosten — *to cost*

sich etwas kosten lassen — *to be prepared to pay good money for.*
Einige sind bereit, sich Qualitätsarbeit etwas kosten zu lassen. *Some are
prepared to pay good money for quality work.*

auf seine Kosten kommen — *to get one's money's worth; to be satisfied.*
In Bills Ballhaus kam jeder auf seine Kosten. *In Bill's ballroom everyone
was satisfied.*

koste es, was es wolle — *at any cost.*
Der Milliardär wollte das Gemälde, koste es, was es wolle. *The billionaire
wanted the painting, no matter what the cost.*

die Kraft — *strength*

bei Kräften sein — *to feel fit.*
Onkel Otto war lange im Krankenhaus; aber jetzt ist er wieder bei
Kräften. *Uncle Otto was in the hospital for a long time, but he's feeling
fit again.*

wieder zu Kräften kommen — *to regain one's strength.*
Die Krankenschwestern waren froh, dass Onkel Otto wieder zu Kräften
gekommen war. *The nurses were glad that uncle Otto had regained his
strength.*

der Kragen — *collar*

an den Kragen gehen — *to be threatened, endangered.*
Nicht nur im Regenwald geht es vielen Tier- und Pflanzenarten an den
Kragen. *Not only in the rain forest are there many endangered species
of plants and animals.*

der Kragen platzen — *to be the last straw.*
Mir (ihm, ihr, uns, ihnen) platzte der Kragen! *That was the last straw (for
me, him, her, us, them)!*

jemands Kragenweite sein — *to be someone's cup of tea.*
Die kleine Brünette war genau seine Kragenweite. *The little brunette was
just his cup of tea.*

die Krähe — *crow*
  Eine Krähe hackt der anderen kein Auge aus. *One dog does not eat*
    another. (Colleagues stick up for each other.)

die Kreide — *chalk*
  in der Kreide stehen — *to be in debt.*
  Seine Firma steht tief in der Kreide. *His firm is deep in debt.*

der Kreis — *circle*
  jemandem dreht sich alles im Kreis — *someone is dizzy/tipsy.*
  Schon nach dem ersten Schnaps drehte sich ihm alles im Kreis. *He felt*
    dizzy after just one whisky.

  den Kreis (schon) eckig kriegen — *to iron out a difficult problem,*
    square the circle.
  Sie glauben sie werden den Kreis schon eckig kriegen, aber sie sind wohl
    etwas blauäugig. *They think they're going to be able to solve their*
    thorny problem, but they're probably a bit naïve.

  Kreise ziehen — *to have repercussions, make waves.*
  Die Schmiergeldaffäre zieht immer weitere Kreise. *That bribery scandal*
    is having ever wider repercussions.

das Kreuz — *cross*
  ein Kreuz mit etwas haben — *to have a burden to bear.*
  Mit seinem Geschäft hat er ein Kreuz. *His business is a heavy burden to him.*

  mit jmdm. über Kreuz sein/stehen — *to be at cross purposes/on bad*
    terms with.
  Seit langem steht er mit uns über Kreuz. *He's been on the outs with us for*
    some time.

  zu Kreuze kriechen — *to eat humble pie.*
  Bismarck weigerte sich, zu Kreuze zu kriechen. *Bismarck refused to eat*
    humble pie.

das Kriegsbeil — *hatchet*
  Wir hatten das Kriegsbeil begraben, aber Lisa grub es wieder aus. *We had*
    buried the hatchet but Lisa dug it up again.

der Kriml — *whodunit; crime novel*

Agathe hat zahlreiche Krimis geschrieben. *Agatha has written numerous whodunits.*

---

die Krippe — *crib; feeding trough* (**Futterkrippe**)

an der Krippe sitzen — *to have a cushy job, feed at the trough.*

Alle glauben, ich sitze an der Krippe, aber schuften muss ich. *Everyone thinks I've got a cushy job, but I have to slave away.*

sich an die Krippe drängen — *to jockey for position.*

Die Chefin weiß, dass die Abteilungsleiter sich an die Krippe drängen und amüsiert sich darüber. *The boss knows the department chiefs are jockeying for position and she's amused.*

---

die Krone — *crown*

allem die Krone aufsetzen — *to take the cake.*

Das setzt allem die Krone auf! *That takes the cake! (That beats all!)*

in die Krone steigen — *to go to one's head.*

Der Champagner, nicht der Erfolg, stieg ihr in die Krone. *The champagne, not her success, went to her head.*

---

der Kuckuck — *cuckoo*

zum Kuckuck schicken — *to send away.*

Schick sie alle zum Kuckuck, wir haben keine Zeit. *Send them all away; we have no time.*

sich als Kuckucksei erweisen — *to turn out to be a liability.*

Die Erbschaft erwies sich als Kuckucksei. *The inheritance turned out to be a liability.*

---

die Kuh — *cow*

die Kuh fliegen lassen — *to have a blast.*

Beim Tanz haben wir alle die Kuh fliegen lassen. *We all had a blast at the dance.*

die Kuh vom Eis bringen — *to solve a difficult problem.*

Glauben Sie, dass wir je die Kuh vom Eis bringen werden? *Do you think we'll ever solve this difficult problem?*

der Kuhhandel — *shady horse trading; dirty deal.*

Der Senator verneinte, dass es sich um einen Kuhhandel handelte. *The senator denied that it was a dirty deal.*

auf keine Kuhhaut gehen — *to be beyond belief.*

Die Gräueltaten der Kriegsteilnehmer gehen auf keine Kuhhaut. *The atrocities of the belligerents are beyond belief.*

---

der Kulturbeutel — *shaving/grooming kit*

Sein einziges Gepäck war ein Kulturbeutel und ein Flachmann. *His only baggage was a shaving kit and a hip flask.*

---

die Kunst — *art*

Das ist keine Kunst! *There's nothing to it.*

Was macht die Kunst? *How are things?*

---

der Kurs — *course, rate*

hoch im Kurs stehen — *to be selling at a high price; to have a high opinion of.*

Deutsche Aktien stehen jetzt hoch im Kurs. *German stocks are selling at a high price now.*

Er steht bei ihr hoch im Kurs. *She has a high opinion of him.*

---

kurz — *short*

binnen Kurzem — *in a short time; shortly.*

Binnen Kurzem ist sie wieder da. *She'll be back shortly.*

den Kürzeren ziehen — *to lose; to get the worst of.*

Er machte erneut einen Prozess und zog wieder den Kürzeren. *He sued again and lost again.*

kurz und gut — *in short.*

Ich kann Ihnen keinen Kuchen backen, weil mir Butter, Eier, Mehl fehlen—kurz und gut alles, was zum Backen nötig ist. *I can't bake a cake for you because I haven't got butter, eggs, flour—in short, everything necessary for baking.*

seit Kurzem — *a short time ago.*

Erst seit Kurzem sind wir angekommen. *We arrived just a short time ago.*

Über Kurz oder lang — *sooner or later.*

über Kurz oder lang werden wir's schaffen. *We'll manage it sooner or later.*

vor Kurzem — *a short time ago.*

Bis vor Kurzem hat er bei Siemens gearbeitet. *Until a short time ago he worked for Siemens.*

zu kurz kommen — *not to get one's share.*

Du hast immer Angst, dass du zu kurz kommst. *You're always afraid you won't get your share.*

L

lachen — *to laugh*

Das ich nicht lache! *Don't make me laugh!*

sich einen Ast lachen — *to double over with laughter.*

Bei seinen Geschichten lachten wir uns einen Ast. *We doubled over with laughter listening to his stories.*

Wer zuletzt lacht, lacht am besten. *Who laughs last, laughs best.*

---

der Lack — *varnish*

Der Lack ist ab. *The bloom is off the rose.*

Die Sache hat nicht mehr ihren alten Reiz — der Lack ist ab. *The matter no longer has its old charm. The bloom is off the rose.*

---

laden — *to load*

schief geladen haben — *to be drunk, loaded.*

Gestern Abend hat er wieder schief geladen. *He was loaded again last night.*

---

der Laden — *store*

Der Laden läuft. *Business is good.*

den Laden schmeißen — *to run a very efficient business; to keep things moving smoothly.*

Ich weiß nicht, ob ich weiterhin den Laden ganz allein schmeißen kann.
I don't know if I can continue to run the business efficiently all alone.

Tante-Emma-Laden — *Mom and Pop store.*
Wir würden gern auf dem Land wohnen, und einen Tante-Emma-Laden
aufmachen. *We'd like to live in the country and open a Mom and Pop
store.*

---

der Ladenhüter — *slow seller*
In unserem Winterschlussverkauf versuchen wir, die Ladenhüter
loszuwerden. *In our winter clearance sale we try to get rid of the slow
sellers.*

---

die Lage — *position*
in der Lage sein — *to be able to, be in a position to.*
Tante Erna ist nicht in der Lage, alles im Haus allein zu tun. *Aunt Erna
isn't able to do everything in the house alone.*

---

die Lampe — *lamp*
einen auf die Lampe gießen — *to wet one's whistle.*
Während der Predigt hatte er große Lust, sich einen auf die Lampe zu
gießen. *During the sermon he really felt like wetting his whistle.*

---

lang — *long*
lang und breit — *at great length; in great detail.*
Sie erklärte uns ihren Computer lang und breit; trotzdem verstanden wir
nichts. *She explained her computer to us in great detail, but we still
didn't understand anything.*

---

die Länge — *length*
sich in die Länge ziehen — *to go on and on.*
Der Film über den Hundertjährigen Krieg zog sich in die Länge. *The
movie about the Hundred Years' War went on and on.*

---

die Lanze — *lance*
eine Lanze brechen für — *to go to bat for.*
Er brach eine Lanze für die Ideen seiner Freundin. *He went to bat for his
friend's ideas.*

---

der Lappen — *cloth, rag*
  durch die Lappen gehen — *to slip through one's fingers.*
  Die Terroristen gingen den Soldaten durch die Lappen. *The terrorists slipped through the soldiers' fingers.*

  sich auf die Lappen machen — *to get underway.*
  Du musst dich jetzt auf die Lappen machen. *You've got to get underway now.*

der Lärm — *noise*
  Viel Lärm um nichts. *Much ado about nothing.*

lassen — *to let, allow*
  etwas lassen — *to stop.*
  Lass doch das Rauchen; es schadet nur deiner Gesundheit. *Stop smoking; it's harmful to your health.*

  gut sein lassen — *to let pass.*
  Es stimmt nicht genau, aber wir können's schon gut sein lassen. *It's not exact, but we can let it pass.*

  lassen müssen — *to have to give/grant.*
  Eines muss man ihm lassen—tanzen kann er gut. *You've got to give him that—he dances well.*

  In Ruhe lassen — *to leave alone.*
  Lass mich in Ruhe mit deinen ewigen Schimpfereien. *Leave me alone with your endless complaining.*

  lassen + infinitive — *to have something done.*
  Sie ließ sich ein neues Kleid machen. *She had a new dress made for herself.*

  sich lassen + infinitive — *to be able to be done.*
  Lässt sich das jetzt machen? *Can that be done now?*
  Lassen Sie sich's gut gehen! *Take it easy. Take care of yourself.*
  Das lässt sich leicht sagen. *That's easy to say.*
  Hier lässt es sich leben! *Life is good here.*
  Es lässt sich nicht leugnen, dass er Geld unterschlagen hat. *There's no hiding the fact that he embezzled money.*

die Last — *load, burden*

   zu Lasten gehen — *to charge*.

   Die Versandkosten gehen zu Lasten der Kunden. *Customers must pay the shipping charges*.

   zur Last fallen — *to be troublesome; to inconvenience*.

   Hoffentlich fällt euch unser Besuch nicht zu sehr zur Last. *We hope our visit isn't too much of an inconvenience for you*.

   Ihr fallt uns gar nicht zur Last; wir freuen uns euch zu sehen. *You're not inconveniencing us at all; we're glad to see you*.

---

das Latein — *Latin*

   mit seinem Latein am Ende sein — *not know what more to do*.

   Die Ärzte waren mit ihrem Latein am Ende. *The doctors didn't know what to do any more*.

---

laufen — *to run*

   auf dem Laufenden halten — *to keep informed*.

   Unser Spion hielt uns über die Rüstungspläne auf dem Laufenden. *Our spy kept us informed about armament plans*.

   wie am Schnürchen laufen — *to run like clockwork*.

   Als sie Abteilungsleiterin war, lief alles wie am Schnürchen. *When she was department head, everything ran like clockwork*.

   wie geschmiert laufen — *to run smoothly*.

   Alles lief, wie geschmiert. *Everything ran smoothly*.

---

die Laune — *mood*

   gute/schlechte Laune haben — *to be in a good/bad mood*.

   Er hat heute wieder schlechte Laune. *He's in a bad mood again today*.

   (nicht) bei Laune sein —*(not) to be in a good mood*.

   Wenn sie bei Laune ist, wird's vielleicht klappen. *If she's in a good mood, it may work out*.

---

das Leben — *life*

   am Leben sein — *to be alive*.

   Ihre Großeltern sind noch am Leben. *Her grandparents are still alive*.

auf Leben und Tod kämpfen — *to be engaged in a life-and-death struggle; to fight to the finish.*

In allen seinen Filmen muss er auf Leben und Tod kämpfen. *In all his movies he has to fight to the finish.*

aus dem Leben gegriffen — *realistic, true to life.*

Aus dem Leben gegriffene Filme gefallen Blanche nicht. *Blanche doesn't like realistic movies.*

ins Leben rufen — *to bring into being; to found.*

Sie hat eine neue Zeitschrift ins Leben gerufen. *She founded a new periodical.*

Leben in die Bude bringen — *to liven the place up.*

Wenn Fritz nur hier wäre, würde er ein bisschen Leben in die Bude bringen. *If Fritz were only here, he'd liven up the place a bit.*

---

leben — *to live*

Leben und leben lassen ist sein Motto. *Live and let live is his motto.*

wie die Made im Speck leben — *to live off the fat of the land.*

Sie sind reich geworden und leben jetzt wie die Made im Speck. *They got rich and are now living off the fat of the land.*

---

die Leber — *liver*

frei von der Leber weg reden — *to speak freely, frankly.*

Frei von der Leber weg hab ich ihm meine Meinung gesagt. *I frankly told him my opinion.*

---

die Leberwurst — *liver sausage*

die beleidigte Leberwurst spielen — *to pout, to have a chip on one's shoulder.*

Meine Kritik war wohlwollend, aber jetzt spielt er die beleidigte Leberwurst. *My criticism was well meaning, but now he's pouting.*

---

leer — *empty*

ins Leere gehen — *to fall on deaf ears; come to nothing.*

Meine Vorschläge gingen ins Leere. *My suggestions fell on deaf ears.*

---

der Leib — *body*

am eigenen Leib — *personally.*
Hunger und Vertreibung haben sie am eigenen Leib erfahren. *They've experienced hunger and expulsion personally.*

bei lebendigem Leibe verbrennen — *to burn alive.*
Die Inquisition verbrannte angebliche Ketzer bei lebendigem Leib. *The inquisition burned alleged heretics alive.*

mit Leib und Seele — *dedicated.*
Sie is mit Leib und Seele Lehrerin. *She is a dedicated teacher.*

zu Leib gehen/rücken — *to tackle.*
Die Präsidentin wollte vielen schweren Sozialproblemen zu Leibe rücken. *The president wanted to tackle many severe social problems.*

die Leib- und Magenspeise — *favorite dish.*
Der Professor behauptete, Berliner Buletten wären Zilles Leib- und Magenspeise gewesen. *The professor declared that rissole was Zille's favorite dish.*

das Leibgericht — *favorite dish.*
Er behauptete auch, Wiener Schnitzel wäre Artur Schnitzlers Leibgericht gewesen. *He also claimed that breaded veal cutlet was Artur Schnitzler's favorite dish.*

leiblich — *physical*

Die leibliche und die Adoptivmutter stritten sich um das Kind. *The biological and the adoptive mother quarreled over the child.*

das leibliche Wohl — *food; creature comforts.*
In der Pension unserer Tante wird bestens für das leibliche Wohl gesorgt. *In our aunt's rooming house creature comforts are well provided for.*

die Leiche — *corpse*

eine Leiche im Keller haben — *to have a skeleton in the closet.*
Die Reporterin war sicher, dass der Senator mehr als eine Leiche im Keller hatte. *The reporter was sure the senator had more than one skeleton in the closet.*
Nur über meine Leiche! *Over my dead body!*

über Leichen gehen — *to be utterly ruthless.*

Um ihre Karriere zu fördern, war die Reporterin bereit, über Leichen zu gehen. *To further her career, the reporter was prepared to be utterly ruthless.*

der Leichenschmaus — *funeral banquet, wake.*

Sein Geschäft geht schlecht, aber noch ist es nicht Zeit für einen Leichenschmaus. *His business is doing badly but it's too early to bury it.*

---

leid — *sorry*

es leid sein — *to be tired of.*

Sie war es leid, immer dieselben Vorwürfe zu hören. *She was tired of listening to the same reproaches.*

leidtun — *to be sorry.*

Bei der Prüfung tat es ihr leid, *Die Leiden des Jungen Werther* nicht gelesen zu haben. *At the exam she was sorry she hadn't read* The Sufferings of Young Werther.

---

leiden — *to suffer*

nicht leiden können — *to be unable to stand.*

Deinen Onkel kann ich nicht leiden. *I can't stand your uncle.*

gern/gut leiden können/mögen — *to like.*

Aber deine ganze Verwandschaft kann ich gut leiden. *But I like all your relatives.*

---

der Leim — *glue*

auf den Leim gehen — *to be taken in.*

Fast alle gingen dem Quecksalber auf den Leim. *Almost everyone was taken in by the quack.*

aus dem Leim gehen — *to come unglued.*

Der Stuhl ist wieder aus dem Leim gegangen. *The chair has come unglued again.*

aus dem Leim gehen — *to put on a lot of weight.*

Nach dem Militärdienst ging er aus dem Leim. *After military service he put on a lot of weight.*

---

die Leine — *rope, leash*
  an der Leine halten — *to keep a tight rein on.*
  Der Parteichef versuchte, die Mitglieder an der Leine zu halten. *The leader of the party tried to keep a tight rein on the members.*

  Leine ziehen — *to clear off, beat it.*
  Kurz darauf zog er Leine. *Shortly after that, he cleared off.*

---

leise — *quiet*
  Bei leiser Musik und leisem Regen kochte leise sein Abendessen. *His dinner simmered gently as soft music played and gentle rain fell.*

  leiser stellen — *to turn down.*
  Trotzdem bat ihn sein Nachbar, die Musik leiser zu stellen. *Still, his neighbor asked him to turn down the music.*

---

der Leisten — *shoemaker's last*
  alles über einen Leisten schlagen — *to lump together.*
  Man kann alle ihre Anhänger nicht über einen Leisten schlagen. *You can't lump together all her devotees.*

  bei seinem Leisten bleiben — *to stick to one's trade and not venture into other areas.*
  Hans Sachs dachte an das Sprichwort: "Schuster bleib bei deinem Leisten!" *Hans Sachs thought of the proverb, "Cobbler stick to your last."*
  Dichter, bleib bei deinem Geistesleisten und lass die Politik! *Poet, stay with your spiritual trade and leave politics alone.*

---

leisten — *to work; to accomplish*
  einen Beitrag leisten — *to make a contribution.*
  Unser Verein wollte einen Beitrag zur Völkerverständigung leisten. *Our club wanted to make a contribution to better understanding among peoples.*

  einen Eid leisten — *to swear an oath.*
  Siegfried vergaß, dass er einen Eid geleistet hatte. *Siegfried forgot that he had sworn an oath.*

  sich leisten — *to treat/permit oneself.*
  Herr Weintraub leistet sich jeden Luxus. *Mr. Weintraub permits himself every luxury.*

sich etwas leisten können — *to be able to afford.*
Das alles können wir uns nicht leisten. *We can't afford all that.*

---

die Leitung — *telephone line, connection*
eine lange Leitung haben — *to be slow on the uptake.*
Dein Bruder hat eine lange Leitung. *Your brother is slow on the uptake.*

---

letzt — *last*
bis aufs Letzte; bis zum Letzten — *totally, to the utmost.*
Die Einbrecher hatten die Wohnung bis aufs Letzte ausgeraubt. *The burglars cleaned out the apartment totally.*
Sie verteidigte ihn bis zum Letzten. *She defended him to the utmost.*

bis ins Letzte — *in every detail.*
Wir wollen die Rechnung bis ins Letzte überprüfen. *We want to check the bill in every detail.*

die Letzten Dinge — *death and eternity.*
Die Mystikerin sprach von den Letzten Dingen und möglichen Reinkarnationen. *The mystic spoke of death, eternity, and possible reincarnations.*

in der letzten Zeit — *recently.*
In der letzten Zeit gibt es erneuertes Interesse dafür. *There has been renewed interest in it recently.*

letzten Endes — *in the last analysis.*
Letzten Endes musst du die Verantwortung dafür tragen. *In the last analysis you'll have to take responsibility for it.*

---

das Licht — *light*
Beim Unterrichten ist ihr manches Licht über das Fach aufgegangen. *When teaching, she gained many insights into the subject.*

das Licht der Welt erblicken — *to be born.*
Die jetzige Schlossherrin erblickte das Licht der Welt in einem Berliner Hinterhof. *The present owner of the castle was born in a Berlin tenement.*

hinters Licht führen — *to fool.*
Es gelang dem Verbrecher, die Polizei hinters Licht zu führen. *The criminal succeeded in fooling the police.*

ein Licht aufstecken — *to put wise*.
Ich versuchte, ihm ein Licht aufzustecken. *I tried to put him wise*.

kein großes Licht sein — *not to be very bright*.
Das Kind ist kein großes Licht, aber ich wollte es der Mutter nicht sagen.
   The child isn't very bright, but I didn't want to say that to his mother.

lichten — *to become lighter*.
Das Geheimnis um die gestohlenen Kunstwerke hat sich gelichtet. *The mystery concerning the stolen works of art has been cleared up*.

---

die Liebe — *love*
   aus Liebe — *for love*.
   Das erste Mal hat sie aus Liebe geheiratet. *The first time, she married for love*.

   bei aller Liebe — *despite all sympathy*.
   Bei aller Liebe kann ich ihm nicht mehr helfen. *However much I sympathize, I can't help him anymore*.

   Die Liebe geht durch den Magen. *The way to a man's heart is through his stomach*.

---

das Lied — *song*
   das gleiche Lied singen — *to repeat the same story; to complain constantly*.
   Er wird nie müde, das gleiche Lied zu singen. *He never tires of telling the same story*.

   ein Lied/Liedchen singen können — *to be able to tell a thing or two about*.
   Von solchen Problemen könnte auch ich ein Lied singen. *I, too, could tell you a thing or two about such problems*.

---

liefern — *to deliver*
   einen Beweis liefern — *to prove*.
   Können Sie den Beweis dafür liefern? *Can you prove that?*

   geliefert sein — *to be sunk; to have had it*.
   Wenn es diesmal seine Schulden nicht zahlen kann, dann ist sein Geschäft geliefert. *If he can't pay his debts this time, his business has had it*.

sich Kämpfe liefern — *to engage in armed conflict.*
Sie liefern sich noch erbitterte Kämpfe. *They're still waging fierce battles.*

liegen — *to lie, be situated; to be*
Das alles liegt noch vor uns. *All that is still before us.*

an etwas /jemandem liegen — *to be due to; to be the responsibility of.*
Dass man die Sänger oft kaum hören konnte, liegt vielleicht an der
Straußschen Musik. *The fact that we often could barely hear the
singers, was perhaps due to Strauss's music.*
Es liegt an Ihnen, ob wir hingehen oder nicht. *It's up to you whether we
go or not.*

liegen — *to appeal.*
"Treu sein, das liegt mir nicht," sang der Tenor. *"Staying faithful doesn't
appeal to me," sang the tenor.*

liegen bleiben — *to stay down; remain unsold, be a non-starter.*
Fallen ist menschlich. Liegen bleiben ist teuflisch. *To fall is human. To
stay down is devilish.*
Wir hofften auf Publikumsrenner, aber die meisten Waren sind uns liegen
geblieben. *We hoped for runaway sales, but most of these goods are still
on our hands.*

Lieschen Müller — *the average person*
Das Werk ist zugleich hohe Kunst und für Lieschen Müller zugänglich.
The work is great art and also accessible to the average person.

die Linie — *line*
auf der ganzen Linie — *all along the line; in every respect.*
Sie haben auf der ganzen Linie Fortschritte gemacht. *You've made
progress in every respect.*

in erster/zweiter Linie — *of primary/secondary importance; primarily/
secondarily.*
"In erster Linie interessiert uns seine Gesundheit: sein Geld spielt nur in
zweiter Linie eine Rolle," erklärten die Verwandten. *"We're primarily
interested in his health; his money is only of secondary importance,"
declared the relatives.*

links — *on the left*

Das Geschäft befindet sich in der nächsten Straße, links. *The store is on the next street, on the left.*

etwas links liegenlassen — *to ignore.*

Die Demonstranten schrieen, dass die Gesellschaft sie links liegengelassen hätte. *The demonstrators screamed that society had ignored them.*

mit links — *with the left hand; with no difficulty.*

Das ist nicht schwer; ich könnte es mit links machen. *That isn't hard; I could do it easily.*

---

die Lippe — *lip*

an den Lippen hängen — *to hang on every word.*

Entzückt hingen ihre Anhänger an den Lippen der Prophetin. *Enraptured, her disciples listened to every word the prophetess uttered.*

nicht über die Lippen bringen können — *to be unable to bring oneself to say.*

Sie brachte es nicht über die Lippen, dass sie ihn nicht mehr liebte. *She couldn't bring herself to say that she didn't love him anymore.*

über die Lippen kommen — *to pass one's lips.*

Kein Wort davon soll mir über die Lippen kommen. *Not a word about it will pass my lips.*

---

das Lob — *praise*

Ein Lob dem Küchenchef. *My/our compliments to the chef.*

über alles Lob erhaben — *beyond all praise.*

Die *Lohengrin* Aufführung war über alles Lob erhaben. *The performance of* Lohengrin *was beyond all praise.*

---

loben — *to praise*

Das lob ich mir! *That's really to my liking!*

Als Goethe dort studierte, sagte er: "Mein Leipzig lob ich mir." *When Goethe studied there he said, "Leipzig is a place really to my liking."*

ein Loblied anstimmen — *to sing the praises of; to praise extravagantly.*

Alle Gäste sangen ein Loblied auf ihre Kochkunst. *All the guests sang the praises of her cooking.*

das Loch — *hole*
  auf dem letzten Loch pfeifen — *to be on one's last legs*.
  Geschäftlich pfeifen wir auf dem letzten Loch. *Our business is on its last legs*.

  ein Loch in den Bauch fragen — *to ply/pester with questions*.
  Ihre Kinder fragen sie ein Loch in den Bauch, aber das stört sie nicht. *Her children ply her with questions, but that doesn't bother her*.

  ein Loch in den Bauch reden — *to talk one's head off*.
  Wir vermeiden ihn, weil er uns immer ein Loch in den Bauch redet. *We avoid him because he always talks his head off at us*.

  ein Loch in den Tag schlafen — *to sleep the day away*.
  Statt zu arbeiten, schläft er wieder ein Loch in den Tag. *Instead of working, he's sleeping the day away again*.

  Löcher in die Luft gucken — *to gaze at space*.
  Ich weiß nicht, ob er ein Genie, ein Idiot oder beides ist, aber er guckt oft Löcher in die Luft. *I don't know whether he's a genius, an idiot, or both, but he often gazes into space*.

---

der Lohn — *wages; reward*
  in Lohn und Brot sein — *to be gainfully employed*.
  In den neuen Fabriken stehen jetzt wieder Tausende in Lohn und Brot. *Thousands are now again gainfully employed in the new factories*.

---

sich lohnen — *to be worthwhile*
  Der Film lohnt sich sehr. *The movie is well worth seeing*.

---

das Los — *lot*
  das große Los ziehen — *to win big, hit the jackpot*.
  Millionen sind mit ihrem Los unzufrieden und hoffen das große Los im Lotto zu ziehen. *Millions are dissatisfied with their lot and hope to win big in the lottery*.

---

das Lot — *perpendicular, plumb line*
  im Lot sein — *to be in order*.
  In ihrem Leben ist jetzt alles wieder im Lot. *Everything is now in order in their lives*.

ins Lot bringen — *to put in order, to straighten out.*
Dem Eheberater gelang es, die Familie ins Lot zu bringen. *The marriage counselor succeeded in straightening out the family.*

---

die Luft — *air*
Wenn die Luft rein ist, komm zu uns. *When the coast is clear, come to us.*

die Luft anhalten — *to hold one's breath.*
Halt doch die Luft an! *Keep quiet!*

in die Luft sprengen — *to blow up.*
Der Terrorist versuchte, die Botschaft in die Luft zu sprengen. *The terrorist tried to blow up the embassy.*

wie Luft behandeln — *to snub; to ignore.*
Warum hast du uns wie Luft behandelt? *Why did you snub us?*

---

die Lüge — *lie*
Lügen haben kurze Beine. *Lies come back to haunt the liar.*

Lügen strafen — *to give the lie to; to prove wrong.*
Durch ihr Benehmen hat sie das üble Gerede Lügen gestraft. *Through her behavior she gave the lie to the vicious gossip.*

---

lügen — *to lie*
wie gedruckt lügen — *to lie like mad; to be an out-and-out liar.*
Sie behauptete, der Senator lüge wie gedruckt. *She declared the senator was an out-and-out liar.*

(sich nicht) lumpen lassen — *(not) to be outdone*
Als Gastgeber ließen sich die Indianer des Nordwestens nicht lumpen. *As hosts, the Northwest Indians would not allow themselves to be outdone.*

---

die Lupe — *magnifying glass*
mit der Lupe suchen müssen — *to be rare.*
Restaurants, die noch Innereiengerichte bieten, muss man mit der Lupe suchen. *Restaurants that still serve giblets are rare.*

unter die Lupe nehmen — *to take a close look at.*
Sherlock Holmes beschloss, das Treiben des Professors unter die Lupe zu nehmen. *Sherlock Holmes decided to take a close look at the professor's doings.*

die Lust — *joy*
  Lust haben — *to feel like.*
  Ich hätte jetzt keine große Lust dazu. *I don't particularly feel like it now.*

lustig — *merry*
  sich lustig machen — *to make fun of.*
  Alle machten sich über sein Kostüm lustig. *They all made fun of his costume.*

M

machen — *to make*
  Das macht nichts. *That doesn't matter.*
  Mach, dass du fortkommst. *See that you get started.*
  Was macht die Arbeit? *How are things at work?*

mächtig — *mighty*
  einen mächtigen Hunger haben — *to be very hungry.*
  Die Arbeiter hatten alle einen mächtigen Hunger auf unsere Currywürste. *The workers were all very hungry for our curry sausages.*
  einer Sprache mächtig sein — *to have a command of a language.*
  Elfriede ist vieler Fremdsprachen mächtig. *Elfriede has a command of many foreign languages.*
  seiner selbst nicht mächtig sein — *to lose control.*
  Als er von dem Betrug erfuhr, war er seiner selbst nicht mächtig. *When he learned of the betrayal, he lost control of himself.*

das Machtwort — *word of command*
　ein Machtwort sprechen — *to lay down the law; to put one's foot down.*
　Warum sprechen die Eltern kein Machtwort? *Why don't the parents put their foot down?*

das Mädchen — *girl*
　Mädchen für alles — *maid of all work; girl (man) Friday.*
　Wir haben ein neues Mädchen für alles im Büro. *We have a new girl (man) Friday in the office.*

madig — *maggot-ridden*
　etwas madig machen — *to ruin.*
　Du hast uns die Party madig gemacht. *You ruined the party for us.*

der Magen — *stomach*
　im Magen haben — *to detest.*
　Sprich nicht von meinem Anwalt, den hab ich im Magen. *Don't talk about my lawyer; I detest him.*

die Makulatur — *spoiled / waste paper*
　Makulatur reden — *to talk nonsense.*
　Die Opposition behauptete, der Präsident rede nur Makulatur. *The opposition alleged that the president was talking nonsense.*

das Mal — *time*
　ein für alle Mal — *once and for all.*
　Ein für alle Mal sag ich dir, ich will nichts damit zu tun haben. *I'm telling you once and for all, I don't want anything to do with it.*

　mit einem Mal — *all of a sudden.*
　Mit einem Mal war sie nicht mehr da. *All of a sudden she wasn't there anymore.*

　zum ersten Mal — *for the first time.*
　Heute tritt sie zum ersten Mal vor die Öffentlichkeit. *She's appearing before the public for the first time today.*

der Mann — *man*

an den Mann bringen — *to know how to market.*
Haydn wusste Bescheid, seine Musik an den Mann zu bringen. *Haydn knew how to market his music.*

auf den Mann dressiert — *trained to attack people.*
Seine Dobermänner sind auf den Mann dressiert. *His dobermans are trained to attack people.*

Ein Mann, ein Wort. *An honest man is as good as his word.*

mit Mann und Maus untergehen — *to go down with all on board.*
Das Schiff ist mit Mann und Maus untergegangen. *The ship went down with all on board.*

seinen Mann stehen — *to demonstrate one's ability; to show one's worth.*
Auch auf diesem technischen Gebiet können Frauen ihren Mann stehen. *In this technical area too, women can demonstrate their ability.*

---

die Manschette — *cuff*
Manschetten haben — *to be afraid.*
Alle glaubten, Zorro hätte vor dem Fechten Manschetten. *Everyone thought Zorro was afraid of fencing.*

---

das Mark — *marrow*
bis ins Mark — *to the quick, core.*
Die erschütternde Nachricht traf uns bis ins Mark. *The shattering news cut us to the quick.*

das Mark aus den Knochen saugen — *to bleed white.*
Uriah gefiel es, seinen Mandanten das Mark auszusaugen. *Uriah enjoyed bleeding his clients white.*

---

das Maß — *measure*
Das Maß ist voll. *Enough is enough.*

ein gerüttelt (und geschüttelt) Maß — *a good measure.*
Wie viele ehemalige Romantiker hat er ein gerüttelt Maß von Zynismus in sich. *Like many former romantics, he has a good measure of cynicism in him.*

in/mit Maßen — *in moderation, moderately.*

Er macht jetzt den Versuch, in Maßen zu leben. *He's making an effort to live moderately now.*

mit zweierlei Maß messen — *to apply different sets of standards.*

Sie warfen dem Richter vor, mit zweierlei Maß zu messen. *They accused the judge of applying two sets of standards.*

über die (alle) Maßen — *extremely.*

Wir waren über die Maßen glücklich, von ihr einen Brief zu bekommen. *We were extremely happy to get a letter from her.*

weder Maß noch Ziel kennen — *to be immoderate, undisciplined.*

Er isst und trinkt zu viel, weil er weder Maß noch Ziel kennt. *He eats and drinks too much because he's undisciplined.*

maßhalten — *to exercise moderation.*

Er hat nie maßhalten gelernt. *He never learned to exercise moderation.*

---

das Maul — *mouth (animals)*

das Maul aufreißen — *to shoot one's mouth off.*

Er hat wieder das Maul weit aufgerissen. *He shot his mouth off again.*

das Maul halten — *to shut one's trap.*

Halt's Maul! *Shut your trap!*

ein schiefes Maul ziehen — *to pull a long face.*

Zieh mir kein schiefes Maul! *Don't pull a long face on me!*

sich das Maul zerreißen — *to gossip viciously.*

Hinter ihrem Rücken haben sie sich das Maul über sie zerrissen. *Behind her back they gossiped viciously about her.*

die Maulsperre kriegen — *to be flabbergasted, speechless.*

Sag's ihr nicht gleich, sonst kriegt sie die Maulsperre. *Don't tell her right away or she'll be flabbergasted.*

---

die Maus — *mouse*

weiße Mäuse sehen — *to see pink elephants.*

Er betrank sich und sah weiße Mäuse. *He got drunk and saw pink elephants.*

---

mein — *my*

    Meine Damen und Herren! *Ladies and gentlemen!*

    mein und dein verwechseln — *to steal.*

    Einige Deutsche behaupten, sie verwechselten manchmal "mir" und
    "mich" aber niemals "mein" und "dein." *Some Germans allege they*
    sometimes confused "me" and "mine," but never "mine" and "thine"
    (yours).

die Meise — *titmouse*

    eine Meise unterm Pony haben — *to have bats in the belfry.*

    Manchmal glaub ich, du hast eine Meise unterm Pony. *Sometimes I think*
    you've got bats in your belfry.

der Meister — *master*

    Es ist noch kein Meister vom Himmel gefallen. *Practice makes perfect.*

    In der Beschränkung zeigt sich erst der Meister. *True champions respond*
    successfully to challenges/limitations.

die Menge — *quantity*

    in rauhen Mengen — *in huge amounts.*

    Vor Jahren aß er alles — und in rauhen Mengen. *Years ago he ate*
    everything, and in huge amounts.

    jede Menge — *loads of.*

    Das Kind hat schon jede Menge Spielzeug. *The child already has loads*
    of toys.

merken — *to notice*

    die Absicht merken und verstimmt werden — *to see what someone is*
    getting at and be displeased.

    In allen seinen Filmen merkt man die propagandistische Absicht und wird
    verstimmt. *In all his movies you can tell he's grinding a propaganda*
    axe, and it's annoying.

das Messer — *knife*

    ans Messer liefern — *to betray, hand over.*

    Der Spitzel hat sie alle ans Messer geliefert. *The spy betrayed them all.*

auf des Messers Schneide stehen — *to be touch and go*.

Ob sie vom Senatsausschuss bestätigt wird, steht auf des Messers Schneide. *It's touch and go whether the senate committee will confirm her.*

bis aufs Messer — *to the bitter end; with no holds barred*.

Die Rivalen kämpften bis aufs Messer. *The rivals fought to the bitter end.*

ins offene Messer laufen — *to play right into someone's hands*.

Mit seinen unbedachten Äußerungen lief er der Opposition ins Messer. *With his ill-considered statements he played right into the opposition's hands.*

---

die Miene — *face; facial expression*

gute Miene zum bösen Spiel machen — *to put a good face on it*.

Wir sind mit dem Abkommen sehr unzufrieden, aber wir versuchen, gute Miene zum bösen Spiel zu machen. *We're very dissatisfied with the agreement, but we're trying to put a good face on it.*

keine Miene verziehen — *not to turn a hair*.

Der Reporter beobachtete die Hinrichtung und verzog keine Miene. *The reporter observed the execution and didn't turn a hair.*

Miene machen — *to show signs of starting*.

Mehrmals machte er Miene, fortzugehen. *Several times he showed signs of starting to leave.*

---

die Miete — *rent*

die halbe Miete sein — *to be halfway to success; half the battle*.

Du hast diese Prüfung gut bestanden; das ist schon die halbe Miete. *You've done well on this exam; that's half the way there (to your goal).*

---

die Mine — *explosive mine*

alle Minen springen lassen — *to go all out*.

Wir lassen alle Minen springen, um den Auftrag zu bekommen. *We're going all out to get the contract.*

eine Mine legen — *to plot, cook up a surprise*.

Was hast du wieder für eine kleine Mine gelegt? *What little surprise have you cooked up now?*

---

mir — *to me*

mir nichts, dir nichts — *just like that.*

Mir nichts, dir nichts ist sie ausgezogen. *She moved out just like that.*

wie du mir, so ich dir — *to repay in kind.*

Du willst dich für einen Heiligen ausgeben, trotzdem sagst du: "Wie du mir, so ich dir." *You want to pass yourself off as a saint, yet you say, "as you do unto me, I do unto you."*

---

mithalten — *to keep up with; to be up to*

Der Tristan versuchte mit der Isolde mitzuhalten, aber seine Stimme versagte ihm. *The Tristan tried to keep up with the Isolde, but his voice gave out.*

Ich würde gerne das Matterhorn ersteigen, aber meine Beine halten nicht mehr mit. *I'd love to climb the Matterhorn, but my legs aren't up to it anymore.*

---

mitmachen — *to take part in*

Er wollte den Krieg nicht mehr mitmachen und wurde fahnenflüchtig. *He didn't want to take part in the war anymore and deserted.*

---

der Mittag — *noon*

Mittag machen — *to take a break for lunch.*

Genug gearbeitet! Jetzt machen wir Mittag. *That's enough work. We'll take a break for lunch now.*

zu Mittag essen — *to eat lunch.*

Nach dem Sektfrühstück hatten wir keine Lust zu Mittag zu essen. *After the champagne breakfast we didn't feel like eating lunch.*

---

mogeln — *to cheat*

die Mogelpackung — *deceptive packaging; sham.*

Die Senatorin hielt die Versprechungen der Regierung, keine Steuern zu erhöhen, für Mogelpackung. *The senator thought the government's promises not to raise taxes were a sham.*

---

das Moment — *factor*
  das auslösende Moment sein — *to trigger.*
  Die Scheidung war das auslösende Moment seines Wahnsinns. *The*
    divorce triggered his madness.

---

der Moment — *moment*
  einen lichten Moment (lichte Momente) — *lucid interval(s).*
  Dann und wann hat er einen lichten Moment. *Now and then he has a lucid*
    interval.

  jeden Moment — *(at) any moment.*
  Jeden Moment kann sie zurückkommen. *She can come back any moment.*

---

die Morgenluft — *morning air*
  Morgenluft wittern — *to see one's chance.*
  Die Opposition witterte Morgenluft. *The opposition saw its chance.*

---

die Morgenstunde — *early morning hour(s)*
  Morgenstund hat Gold im Mund. Wer verschläft sich geht zugrund. *The*
    morning hours are wonderful for getting things done. Oversleepers
    come to grief.

---

das Moos — *moss*
  Moos ansetzen — *to get old.*
  Ohne Selbstironie, stellte er fest, dass seine Schulfreunde Moos angesetzt
    hatten. *Without irony, he determined that his school friends had*
    gotten old.

---

die Mücke — *gnat*
  aus einer Mücke einen Elefanten machen — *to make a mountain out of*
    a molehill.
  Wie gewöhnlich, machst du aus einer Mücke einen Elefanten. *As usual,*
    you're making a mountain out of a molehill.

  die Mücke machen — *to clear out, scram.*
  Mach schnell die Mücke, dass der Chef dich nicht erwischt. *Clear out fast*
    so the boss doesn't catch you.

---

der Muckefuck — *watery coffee; coffee substitute*

Ohne zu mucken, trank der Patient den Muckefuck. *Without grumbling, the patient drank his watery coffee.*

die Mucken — *whims*

seine Mucken haben — *to have one's moods, be temperamental; not to run right (machines).*

Mein Bruder hat seine Mucken. *My brother has his moods.*

Besonders im Winter hat der Wagen seine Mucken. *The car is a bit temperamental, especially in the winter.*

der Mund — *mouth*

aus dem Mund riechen — *to have bad breath.*

Gib auch mir etwas Knoblauch, damit wir beide aus dem Mund riechen. *Give me some garlic too, so that we can both have bad breath.*

den Mund voll nehmen — *to talk big.*

Er taugt wenig, aber er nimmt gern den Mund voll. *He's not good for much, but he likes to talk big.*

in aller Munde sein — *to be widely talked about.*

Nach ihrem Olympiasieg war sie in aller Munde. *After her Olympic victory, she was talked about everywhere.*

nach dem Mund reden — *to be a yes person; to tell someone what they want to hear.*

Alle redeten dem verrückten Diktator nach dem Munde. *They all told the crazy dictator what he wanted to hear.*

nicht auf den Mund gefallen sein — *not to be at a loss for words.*

Normalerweise bist du nicht auf den Mund gefallen. *Usually you're not at a loss for words.*

wie aus einem Munde — *as if with one voice.*

Die Abgeordneten riefen wie aus einem Munde: "Verrat!" *The congresspersons cried as if with one voice, "Treason!"*

mundtot machen — *to silence.*

Die Dissidenten wurden mundtot gemacht. *The dissidents were silenced.*

das Mündel — *ward (person under a guardian's care)*
    mündelsicher — *gilt-edged, blue chip.*
    Selbst ihre mündelsicher geglaubten Wertpapiere sind jetzt wertlos. *Even
    their supposedly gilt-edged securities are now worthless.*

---

die Münze — *coin*
    für bare Münze nehmen — *to take at face value.*
    Seine Schwärmereien sind nicht für bare Münze zu nehmen. *His effusions
    aren't to be taken at face value.*

    in/mit gleicher Münze heimzahlen — *to pay back in kind.*
    Diese Frechheit werde ich dir in gleicher Münze heimzahlen. *I'll pay you
    back in kind (in your own coin) for that impudence.*

    klingende Münze — *hard cash.*
    Hier musst du mit klingender Münze bezahlen, mein Freund. *You've got
    to pay with hard cash here, my friend.*

---

die Muse — *muse*
    die leichte Muse — *light entertainment; operettas; musical comedies.*
    In unserem Opernhaus wird die leichte Muse nicht vernachlässigt. *In our
    opera house operettas are not neglected.*

    von der Muse geküsst werden — *to be inspired.*
    Seit langem ist er nicht von der Muse geküsst worden. *He hasn't been
    inspired for some time.*

    musisch veranlagt — *to be artistic.*
    Sie ist ein musisch veranlagter Mensch. *She's a very artistic person.*

N

der Nabel — *navel*
    der Nabel der Welt — *the hub of the universe.*
    Viele Orte halten sich noch für den Nabel der Welt. *Many places still
    think they're the hub of the universe.*

die Nabelschau — *navel contemplation; ego trip.*
Der Film ist mehr als eine selbstgefällige Nabelschau. *The movie is more than a self-satisfied ego trip.*

---

nach — *after*
  nach und nach — *gradually, little by little.*
  Nach und nach wurde uns alles klar. *Gradually everything became clear to us.*

  nach wie vor — *still, as always.*
  Nach wie vor ist er ein Publikumsliebling. *He's still popular with the public.*

  nach — *according to, by.*
  Ich kenne ihn nur dem Namen nach. *I know him only by name.*

  nach Adam Riese — *correctly calculated; according to my arithmetic.*
  Nach Adam Riese macht das 50 nicht 60 Euro. *According to my arithmetic, that makes 50, not 60 euros.*

  im Nachhinein — *after the event; with hindsight.*
  Im Nachhinein ist man natürlich immer klüger. *Of course one is always wiser after the event.*

---

nachsehen — *to go (look and) see*
  das Nachsehen bleiben — *to be duped/disadvantaged.*
  Der Direktor verschwand mit dem Geld und den Aktionären blieb das Nachsehen. *The director disappeared with the money, and the shareholders were left holding the bag.*

---

nächst — *next*
  Jeder ist sich selbst der Nächste. *Everyone looks out for number one. (Charity begins at home.)*

  die Nächstenliebe — *love of one's fellow (hu)man; philanthropy.*
  Im Alter entdeckte der Milliardär die Nächstenliebe. *In old age the billionaire discovered philanthropy.*

---

nachstehen — *to lag behind*
  in nichts nachstehen — *to be in no way inferior.*
  Dieses Modell steht den anderen in nichts nach. *This model is in no way inferior to the others.*

---

die Nacht — *night*

bei Nacht und Nebel — *under cover of darkness.*
Bei Nacht und Nebel schlich er in das Schloss. *Under cover of darkness he sneaked into the castle.*

die Nacht um die Ohren schlagen — *to stay up all night.*
Er hat sich wieder die Nacht um die Ohren geschlagen. *He stayed up all night again.*

---

das Nachthemd — *nightshirt*

ein aufgeblasenes Nachthemd sein — *to be a pretentious fool/a stuffed shirt.*
Onkel Otto ist doch alles andere als ein aufgeblasenes Nachthemd. *Uncle Otto is really anything but a pretentious fool.*

---

die Nachtigall — *nightingale*

Nachtigall, ich hör dir trapsen! *I know what you're after!*

---

der Nacken — *neck*

jemandem im Nacken sitzen — *to be breathing down one's neck; to threaten.*
Ich half ihm, sein Geschäft auf die Beine zu bringen, und jetzt sitzt mir seine Konkurrenz im Nacken. *I helped him to start up his business, and now competition from him is threatening me.*

den Nacken steifhalten — *to keep one's chin up.*
Im Moment geht das Geschäft schlecht, aber ich halte noch den Nacken steif. *At the moment business is bad, but I'm still keeping my chin up.*

den Nacken steifen/stärken — *to give moral support; to comfort.*
Nach dem Tod seiner Frau versuchten wir, ihm den Nacken zu stärken. *After his wife's death, we tried to comfort him.*

---

die Nadel — *needle*

Man konnte eine Nadel fallen hören. *One could hear a pin drop.*

die/eine Nadel im Heuschober/Heuhaufen suchen — *to look for a needle in a haystack.*
Du suchst ein geräumiges, trotzdem billiges Hotelzimmer in Wien? Das ist wie eine Nadel im Heuschober suchen. *You're looking for a spacious*

yet inexpensive hotel room in Vienna? That's like looking for a needle in a haystack.

mit der heißen Nadel genäht — *done hurriedly/carelessly.*
In der letzten Zeit ist nicht nur ihre Näharbeit mit der heißen Nadel genäht. *Recently, it's not just her sewing that's been done carelessly.*

---

der Nagel — *nail*

an den Nagel hängen — *to give up.*
Wegen der Knieverletzung musste er den Sport an den Nagel hängen. *Because of a knee injury, he had to give up sports.*

auf den Nägeln brennen — *to be urgent.*
Das Problem brennt uns allen auf den Nägeln. *We all consider the problem urgent.*

auf den Nägeln brennend liegen — *to be of great concern/urgency.*
Dieses Thema liegt uns brennend auf den Nägeln. *This subject is of great concern to us.*

den Nagel auf den Kopf treffen — *to hit the nail on the head.*
Diesmal hast du den Nagel auf den Kopf getroffen. *This time you've hit the nail on the head.*

Nägel mit Köpfen machen — *to make a good job of.*
Wir wollen Nägel mit Köpfen machen. *We want to make a good job of it.*

sich etwas unter den Nagel reißen — *to make off with.*
Lass die Sachen nicht so herumliegen, sonst reißt er sie sich unter den Nagel. *Don't let things lie around like that, or he'll make off with them.*

---

nagen — *to gnaw*

am Hungertuch nagen — *to be starving; be destitute.*
"Man hält mich für reich, aber ich nage am Hungertuch!" klagte der Geizhals. *"People think I'm rich, but I'm destitute!" complained the miser.*

---

nah — *near*

aus nah und fern — *from far and wide.*
Unsere Gäste kommen aus nah und fern. *Our guests come from far and wide.*

nahe treten — *to give offense.*

Ohne Ihnen nahe treten zu wollen, muss ich Ihnen doch die Wahrheit sagen. *Without wishing to give offense, I must nevertheless tell you the truth.*

---

die Nahrung — *food*

Nahrung geben — *to fan the flames.*

Die Presseberichte gaben dem Skandal neue Nahrung. *The reports in the press fanned the flames of the scandal.*

---

das Nähkästchen — *sewing kit*

aus dem Nähkästchen plaudern — *to spill the beans.*

Der Senator betrank sich und plauderte aus dem Nähkästchen. *The senator got drunk and spilled the beans.*

---

der Name — *name*

Name ist Schall und Rauch. *What's in a name?*

---

der Narr, die Närrin — *fool*

einen Narren gefressen haben — *to be smitten with.*

Meine Tochter hat an dem Filmstar einen Narren gefressen. *My daughter is smitten with the movie star.*

zum Narren halten — *to fool.*

Mit der erfundenen Geschichte hat der Reporter alle zum Narren gehalten. *With that made-up story the reporter fooled everybody.*

---

die Nase — *nose*

an der Nase herumführen — *to lead by the nose.*

Er hat uns lange genug an der Nase herumgeführt. *He's led us by the nose long enough.*

die Nase in die Bücher stecken — *to buckle down and study.*

Wann steckst du endlich die Nase in die Bücher? *When will you finally buckle down and study?*

die Nase rümpfen — *to turn up one's nose.*

Sie hat eigentlich kein Recht, die Nase über diesen armen Menschen zu rümpfen. *She really has no right to turn up her nose at this unfortunate individual.*

die Nase voll haben — *to be fed up with.*

Von Krieg und Zerstörung hatten sie die Nase voll. *They were fed up with war and destruction.*

die Nase vorn haben — *to be leading.*

Auf dem internationalen Markt haben wir die Nase vorn. *We're leading on the international market.*

die Nase zu tief ins Glas stecken — *to get roaring drunk.*

Er hat die Nase zu tief ins Glas gesteckt. *He got roaring drunk.*

auf der Nase herumtanzen — *to walk all over.*

Er lässt sich von allen auf der Nase herumtanzen. *He lets everybody walk all over him.*

sich die Nase begießen — *to have a few drinks.*

Nach der Arbeit begießt er sich gern die Nase. *After work he likes to have a few drinks.*

sich eine goldene Nase verdienen — *to make a lot of money.*

Mit seinem Elixir hat sich der Scharlatan eine goldene Nase verdient. *With his elixir the charlatan made a lot of money.*

---

nehmen — *to take*

    Woher nehmen und nicht stehlen? *Just where am I supposed to get a hold of that?*

    nicht für voll nehmen — *not to take seriously.*

    Nur weil ich jung und schön bin, nimmt man mich nicht für voll. *Just because I'm young and beautiful, they don't take me seriously.*

---

die Neige — *dregs*

    bis zur Neige auskosten — *to enjoy to the fullest.*

    Sie hat ihren Tennistriumph bis zur Neige ausgekostet. *She enjoyed her tennis triumph to the fullest.*

    bis zur Neige leeren — *to drink to the dregs.*

    Wir haben das Glas voll Muscadet Wein zur Neige geleert. *We drank our glass of Muscadet to the dregs.*

    zur Neige gehen — *to run low.*

    Der Honig geht zur Neige. *The honey is running low.*

zur Neige gehen — *to draw to a close.*

Der Tag ging zur Neige und er war noch nicht gekommen. *The day was drawing to a close, and he hadn't come yet.*

---

neppen — *to rook; to rip off*

sich neppen lassen — *to get ripped off.*

Wir wollen uns von niemand neppen lassen. *We don't want to get ripped off by anyone.*

das Nepplokal — *clip joint.*

Leider sind wir in einem Nepplokal gelandet. *Unfortunately, we wound up in a clip joint.*

---

der Nerv — *nerve*

an den Nerv der Sache rühren — *to get to the heart of the matter.*

Sie hat an den Nerv der Sache gerührt. *She got to the heart of the matter.*

einen sonnigen Nerv haben — *to be naive and foolish.*

Wenn du weiterhin daran glauben willst, hast du einen ganz sonnigen Nerv. *If you choose to continue to believe that, then you're quite naive and foolish.*

den letzten Nerv rauben — *to drive up the wall.*

Mit seiner Trunksucht raubt er mir den letzten Nerv. *He's driving me up the wall with his drinking.*

nerven — *to get on one's nerves.*

Sein Benehmen nervt mich. *His behavior gets on my nerves.*

---

die Nessel — *nettle*

sich in die Nesseln setzen — *to get into hot water.*

Tu's nicht; du wirst dich nur in die Nesseln setzen. *Don't do it; you'll just get into hot water.*

---

neu — *new*

aufs Neue — *(once) again.*

Leider muss ich Sie aufs Neue darauf aufmerksam machen. *Unfortunately, I must once again bring it to your attention.*

von Neuem — *(all over) again*.

Wir sollten eigentlich alles von Neuem beginnen. *We really ought to make a fresh start*.

---

neun(e) — *nine*

Ach, du grüne Neune! — *Oh, for heaven's sake!/Well I'll be darned!*

Ach, du grüne Neune, der Hund ist wieder fortgelaufen! *Oh, for heaven's sake, the dog's run off again!*

Verrückt und fünf ist neune! — *The world is full of madness!/The crazies are out there!*

Opa will snowboarden gehen—verrückt und fünf ist neune! *Gramps wants to go snowboarding—he's gone off the deep end!*

---

das Nichts — *nothingness*

aus dem Nichts — *from nothing*.

Das einst blühende Unternehmen hat er aus dem Nichts aufgebaut. *He built up his once flourishing enterprise from nothing*.

vor dem Nichts stehen — *to be facing ruin*.

Jetzt steht er vor dem Nichts. *Now he is facing ruin*.

---

nichts — *nothing*

für nichts und wieder nichts — *for nothing at all; in vain*.

Für nichts und wieder nichts hat er gearbeitet. *He's worked in vain*.

---

die Niere — *kidney*

an die Nieren gehen — *to stir deeply*.

Die Fernsehbilder von den Kriegsopfern gingen uns an die Nieren. *The TV pictures of the war victims stirred us deeply*.

---

die Niete — *rivet*

alles, was nicht niet- und nagelfest ist — *everything that isn't nailed or screwed down*.

Die abziehenden Soldaten nahmen alles mit, was nicht niet- und nagelfest war. *The departing soldiers took with them everything that wasn't nailed or screwed down*.

nicht alle Nieten an der Hose haben — *not to have all one's marbles*.
Sein Benehmen ist mir unerklärlich; der hat wohl nicht alle Nieten an der
Hose. *I can't understand his behavior; he probably hasn't got all his
marbles*.

---

das Niveau — *level*
  an Niveau einbüßen — *to decline in quality*.
  Das Restaurant hat an Niveau eingebüßt, doch sind die Preise gestiegen.
  The restaurant has declined in quality but the prices have gone up.

  Niveau haben — *to be of quality*.
  Die Sendung über Händel in Halle und Hannover hatte hohes Niveau. *The
  program about Händel in Halle and Hanover was of high quality*.

---

das Nickerchen — *nap*
  ein Nickerchen halten/machen — *to take a nap*.
  Jeden Nachmittag macht er sein Nickerchen. *Every afternoon he takes his
  nap*.

---

auf Nimmerwiedersehen verschwinden — *to disappear forever*
  Der Betrüger nahm das Geld und verschwand auf Nimmerwiedersehen. *The
  con-man took the money and disappeared forever*.

---

die Not — *need; emergency*
  Not bricht Eisen. *Necessity is the mother of invention*.

  Spare in der Zeit, dann hast du in der Not. *Save beforehand; then you'll
  be provided for when you need it*.

  nottun — *to need, be needed*.
  In diesem Betrieb tut eine Reform not. *This company needs reform*.

---

der Notnagel — *last resort, fill in, stopgap*
  Leider halten die meisten Jugendlichen ein Job in der Landwirtschaft
  für eine Notnagel für Schlusslichter. *Unfortunately, most young people
  think a job on the farm is a last resort for those at the bottom of
  the class*.

---

die Null — *zero*

in Null Komma nichts — *in no time at all*.
In Null Komma nichts kam sie zurück. *In no time at all she returned*.

Null Komma nichts erreichen — *to get nowhere at all*.
Bei den Beamten hat er Null Komma nichts erreicht. *He got nowhere at
all with the officials*.

nullachtfünfzehn — *run-of-the-mill, humdrum*.
Meiner Ansicht nach war die Vorstellung alles andere als nullachtfünfzehn.
In my opinion the performance was anything but humdrum.

die Null-Bock-Generation — *turned-off generation*.
Sie sagten, sie gehörten der Null-Bock-Generation an. *They said they
belonged to the dropout generation*.

die Nulldiät — *starvation diet*.
Er ging auf Nulldiät. *He went on a starvation diet*.

zum Nulltarif — *free of charge*.
Er hält sich berechtigt, zum Nulltarif zu fahren. *He thinks he's entitled to
ride free of charge*.

---

die Nummer — *number*

auf Nummer Sicher gehen — *to play it safe*.
Die meisten Wähler wollten auf Nummer Sicher gehen. *Most voters
wanted to play it safe*.

eine dicke Nummer haben — *to be well thought of*.
Bei allen Nachbarn hat er eine dicke Nummer. *He's well thought of by all
the neighbors*.

---

oben — *above*

oben nicht ganz richtig sein — *to be not quite right in the head (upstairs)*.
Ich glaube er ist oben nicht ganz richtig. *I don't think he's quite right in
the head*.

von oben herab — *condescendingly.*

Ehe sie ihn heiratete, behandelte sie ihren Chauffeur von oben herab.
Before she married him she treated her chauffeur condescendingly.

obenhinaus wollen — *to be a social climber.*

Einst wollte sie obenhinaus, jetzt aber lebt sie nur der Liebe. *Once she was a social climber, now she lives only for love.*

---

ober — *upper*
die oberen Zehntausend — *the upper crust.*
Suzannes Galerie ist für die oberen Zehntausend. *Suzanne's gallery is for the upper crust.*

---

offen — *open*
offen gesagt — *frankly speaking.*
Offen gesagt, glaub ich das nicht. *Frankly speaking, I don't believe that.*

offene Türen einrennen — *to fight battles already won.*
Wir sind ganz deiner Meinung; du rennst nur offene Türen ein. *We agree with you completely; you're fighting a battle already won.*

---

das Ohr — *ear*
bis über beide Ohren in Schulden stecken — *to be up to one's neck in debt.*
Bis über beide Ohren steckt er in Schulden. *He's up to his neck in debt.*

bis über beide Ohren verliebt sein — *to be very much in love.*
Einst waren sie bis über beide Ohren in einander verliebt. *Once they were very much in love with each other.*

bis über die Ohren rot werden — *to blush all over.*
Er wurde bis über die Ohren rot. *He blushed all over.*

die Ohren steif halten — *to maintain morale.*
Halt die Ohren steif! *Keep smiling!//Keep a stiff upper lip!*

etwas hinter den Ohren haben — *to be smart.*
Sie hat was hinter den Ohren. *She's got something upstairs.*

etwas hinter die Ohren schreiben — *to be sure to remember; to take due note of.*

Vor Mitternacht musst du zu Hause sein — schreib dir das hinter die
Ohren. *You must be home before midnight. Be sure to remember that.*

ganz Ohr sein — *to be all ears.*
Wenn geklatscht wird, ist er immer ganz Ohr. *Whenever anyone gossips,
he's always all ears.*

jemandem die Ohren langziehen — *to give s.o. a good talking-to/an
earful.*
Dem Lausbuben hat Mutti ganz schön die Ohren langgezogen. *Mom gave
that rotten kid a good talking-to.*

**jemandem in den Ohren liegen/jemandem mit etwas auf den Ohren
liegen** — *to nag; importune someone.*
Ach, wenn er nur aufhören würde, mir mit seinen Theorien endlos in den
Ohren zu liegen. *Oh, if he'd only quit going on and on about his theories.*

sich aufs Ohr legen/hauen — *to turn in, hit the hay.*
Ich leg mich jetzt ein bisschen aufs Ohr. *I'm going to have a little lie
down now.*

übers Ohr hauen — *to cheat.*
Prüfen Sie die Echtheit genau, damit Sie nicht übers Ohr gehauen werden.
Check the authenticity carefully, so that you aren't cheated.

viel um die Ohren haben — *to have a lot to do.*
Diese Woche hatte ich viel um die Ohren. *I had a lot to do this week.*

---

das Öl — *oil*
Öl auf die Wogen gießen — *to pour oil on troubled waters.*
Sie goß Öl auf die Wogen und setzte dem Streit ein Ende. *She poured oil
on troubled waters and put an end to the quarrel.*

Öl ins Feuer gießen — *to add fuel to the flames.*
Die Reporterin wusste, dass der Artikel Öl ins Feuer gießen würde. *The
reporter knew that the article would add fuel to the flames.*

ölen — *to lubricate*
wie geölt — *like clockwork.*
Alles lief wie geölt. *Everything went like clockwork.*

---

die Olympiade — *Olympic Games*

Auf der Olympiade gewann sie Gold. *She won a gold medal at the Olympics.*

olympiaverdächtig — *Olympics material; outstanding in sports.*

Unsere Kleine ist immer auf der Piste; sie ist wohl olympiaverdächtig. *Our little daughter is always on the ski lanes; she's Olympics material.*

der Olympionike, die Olympionikin — *Olympics victor/participant.*

Er treibt gern Sport, aber Olympionike wird er wohl nie. *He loves sports, but it's doubtful he'll ever make the Olympics.*

---

die Oper — *opera*

ein Opernnarr sein — *to be avidly fond of the opera.*

Er ist zugleich Opernnarr und Leseratte. *He's both a bookworm and an opera nut.*

Opern quatschen — *to talk too much.*

Quatsch keine Opern! *Don't talk so much.*

Otto Normalverbraucher — *the average person; John Q. Public*

Würde so etwas Otto Normalverbraucher ansprechen? *Would something like that appeal to the average person?*

P

pachten — *to lease*

Glauben Sie, die Straße für sich gepachtet zu haben? *Do you think you own the street?*

---

das Päckchen — *small parcel*

sein Päckchen (zu tragen) haben — *to have one's cross (to bear); to have one's troubles.*

Jeder hat sein Päckchen (zu tragen). *Everyone has his troubles.*

---

die Palme — *palm tree*

auf die Palme bringen — *to drive up the wall.*

Sein moralinsaueres Benehmen bringt mich auf die Palme. *His holier-than-thou behavior drives me up the wall.*

---

der Pantoffel — *slipper*
unter dem Pantoffel stehen — *to be henpecked.*
Lange Jahre stand er unter dem Pantoffel. *He was henpecked for many years.*

der Pantoffelheld — *henpecked husband.*
Man nannte ihn einen Pantoffelhelden, aber er war glücklich. *They called him henpecked, but he was happy.*

---

der Pappenstiel — *trifle*
für einen Pappenstiel — *for a song.*
Sie hat den Wagen für einen Pappenstiel gekauft. *She bought the car for a song.*

---

die Parade — *parade*
in die Parade fahren — *to oppose vigorously.*
Sie fuhr dem Senator oft in die Parade. *She often opposed the senator.*

---

die Partei — *political party*
es mit beiden Parteien halten — *to keep a foot in both camps.*
Er versucht es, mit beiden Parteien zu halten. *He's trying to keep a foot in both camps.*

Partei ergreifen — *to take sides; to take a stand.*
Sehr früh ergriff sie für den Umweltschutz Partei. *Very early on she took a stand for environmental protection.*

---

die Partie — *part; game*
eine gute Partie sein — *to be a good match.*
Ihre Mutter nannte ihn eine gute Partie, aber sie wollte nichts von ihm wissen. *Her mother called him a good match, but she didn't want anything to do with him.*

mit von der Partie sein — *to join in.*
Wenn wir aufs Land gingen, war sie oft mit von der Partie. *When we went to the country, she often joined us.*

---

die Pauke — *kettle drum*
  auf die Pauke hauen — *to have a blast.*
  Gestern Abend haben wir auf die Pauke gehauen. *Last night we had a blast.*

  auf die Pauke hauen — *to blow one's own trumpet.*
  Seitdem er das Vermögen geerbt hat, haut er auf die Pauke. *Ever since he inherited the fortune he's been blowing his own trumpet.*

---

das Pech — *pitch; bad luck*
  Pech im Spiel, Glück in der Liebe. *Unlucky at cards, lucky in love.*

---

der Pechvogel — *unlucky person*
  Dein Bruder hat wieder einen Unfall gehabt? Er ist ein richtiger Pechvogel. *Your brother had another accident? He's a walking disaster area.*

---

die Pelle — *skin; peel*
  auf die Pelle rücken — *to harrass, be after.*
  Er rückt mir dauernde auf die Pelle, damit ich Geld bei ihm anlege. *He's always after me to invest money with him.*

  von der Pelle gehen — *to leave in peace.*
  Er will mir nicht von der Pelle gehen. *He won't leave me in peace.*

---

der Pelz — *fur; pelt*
  eins auf den Pelz geben — *to tan someone's hide.*
  Sie drohen oft, den Kindern eins auf den Pelz zu geben, aber es bleibt bei der Drohung. *They often threaten to tan their kids' hides, but threatening is all they do.*

---

perfekt — *perfect; a done deal*
  Das Abkommen ist perfekt. *The agreement is a done deal.*

---

die Pfanne — *frying pan*
  in die Pfanne hauen — *to pan.*
  Das Stück wurde von den meisten Kritikern in die Pfanne gehauen. *The play was panned by most of the critics.*

---

der Pfeffer — *pepper*

  hingehen, wo der Pfeffer wächst — *to go to hell; get lost.*

  Deine besoffenen Kumpane sollen hingehen, wo der Pfeffer wächst. *Your drunken buddies can go to hell.*

---

pfeffern — *to season with pepper*

  eine pfeffern — *to whack.*

  Lass mich in Ruh, oder ich pfeffre dir eine. *Leave me alone or I'll whack you.*

  gepfeffert — *steep.*

  Die gepfefferten Preise for Spitzenweine können wir nicht zahlen. *We can't pay the steep prices for top-quality wines.*

  gepfeffert — *racy; spicy.*

  Beim Gewürztraminertrinken erzählen sie sich gepfefferte Geschichten. *While drinking Gewürztraminer they tell spicy stories.*

---

pfeifen — *to whistle*

  auf etwas pfeifen — *not to care a damn about.*

  Wir pfeifen auf seine Befehle. *We don't care a damn about his orders.*

---

der Pfeil — *arrow*

  alle seine Pfeile verschossen haben — *to have used up all one's arguments.*

  Alle glaubten, die Anwältin hätte ihre Pfeile verschossen. *Everyone thought the lawyer had used up all her arguments.*

---

der Pfennig — *penny, cent*

  Wer den Pfennig nicht ehrt, ist des Talers nicht wert. *Whoever doesn't respect the penny doesn't deserve the dollar.*

  auf den Pfennig genau — *correct to the last cent.*

  Die Rechnung stimmte auf den Pfennig genau. *The bill was correct to the last cent.*

  auf Heller und Pfennig — *down to the last cent/detail.*

  Er hatte alles auf Heller und Pfennig gerechnet. *He had figured everything out down to the last detail.*

bis auf den letzten Pfennig — *down to the last cent*.

Er hat alles verloren, bis auf den letzten Pfennig. *He lost everything, down to the last cent.*

---

das Pferd — *horse*

das Pferd am Schwanz aufzäumen — *to make a false start*.

Vielleicht wäre das Projekt besser gelungen, wenn er das Pferd nicht am Schwanz aufgezäumt hätte. *Perhaps the project would have worked out better if he hadn't made a false start of it.*

die Pferde durchgehen — *to lose control, composure*.

Wenn man dieses Thema berührt, gehen ihm die Pferde durch. *When that subject comes up, he loses control.*

einen vom Pferd erzählen — *to tell a fish story, a fib*.

Er hat dir wohl wieder einen vom Pferd erzählt. *He probably told you a fib again.*

keine zehn Pferde — *wild horses*.

Keine zehn Pferde bringen mich wieder in sein Restaurant. *Wild horses couldn't get me to go back to his restaurant.*

mit jemandem Pferde stehlen können — *to be game for anything*.

Die beiden sind alte Schulkameraden, mit denen man Pferde stehlen kann. *Both are old school chums who are game for anything.*

---

der Pferdefuß — *horse's foot*

einen Pferdefuß haben — *to have a (hidden) disadvantage/drawback*.

Erst nach Unterzeichnung des Kaufvertrags, sah er ein, dass das Haus einen Pferdefuß hatte. *Only after signing the sales contract did he realize that the house had a drawback.*

---

der Pfifferling — *chanterelle mushroom*

keinen Pfifferling wert sein — *to be worthless*.

Sie behauptete, die Versprechungen des Senators wären keinen Pfifferling wert. *She alleged the senator's promises were worthless.*

---

das Pflaster — *sticking plaster; pavement*

ein heißes Pflaster — *a dangerous spot*.

ein teures Pflaster — *an expensive district.*

Dieser Gangster wohnt in Hamburg-Blankenese, ein teures und jetzt auch
ein heißes Pflaster. *That gangster lives in Hamburg-Blankenese, an
expensive area, and now a dangerous one, too.*

piepen — *to peep, chirp*

Bei dir piept's wohl! Du hast einen Vogel! *You must be off your rocker.
You're bonkers!*

Der Film war zum Piepen! *The movie was a scream/hoot!*

die Pike — *pike*

von der Pike auf dienen/lernen — *to start at the bottom and work one's
way up.*

Er sollte im Geschäft seines Vaters von der Pike auf dienen. *He was
supposed to work his way up in his father's business.*

die Piksieben — *seven of spades*

dastehen wie Piksieben — *to stand there looking stupid.*

Keiner bewegte sich; alle standen da wie Piksieben. *No one moved; they
all stood there looking stupid.*

die Pistole — *pistol*

die Pistole auf die Brust setzen — *to hold a gun to someone's head.*

Niemand setzte ihm eine Pistole auf die Brust; er tat es aus freien
Stücken. *No one put a gun to his head; he did it of his own accord.*

wie aus der Pistole geschossen — *unhesitatingly.*

Wie aus der Pistole geschossen antwortete sie auf alle Fragen. *She
answered all questions unhesitatingly.*

die Platte — *record*

die alte Platte laufen lassen — *to put on the same broken record.*

Er lässt immer die alte Platte laufen. *He always puts on the same broken
record.*

die Platte kennen — *to have heard it before.*

Die Platte kennen wir schon. *We've heard that tune before.*

die Platte putzen — *to make oneself scarce.*

Ohne dass es die anderen merkten, putzte er die Platte. *Without the others' noticing, he made himself scarce.*

eine andere Platte auflegen — *to put another record on; to change the subject.*

Leg doch 'ne andere Platte auf — das alles kennen wir schon. *Put on another record. We know all that.*

der Platz — *place*

am Platz sein — *to be fitting.*

An diesem Feiertag ist es am Platz, dass wir an unsere verstorbenen Kameraden denken. *On this holiday it is fitting that we think of our dead comrades.*

der Platzhirsch — *the dominant stag; the boss, the big cheese.*

Er hält sich für den Platzhirsch hier. *He thinks he's the boss around here.*

das Porzellan — *porcelain*

das Porzellan zerschlagen — *to cause a lot of trouble.*

Mit seinen Beschuldigungen hat er viel Porzellan zerschlagen. *His accusations caused a lot of trouble.*

die Post — *mail; post office; mail coach* (**Postkutsche**)

Jetzt geht die Post ab! *It's time to get going now!*

In dem Film geht richtig die Post ab. *There's plenty of action in that movie.*

Wir hätten gerne größere Marktanteile in China—dort wird die Post abgehen! *We'd like a larger share of the market in China—that's where the action will be!*

der Posten — *post, position*

auf verlorenem Posten stehen — *to be fighting for a lost cause.*

Nicht alle Anhänger des Kreationismus wissen, dass sie auf verlorenem Posten stehen. *Not all devotees of creationism know that they're fighting for a lost cause.*

der Pott — *pot*
zu Pott(e) kommen — *to get to the point; to make up one's mind.*
Nixon bat Eisenhower zu Potte zu kommen. *Nixon asked Eisenhower to make up his mind.*

der Pranger — *pillory*
an den Pranger stellen — *to pillory.*
Die Presse stellte den Senator an den Pranger. *The press pilloried the senator.*

die Probe — *test*
auf die Probe stellen — *to put to the test.*
Ihre Liebe wurde auf die Probe gestellt. *Their love was put to the test.*

auf Probe — *on a trial basis.*
Könnten Sie mich vielleicht auf Probe einstellen? *Could you maybe hire me on a trial basis?*

die Probe aufs Exempel machen — *to decide by trying.*
Ob meiner der beste Apfelstrudel ist? Machen Sie die Probe aufs Exempel! *As to whether mine is the best apple strudel, try some and decide!*
Probieren geht über Studieren. *The proof of the pudding is in the eating.*

das Profil — *profile*
Profil haben — *to have a distinctive image.*
Unter den Wählern hat er Profil. *He has a distinctive image among the voters.*

sich profilieren — *to make one's name/mark.*
Auf der Schule profilierte er sich mehr als Athlet denn als Schüler. *In school he made more of a name for himself as an athlete than as a student.*

das Protokoll — *written record*
das Protokoll führen — *to take the minutes.*
Bei der CIA Sitzung führte ein Doppelagent das Protokoll. *A double agent took the minutes at the CIA meeting.*

etwas zu Protokoll geben — *to make a statement (for the record).*
Er gab zu Protokoll, dass er die Ermordete seit zwei Jahren nicht gesehen hätte. *He stated that he hadn't seen the murdered woman for two years.*

der Prozess — *trial; lawsuit*
  den Prozess machen — *to sue.*
  Er drohte, ihnen den Prozess zu machen. *He threatened to sue them.*

  kurzen Prozess machen — *to make short work of.*
  Die Tennis Weltmeisterin machte mit der Konkurrenz kurzen Prozess. *The world champion tennis player made short work of the competition.*

---

der Pudel — *poodle*
  Das war also des Pudels Kern! *So that's what was behind the matter!*

  wie ein begossener Pudel — *crestfallen.*
  Wie ein begossener Pudel zog er ab. *He went off crestfallen.*

  sich pudelwohl fühlen — *to feel on top of the world.*
  In der neuen Wohnung im Hochhaus fühlte sie sich pudelwohl. *In the new apartment in the high-rise she felt on top of the world.*

---

das Pulver — *powder; gunpowder*
  das Pulver nicht erfunden haben — *not to be very bright.*
  Er hat das Pulver nicht erfunden, aber sein Vater ist reich. *He's not particularly bright, but his father's rich.*

  sein Pulver verschossen haben — *to have used up one's ammunition.*
  Er konnte wenig mehr sagen, denn er hatte schon sein Pulver verschossen. *He couldn't say much more, for he'd already used up his ammunition.*

---

der Punkt — *point; period*
  auf den Punkt bringen — *to sum up; to put in a nutshell.*
  Um es auf den Punkt zu bringen, wenn wir keine Lohnerhöhung bekommen, streiken wir. *To put it in a nutshell, if we don't get a wage raise, we'll go on strike.*

  der springende Punkt — *the essential factor; the main thing.*
  Ja, schön ist es, aber zu teuer — das ist der springende Punkt. *Yes, it's nice, but too expensive; that's the main thing.*

  den toten Punkt überwinden — *to get one's second wind.*
  Ein Schluck Schnaps half ihm, den toten Punkt zu überwinden. *A swig of schnapps helped him get his second wind.*

ohne Punkt und Komma reden — *to talk nonstop.*
Da verstummte er, obwohl er gewöhnlich ohne Punkt und Komma redet.
He fell silent then, although he usually talks nonstop.

die Puppe — *doll*
  bis in die Puppen — *for a long time; till all hours.*
  Sie tanzten bis in die Puppen. *They danced till all hours.*

  die Puppen tanzen lassen — *to let it all hang out.*
  Gestern abend vergaß er seine Hemmungen und ließ alle Puppen tanzen.
  Last night he forgot his inhibitions and let it all hang out.

  die Puppen tanzen lassen — *to kick up a fuss.*
  Wenn wir seinen Befehlen nicht genau gehorchen, wird er die Puppen
  tanzen lassen. *If we don't obey his orders exactly, he will kick up a fuss.*

putzen — *to clean*
  jmdn. herunterputzen — *to put s.o. down.*
  Ihm macht's Spaß, alle herunterzuputzen. *He enjoys putting everybody
  down.*

die Qual — *torment*
  Wer die Wahl hat, hat die Qual. *It's terrible making up your mind when
  there's so much to choose from.*

der Quark — *sour curd cheese*
  Getretener Quark wird breit, nicht stark. *Under pressure jellyfish
  (weaklings) get wider, not stronger.*

  seine Nase in jeden Quark stecken — *to stick one's nose in everywhere.*
  Er fühlt sich bemüßigt, seine Nase in jeden Quark zu stecken. *He feels
  obliged to stick his nose in everywhere.*

quasseln — *to babble; chatter*
   Quasselwasser getrunken haben — *to chatter on and on.*
   Er schien Quasselwasser getrunken zu haben und ließ keinen zu Wort
     kommen. *He chattered on and on and didn't let anyone get a word in*
     edgewise.

---

das Quecksilber — *mercury, quicksilver*
   Quecksilber im Leib haben — *to have ants in one's pants.*
   Jungen in seinem Alter haben Quecksilber im Leib. *Boys his age have*
     ants in their pants.

---

quer — *sideways*
   Die Kunstziele des Bauhaus standen dem breiten Publikum quer. *The*
     artistic goals of the Bauhaus were at odds with the public at large.

   quer durch — *straight through.*
   Die Karnevalstimmung geht quer durch die Stände. *The carnival*
     atmosphere cuts across class lines.

   der Querdenker — *independent thinker; maverick.*
   Von Dogmen will er nichts wissen; er ist Querdenker. *He wants nothing to*
     do with dogmas; he's an independent thinker.

   in die Quere kommen — *to get in someone's way.*
   Keiner soll mir jetzt in die Quere kommen. *Just don't let anybody get in*
     my way now.

   quer schießen — *to make trouble, raise objections.*
   Wir glaubten alle, eine Lösung gefunden zu haben, aber natürlich musste
     Gero wieder quer schießen. *We all thought we'd found a solution, but of*
     course Gero had to raise objections again.

   der Quertreiber — *troublemaker.*
   Der wirkliche Quertreiber ist Fritz, der seine Querflöte zu ungelegener
     Zeit spielt. *The real troublemaker is Fritz, who plays his transverse*
     flute at inopportune times.

---

der Quirl — *kitchen blender*
   ein Quirl sein — *to be a real live wire.*
   Kai ist ein richtiger Quirl. *Kai is a real live wire.*

---

der Rabe — *raven*

ein weißer Rabe — *a great rarity; very unusual.*

Er sieht niemals fern, und gilt bei seinen Schulkameraden als ein weißer Rabe. *He never watches television, and his schoolmates think he's very unusual.*

klauen wie ein Rabe — *to pinch everything one can lay one's hands on.*

Überall wo Hedi hingeht, klaut sie wie ein Rabe. *Everywhere Hedi goes she pinches everything she can lay her hands on.*

schwarz wie ein Rabe — *black as pitch.*

Draußen war es schwarz wie ein Rabe. *Outside it was black as pitch.*

---

die Rabenmutter — *cruel and uncaring mother*

Die Milliardärin sagte, ihre Mutter wäre eine Rabenmutter. *The billionairess said her mother was cruel and uncaring.*

---

die Rache — *revenge*

Rache ist süß/Blutwurst. *Revenge is sweet.*

---

das Rad — *wheel*

das fünfte Rad am Wagen sein — *to be a fifth wheel.*

Ich hatte keine Lust das fünfte Rad am Wagen zu sein und blieb zu Hause. *I had no wish to be a fifth wheel and stayed home.*

unter die Räder kommen — *to get run over.*

Die Kinder kamen fast unter die Räder des Lkws. *The children almost got run over by the truck.*

unter die Räder kommen — *to go to rack and ruin; go to the dogs.*

Trotz, oder vielleicht wegen seiner Begabungen, kam er unter die Räder. *Despite, or perhaps because of, his talents, he went to the dogs.*

---

das Rädchen — *small wheel, cog*

ein Rädchen zuviel haben — *to be cuckoo, weird.*

Einige glauben, er hat ein Rädchen zuviel. *Some think he's weird.*

nur ein Rädchen im Getriebe sein — *to be a mere cog in the machinery.*
Der Beamte behauptete, er wäre nur ein Rädchen im Getriebe gewesen.
The official declared he was a mere cog in the machinery.

das Radieschen — *radish*
    die Radieschen von unten betrachten — *to push up daisies.*
Es störte die pantheistische Botanikerin nicht im geringsten, dass sie eines
    Tages die Radieschen von unten betrachten würde. *It didn't in the least
    disturb the pantheistic botanist that one day she'd be pushing up daisies.*

das Rampenlicht — *the footlights*
    im Rampenlicht stehen — *to be in the limelight.*
Sie träumt davon, im Rampenlicht zu stehen. *She dreams of being in the
    limelight.*

der Rang — *rank*
    alles, was Rang und Namen hat — *anybody who is anybody.*
Alles, was in der Stadt Rang und Namen hatte, erschien für die
    Erstaufführung. *Anyone who was anyone in the city appeared for the
    first performance.*

    den Rang ablaufen — *to surpass.*
Der Werbung nach läuft dieses neue Waschmittel allen anderen den Rang
    ab. *According to the commercials, this new detergent surpasses all the
    others.*

    ersten Ranges — *of the greatest importance.*
Für uns ist das eine Entscheidung ersten Ranges. *For us that is a decision
    of the greatest importance.*

rasten — *to rest*
    Wer rastet, der rostet. *Use it or lose it.*

der Rat — *advice*
Da ist guter Rat teuer. *This is a difficult situation to find a solution for.*

    keinen Rat wissen — *to know no way out of a situation; to be at one's
    wit's end.*
Er wusste keinen Rat mehr, und sah sich gezwungen, das Geschäft zu
    verkaufen. *He knew no other way out and sold the business.*

mit Rat und Tat — *with moral and practical support.*
Unsere Freunde standen uns mit Rat und Tat zur Seite. *Our friends stood
by us offering moral and practical support.*

mit sich zu Rate gehen — *to think over carefully.*
Wir müssen erst mit uns zu Rate gehen, bevor wir Ihr Angebot annehmen
können. *We'll have to think it over carefully before we can accept
your offer.*

zu Rate ziehen — *to consult.*
Sie haben eine Fachärztin zu Rate gezogen. *They consulted a specialist.*

---

der Raubbau — *ruthless exploitation*
Raubbau mit seiner Gesundheit treiben — *to undermine one's health.*
Um sein Geschäft aufzubauen, trieb er mit seiner Gesundheit Raubbau. *In
building up his business he undermined his health.*

die Raupe — *caterpillar*
Raupen im Kopf haben — *to have odd ideas.*
Mit 80 Jahren will er wieder zur See fahren. Na, er hat ja immer Raupen
im Kopf gehabt. *At 80 he wants to go to sea again. Well, he's always
had odd ideas.*

---

rechnen — *to reckon; calculate*
gut/schlecht rechnen können — *to be good/bad at figures.*
Käthi kann gut rechnen, besser als ihr Bruder. *Käthi is good at figures,
better than her brother.*

sich rechnen — *to show a profit; pay off.*
Das Projekt ist teuer, aber in wenigen Jahren wird es sich rechnen. *The
project is expensive, but in a few years it will show a profit.*

---

die Rechnung — *calculation*
auf eigene Rechnung — *at one's own risk.*
Er hat es auf eigene Rechnung getan. *He did it at his own risk.*

auf seine Rechnung kommen — *to get one's money's worth.*
In dem Restaurant kommt jeder auf seine Rechnung. *All get their money's
worth in that restaurant.*

einen Strich durch die Rechnung machen — *to ruin plans*.
Wir wollten aufs Land, aber der Wettergott hat uns einen Strich durch die
Rechnung gemacht. *We wanted to go to the country, but the weather
ruined our plans.*

---

recht — *right*
jemandem recht geben — *to admit that someone is right*.
Ich musste ihr recht geben. *I had to admit that she was right.*

recht behalten — *to be proved right*.
Also hat sie doch recht behalten. *So she was proved right anyway.*

recht haben — *to be right*.
Die Partei hatte nicht immer recht. *The party wasn't always right.*

Was dem einen recht ist, ist dem anderen billig. *What is justice for one
person is justice for another, too.*

---

reden — *to speak*
reden wie einem der Schnabel gewachsen ist — *to talk freely and easily*.
In der Kiezkneipe kann der Chef reden, wie ihm der Schnabel gewachsen
ist. *In that neighborhood bar the boss can talk freely and easily.*

---

der Regen — *rain*
ein warmer Regen — *a windfall*.
Er hofft auf einen warmen Regen. *He's hoping for a windfall.*

im Regen stehen lassen — *to leave in the lurch*.
Er ließ seine Familie im Regen stehen. *He left his family in the lurch.*

vom Regen in die Traufe kommen — *to go from the frying pan into
the fire*.
Wir zogen um und kamen vom Regen in die Traufe. *We moved and went
from the frying pan into the fire.*

---

der Regenbogen — *rainbow*
die Regenbogenpresse — *gossip/scandal/romance print media*.
In der Regenbogenpresse steht viel über Filmstars, Politiker und Adlige.
In scandal sheets there's a lot about movie stars, politicians, and royals.

---

das Register — *register, index; organ stop*

  alle Register ziehen/alle Register spielen lassen — *to pull out all the stops.*

  Um den Vertrag zu bekommen, mussten wir alle Register ziehen. *We had to pull out all the stops to get the contract.*

  andere Register ziehen — *to take a different approach.*

  Sie werden immer unverschämter; wir müssen jetzt andere Register ziehen. *They're growing more and more brazen; we'll have to take a different tack.*

---

reichen — *to reach; to be/have enough*

  Die Demonstranten schrien: "Uns reicht's!" *The demonstrators shouted, "We've had enough!"*

---

die Reihe — *row*

  an der Reihe sein — *to be someone's turn.*

  Jetzt bist du an der Reihe. *It's your turn now.*

  an die Reihe kommen — *to get one's turn.*

  Wann komme ich an die Reihe? *When do I get my turn?*

  aus der Reihe tanzen — *to be different.*

  In der Militärschule durfte niemand aus der Reihe tanzen. *In military school no one was allowed to be different.*

  nicht alle in der Reihe haben — *not to be all there.*

  Ich glaube, er hat nicht alle in der Reihe. *I don't think he's all there.*

  wieder in die Reihe kommen — *to get back on one's feet again.*

  Ich hoffe, bald wieder in die Reihe zu kommen. *I hope to get back on my feet again soon.*

---

rein — *pure, clear*

  ins Reine kommen — *to sort/straighten out.*

  Sie versucht, mit ihren inneren Konflikten ins Reine zu kommen. *She's trying to sort out her inner conflicts.*

  reinen Wein einschenken — *to be honest, forthcoming.*

  Die Politiker müssen uns reinen Wein einschenken. *The politicians must be more honest with us.*

reinsten Wassers — *through and through*.
Sie ist eine Dichterin reinsten Wassers. *She's a poet through and through*.

die Reise — *trip*
eine Reise machen — *to take a trip*.
Jedes Jahr machen wir eine Reise in die Berge. *Every year we take a trip to the mountains*.

sich auf die Reise machen — *to start (out) on a trip*.
Bald machen wir uns auf die Reise. *We'll be starting out soon*.

viel auf Reisen sein — *to be away; to travel*.
Geschäftlich ist er viel auf Reisen. *He travels a lot on business*.

der Reiter — *horseman, rider; cavalryman*
der Paragraphenreiter — *stickler for the rules, pedant*.
Der Chef ist kein Paragraphenreiter; manchmal lässt er auch fünf gerade sein. *The boss is no petty bureaucrat; sometimes he bends the rules a little*.

der Spitzenreiter — *front-runner, top seller; number-one hit*.
Das altbekannte Waschmittel ist nicht mehr Spitzenreiter. *The well-known old detergent isn't the market leader anymore*.

der Vorreiter — *avant-gardist, pioneer*.
Sein Unternehmen war Vorreiter bei der Unterstützung junger Künstler. *Our company was a trailblazer in the support of young artists*.

das Rennen — *race*
Das Rennen ist gelaufen. *The race is over (the matter is settled)*.

das Rennen machen — *to win the race*.
Jede der drei Parteien sagte, sie würde das Wahlrennen machen. *Each of the three parties said they'd win the electoral race*.

die Rente — *pension*
in Rente gehen — *to retire*.
Seit Jahren denkt er daran, in Rente zu gehen. *For years he's been thinking of retiring*.

sich rentieren — *to be profitable*
   Sie glauben, dass die Magnetschwebebahn sich rentieren wird. *They*
    believe the magnetic levitation train will be profitable.

der Rest — *rest, remainder*
   den Rest geben — *to wipe out, finish off.*
   Die Gier nach Kaviar hat dem europäischen Stör fast den Rest gegeben.
    Greed for caviar has almost wiped out the European sturgeon.

riechen — *to smell*
   etwas nicht riechen können — *not be able to know.*
   Ich konnte nicht riechen, dass er ein Spion war. *How was I supposed to*
    know that he was a spy?

   nicht riechen können — *not to be able to stand.*
   Sie kann ihn nicht riechen. *She can't stand him.*

der Riecher — *smeller; nose*
   den richtigen Riecher (einen guten Riecher) haben — *to have a*
    sense/instinct for.
   Ich hatte den richtigen Riecher und wusste, dass es Schwindel war. *I had*
    the right instinct and knew that it was a swindle.

der Riemen — *belt*
   den Riemen enger schnallen — *to tighten one's belt.*
   Im Krieg mussten wir uns den Riemen enger schnallen und dabei wurden
    wir gesünder. *In the war we had to tighten our belts and were healthier*
    for it.

   sich am Riemen reißen — *to pull oneself together.*
   Wenn du dich am Riemen reißt, besteht noch Hoffnung für dich. *If you*
    pull yourself together there's still hope for you.

   sich kräftig in die Riemen legen — *to put one's nose to the grindstone.*
   Wenn ihr euch kräftig in die Riemen legt, werden wir noch vor Abend
    fertig. *If you put your nose to the grindstone, we'll be done before*
    evening.

der Ritt — *ride*
    auf einen Ritt — *all at once.*
    Du brauchst den Kuchen nicht auf einen Ritt aufzuessen. *You don't have to eat up the cake all at once.*

der Rock — *skirt; jacket*
    Der letzte Rock hat keine Taschen. *You can't take it with you.*

die Rolle — *roll*
    aus der Rolle fallen — *to behave inappropriately.*
    Bei seinem Empfang betrank sich der Botschafter und fiel aus der Rolle. *At his reception the ambassador got drunk and behaved inappropriately.*

    eine Rolle spielen — *to be of importance.*
    Ihre Unterstützung hat eine entscheidende Rolle gespielt. *Her support was of crucial importance.*

röntgen — *to take X-rays*
    Man hat geröngt, aber nichts gefunden. *They took X-rays but found nothing.*

das Ross — *horse; steed*
    auf dem hohen Ross sitzen — *to lord it over others.*
    Sie sind reich und sitzen gern auf dem hohen Ross. *They're rich and like to lord it over others.*

    Ross und Reiter nennen — *to name names.*
    Warum nennt die Zeitung Ross und Reiter nicht? *Why doesn't the newspaper name names?*

    die Rosskur — *drastic measure/remedy.*
    Er will den Betrieb einer Rosskur unterziehen. *He wants to apply drastic measures to save the company.*

rot — *red*
    auf der roten Liste stehen — *to be endangered.*
    Viele Tierarten stehen auf der roten Liste. *Many species are endangered.*

die rote Laterne tragen — *to be last.*

Wirtschaftlich trägt unser Bundesland noch die rote Laterne.
Economically, our state still brings up the rear.

Heute rot, morgen tot. *Here today, gone tomorrow. (Today in the pink, tomorrow in the drink.)*

---

der Rubel — *Russian ruble*

Der Rubel rollt. *Business is booming.*

---

das Ruder — *rudder; oar*

am Ruder sein — *to be in power.*

Trotz Unruhen ist der Diktator noch am Ruder. *Despite disturbances, the dictator is still in power.*

das Ruder (he)rumreißen — *to right a course, reverse a trend.*

Die Präsidentin will alles versuchen, vor der Wahl das Ruder noch herumzureißen. *The president wants to do all she can to reverse the trend before the elections.*

das Ruder in der Hand haben — *to be in control.*

Sie hat noch das Ruder in der Hand—aber wie lange noch? *She's still in control—but for how long?*

---

der Ruf — *call; reputation*

Ist der Ruf erst ruiniert, lebt man völlig ungeniert. *Once your reputation's ruined, you can do as you please./If you've got the name, you might as well have the game.*

---

rufen — *to call*

wie gerufen kommen — *to come at just the right moment.*

Du kommst wie gerufen! *You've come just at the right moment.*

---

der Rufmord — *character assassination*

Der Filmstar drohte, den Journalisten wegen Rufmord zu verklagen.
The movie star threatened to sue the Journalist for character assassination.

---

die Ruhe — *calm*

   Immer mit der Ruhe! *Just take it easy. Don't panic.*

   in aller Ruhe — *quite calmly.*

   In aller Ruhe erörterten wir die Lage. *We discussed the situation quite calmly.*

   aus der Ruhe bringen — *to make nervous.*

   Jetzt hast du mich wieder aus der Ruhe gebracht. *Now you've made me nervous again.*

   sich zur Ruhe setzen — *to retire.*

   Sie will sich noch nicht zur Ruhe setzen. *She doesn't want to retire yet.*

---

der Ruhestand — *retirement*

   in den Ruhestand treten — *to retire.*

   Mit 48 Jahren ist er schon in den Ruhestand getreten. *He retired at 48.*

---

rund — *round*

   rund um die Uhr — *round-the-clock.*

   Diese Patienten brauchen Pflege rund um die Uhr. *These patients require round-the-clock care.*

---

die Runde — *round*

   die Runde machen — *to make the rounds.*

   Üble Gerüchte machten die Runde durch die Stadt. *Nasty rumors made the rounds in the city.*

   eine runde Kugel schieben — *to have a cushy job.*

   Jahrelang schob Lars eine runde Kugel im Auswärtigen Amt. *For years Lars had a cushy job in the State Dept./Foreign Office.*

   eine Runde schmeißen — *to buy a round of drinks.*

   Gestern hat er allen eine Runde Bier geschmissen. *Yesterday he bought a round of beer for everybody.*

   über die Runden kommen — *to make ends meet.*

   Mit seinem so niedrigen Gehalt kommt seine Familie kaum über die Runden. *His family scarcely makes ends meet on his low salary.*

---

die Sache — *thing; matter*

nicht bei der Sache sein — *not to be committed; not to be with it.*

Er ist sehr begabt, scheint aber nicht ganz bei der Sache zu sein. *He's very talented but doesn't seem to be entirely with it.*

zur Sache kommen — *to get to the point.*

Wann kommen Sie endlich zur Sache? *When will you finally get to the point?*

der Sack — *bag*

im Sack haben — *to have in the bag.*

Die Firma glaubte, den Auftrag im Sack zu haben. *The firm thought it had the contract in the bag.*

mit Sack und Pack — *with bag and baggage.*

Sie wollen mit Sack und Pack kommen. *They want to come with bag and baggage.*

säen — *to sow*

dünn gesät — *few and far between.*

Solche Gelegenheiten sind dünn gesät. *Such opportunities are few and far between.*

wie gesät — *spread out in quantity.*

Die Pflaumen lagen auf dem Gras wie gesät. *Quantites of plums were all spread out on the grass.*

der Saft — *juice*

im eigenen Saft schmoren lassen — *to let someone stew in his/her own juices.*

Sie sagte nichts, und ließ ihn im eigenen Saft schmoren. *She said nothing and let him stew in his own juices.*

ohne Saft und Kraft — *insipid; limp.*

Seine Argumente waren ohne Saft und Kraft. *His arguments were limp.*

sagen — *to say*

das Sagen haben — *to say what goes*.

Niemand weiß, ob der Präsident oder der General das Sagen im Land hat.
*No one knows whether it's the president or the general who says what
goes in that country.*

nichts zu sagen haben — *not to mean anything*.

Sein "Nein" hat nichts zu sagen. *His "No" doesn't mean anything.*

sage und schreibe — *really; no kidding*.

Sie hat sage und schreibe 200 Millionen Dollar geerbt. *She inherited 200
million dollars, no kidding.*

unter uns gesagt — *between you and me*.

Unter uns gesagt, ich suche eine andere Stelle. *Between you and me, I'm
looking for another job.*

---

der Salat — *salad*

den Salat haben — *to be in a (fine) fix*.

Jetzt haben wir den Salat; der Wagen springt nicht an. *Now we're in a fix;
the car won't start.*

---

der Salon — *parlor, living-room*

salonfähig — *socially acceptable, presentable*.

Seine radikale Partei ist jetzt salonfähig geworden. *His radical party's
now socially acceptable.*

der Salonkommunist/Salonanarchist — *parlor pink/armchair
revolutionary*.

Dieser Salonkommunist ist millionenschwer. *That parlor pink's got millions.*

der Salontiroler — *armchair yodeler (Northerner/city slicker enthusiastic
about the Alps)*.

Dieser Salontiroler will Unterricht im Jodeln und Skifahren von mir. *That
armchair yodeler wants skiing and yodeling lessons from me.*

---

das Salz — *salt*

nicht das Salz in der Suppe gönnen — *to begrudge everything; not to
want to give someone the time of day*.

Sie gönnen uns nicht das Salz in der Suppe. *They begrudge us everything.*

Salz auf die Wunde streuen — *to rub salt into the wound.*
Musst du noch Salz auf meine Wunde streuen? *Do you have to rub salt into the wound?*

weder Salz noch Schmalz haben — *to have neither wit nor intensity.*
Das Stück hatte weder Salz noch Schmalz. *The play had neither wit nor intensity.*

Sankt-Nimmerleins-Tag — *"Saint Neverly's Day"; Doomsday; never*
bis zum Sankt-Nimmerleins-Tag warten — *to wait forever.*
Bevor ich mich bei ihm entschuldige, kann er bis zum Sankt-Nimmerleins-Tag warten. *He can wait forever before I apologize to him.*

die Sau — *sow*
die Sau rauslassen — *to let it all hang out.*
Wir wollten uns amüsieren und die Sau richtig rauslassen. *We wanted to have a good time and let it all hang out.*

Perlen vor die Säue werfen — *to cast pearls before swine.*
Er bildete sich ein, seine Perlen vor die Säue zu werfen. *In his conceit he thought he was casting his pearls before swine.*

unter aller Sau — *beneath contempt, really rotten.*
Sein Vortrag war unter aller Sau. *His presentation was pathetic.*

sauer — *sour; ticked off*
Die Mannschaft war auf den Schiedsrichter sauer. *The team was ticked off at the umpire.*

saufen — *to drink (animals); to guzzle*
saufen wie ein Loch/Schlauch — *to drink like a fish.*
Onkel Otto säuft wie ein Loch. *Uncle Otto drinks like a fish.*

saugen — *to suck*
sich etwas aus den Fingern saugen — *to make s.t. up; figure out.*
Das wär's also? Nichts mehr? Das hätte ich mir selber aus den Fingern saugen können. *So that's it? Nothing more? I could have come up with that myself.*

in Saus und Braus leben — *to live the life of Riley*

Mit dem gestohlenen Geld lebten sie eine Zeitlang in Saus und Braus. *For a while they lived the life of Riley with the money they stole.*

---

die Sause — *pub crawl*

eine Sause machen — *go barhopping.*

Er machte eine Sause, trank zu viel vom Sauser, und wurde krank. *He went barhopping, drank too much new wine, and got sick.*

---

sausen — *to roar (wind)*

durchs Examen sausen — *to fail an exam.*

Er sauste wieder durchs Examen. *He failed the exam again.*

sausenlassen — *not to bother about; to drop.*

Er bot mir eine Stelle an, aber ich ließ sie sausen. *He offered me a job, but I didn't bother about it.*

---

der Schaden — *damage*

Durch Schaden wird man klug. *One learns by negative experiences. (Experience is the best teacher.)*

Wer den Schaden hat, braucht nicht für Spott zu sorgen. *The laugh is always on the loser.*

zu Schaden kommen — *to be harmed.*

Durch seine Trunksucht ist seine Karriere zu Schaden gekommen. *His career was harmed by his alcoholism.*

---

die Schadenfreude — *malicious pleasure*

Schadenfreude heißt, sich über das Unglück anderer freuen.
"Schadenfreude" means taking malicious pleasure in others' misfortunes.

schadenfroh — *with malicious pleasure.*

Schadenfroh beobachtete Iago den eifersüchtigen Othello. *With malicious pleasure Iago observed jealous Othello.*

---

das Schäfchen — *little lamb*

sein Schäfchen ins Trockene bringen — *to look out for one's own interests.*

Der Börsenmakler brachte sein Schäfchen ins Trockene, ohne sich um seine Auftraggeber zu kümmern. *The stockbroker looked out for his own interests with no concern for his clients.*

---

der Schalk — *imp, jokester*
jemandem sitzt der Schalk im Nacken — *s.o. is impish.*
Diesem Satiriker sitzt der Schalk im Nacken. *That satirist is quite a Merry Devil.*

---

der Schall — *sound*
Schall und Rauch — *meaningless.*
Seine Versprechungen waren nur Schall und Rauch. *His promises were meaningless.*

---

scharf — *sharp*
scharf auf — *keen on; fond of.*
Sie ist scharf auf Gesundheit. *She's keen on (maintaining) health.*
Ich esse gern scharf. *I'm fond of spicy foods.*

scharf schießen — *to use live ammunition; to aim to hit.*
Es wurde scharf geschossen. *They used live ammunition.*

---

der Schatten — *shade; shadow*
über seinen eigenen Schatten springen — *to transcend one's nature/feelings by making a great effort.*
Sie sprang über ihren eigenen Schatten und vergab ihm. *She mastered her feelings and forgave him.*

Über seinen eigenen Schatten kann man nicht springen. *A leopard can't change its spots.*

---

das Schattendasein — *shadowy existence*
ein Schattendasein fristen — *to be insignificant.*
Einst fristete die Umweltschutzpolitik ein Schattendasein; heute steht sie im Mittelpunkt. *Once the political aspects of environmental protection were insignificant; today they're central.*

---

die Schau — *show*
  zur Schau stellen — *to exhibit.*
  Ihre Gemälde werden jetzt in mehreren Galerien zur Schau gestellt. *Her paintings are now on exhibition in several galleries.*

  zur Schau tragen — *to make a show of.*
  Der Heuchler trug seine Frömmigkeit zur Schau.
  The hypocrite made a show of his piety.

---

der Schaum — *foam*
  Schaum schlagen — *to boast, talk big.*
  Wird er's wirklich tun, oder hat er nur Schaum geschlagen? *Will he really do it, or was he just talking big?*

---

die Scheibe — *slice*
  eine Scheibe abschneiden — *to learn a thing or two.*
  Von ihr könntest du dir eine Scheibe abschneiden. *You could learn a thing or two from her.*

---

der Schein — *appearance*
  Der Schein trügt. *Appearances are deceptive.*

  den Schein wahren — *to keep up appearances.*
  Die Geschäftspartner vertragen sich nicht, aber sie versuchen noch, den Schein zu wahren. *The business partners don't get along, but they're still trying to keep up appearances.*

  zum Schein — *as a pretense; to pretend to do.*
  Der Polizeibeamte sollte die Drogen nur zum Schein kaufen. *The policeman was supposed only to pretend to buy the drugs.*

---

der Schickimicki — *trendy; glitzy, fancy-shmantzy*
  Die Nordseeinsel Sylt gilt als Schickimicki. *The North Sea island Sylt is considered trendy.*

---

schießen — *to shoot*
  ausgehen wie das Hornberger Schießen — *to fizzle out.*
  Monatelang gab es viel Rummel, aber schließlich ging alles wie das Hornberger Schießen aus. *For months there was a lot of fuss, but at the end everything fizzled out.*

zum Schießen sein — *to be very funny.*
Diese Komikerin ist wirklich zum Schießen. *This comic is really very funny.*

der Schild — *shield*

auf den Schilde heben — *to make one's leader.*
Die Gruppe suchte einen Helden, den sie auf den Schilde erheben konnte. *The group was looking for a hero they could make their leader.*

etwas Im Schilde führen — *to be plotting; to be up to no good.*
Ich glaube, er führt gegen uns etwas im Schllde. *I think he's plotting against us.*

der Schildbürger — *Gothamite, big fool*

Es stellte sich heraus, dass die vermeintlichen Schildbürger alles andere als Bauernopfer waren. *It turned out that the supposedly foolish villagers were anything but dumb country bumpkins.*

der Schimmer — *gleam; shimmer*

keinen (blassen) Schimmer haben — *to have no (not the faintest) idea.*
Wir hatten keinen Schimmer davon, dass sie heute kommen sollten. *We had no idea they were coming today.*

der Schlag — *blow; stroke*

auf einen Schlag — *all at once; simultaneously.*
Die Gefangenen begannen alle, auf einen Schlag zu schreien. *The prisoners all began shouting simultaneously.*

ein Schlag ins Wasser — *a washout.*
Sein Versuch, den Betrieb zu retten, war ein Schlag ins Wasser. *His attempt to save the company was a washout.*

mit einem Schlag — *suddenly.*
Nach ihrem ersten Film wurde sie mit einem Schlag berühmt. *After her first movie she was suddenly famous.*

Schlag auf Schlag — *in rapid succession.*
Nach dem missglückten Staatsstreich kamen die Nachrichten Schlag auf Schlag. *After the unsuccessful coup, the news came in rapid succession.*

schlagen — *to beat*

Brücken schlagen — *to build bridges; create bonds.*

Wir wollen alle mithelfen, Brücken zwischen den Menschen zu schlagen. *We all want to help in building bridges between people.*

Vorteil schlagen — *to turn to one's advantage.*

Aus allen Lagen weiß er, Vorteil zu schlagen. *He knows how to turn every situation to his own advantage.*

Wurzeln schlagen — *to put down roots.*

Sie haben schon in der neuen Heimat Wurzeln geschlagen. *They've already put down roots in their new homeland.*

---

die Schlange — *snake*

Die Schlange beißt sich in den Schwanz. *This business just keeps going round in circles.*

Schlange stehen — *to wait in line.*

Wir mussten fast eine Stunde Schlange stehen. *We had to wait in line for almost an hour.*

der Schlangenmensch — *contortionist.*

Ich kann's nicht, bin doch kein Schlangenmensch. *I can't do it, I'm no contortionist.*

---

schlecht — *bad*

mehr schlecht als recht — *after a fashion.*

Das Buch langweilte sie und sie las es mehr schlecht als recht. *The book bored her and she read it only after a fashion.*

---

schlechthin — *quintessential(ly); the very embodiment of*

Nietzsche war der individuelle Denker schlechthin. *Nietzsche was the very embodiment of the individualistic thinker.*

---

der Schliff — *cut; polish*

der letzte Schliff — *the finishing touch.*

Es schien ihr, dass der Maler vergessen hatte, dem Gemälde den letzten Schliff zu geben. *It seemed to her that the painter had forgotten to give the painting the finishing touch.*

Schliff backen — *to do a poor job.*
Sie haben mit dem Projekt Schliff gebacken. *They did a poor job on the project.*

schlucken — *to swallow*
eine Kuh/Kröte schlucken müssen — *to have to accept something, make difficult/unpleasant compromises.*
Die Senatoren mussten manche Kröte schlucken, aber sie stimmten doch für den Plan. *The senators had to accept many things they didn't like but nevertheless they voted for the plan.*

der Schlüssel — *key*
schlüsselfertig — *ready to move into.*
Der Makler sagte, das Haus wäre schlüsselfertig. *The real estate agent said the house was ready to move into.*

das Schloss — *lock*
hinter Schloss und Riegel — *behind bars; under lock and key.*
Die Betrogenen freuten sich, dass der Betrüger hinter Schloss und Riegel saß. *The people he cheated were glad the conman was behind bars.*

der Schlot — *chimney*
wie ein Schlot qualmen — *to smoke like a chimney.*
Er weiß, dass es seiner Gesundheit schadet, trotzdem qualmt er wie ein Schlot. *He knows it's harmful to his health, still he smokes like a chimney.*

der Schlotbaron — *industrial tycoon.*
Er gibt sich gern für einen Schlotbaron aus. *He likes to pass himself off as a tycoon.*

der Schluss — *conclusion*
Schluss machen — *to stop; to break off a relationship.*
Erst gegen Mitternacht machten sie Schluss mit dem Lärm. *They stopped making noise only around midnight.*
Sie überlegte sich, wie sie mit ihm Schluss machen könnte. *She pondered how she could break off with him.*

schlüssig — *convincing; logical*
  sich schlüssig werden — *to make up one's mind.*
  Sie konnten sich über ihre Reisepläne nicht schlüssig werden. *They*
  couldn't make up their minds about their travel plans.

---

das Schlusslicht — *taillight*
  Schlusslicht sein — *to be in last position, bring up the rear.*
  Dieses Jahr ist unsere Mannschaft wieder Schlusslicht. *Our team's in last*
  position again this year.

---

schmecken — *to taste*
  "Hat es Ihnen geschmeckt?" fragte die Kellnerin. *"Did you enjoy your*
  meal?" asked the waitress.
  Wie schmeckte Ihnen die Linsensuppe? *How did you like the lentil soup?*

  nach gar nichts schmecken; nicht nach ihm und nicht nach ihr
  schmecken — *to be flat-tasting.*
  Das Gemüse schmeckte nach gar nichts. *The vegetables were flat-tasting.*

  nach mehr schmecken — *to taste like more.*
  Der Nachtisch schmeckt nach mehr. *The dessert tastes like more.*

---

der Schmied — *blacksmith*
  Jeder ist seines Glückes Schmied. *Life is what you make it.*

---

der Schmock — *hack writer*
  Weil sie eifersüchtig waren, nannten sie ihn einen Schmock. *Because they*
  were jealous, they called him a hack writer.

  der Schmöker — *light reading (adventure, romance).*
  Sie liest gern dicke Schmöker. *She likes to read fat, fast-moving books.*

  schmökern — *to bury oneself in a book.*
  Sie wollte schmökern, nicht fernsehen. *She wanted to bury herself in a*
  book instead of watching television.

---

schmettern — *to hurl; bellow*
  einen schmettern — *to belt down alcohol.*
  Er hatte Lust, einen zu schmettern. *He felt like belting one down.*

---

das Schnäppchen — *bargain*
  ein Schnäppchen machen — *to get a bargain.*
  Er glaubte, ein Schnäppchen gemacht zu haben, aber das Gemälde war
    nicht echt. *He thought he'd gotten a bargain, but the painting wasn't*
    genuine.

---

die Schnapsfahne — *boozy breath*
  Bleib mir weg mit deiner Schnapsfahne. *Stay away from me with your*
    boozy breath.

---

die Schnapsidee — *hare-brained scheme*
  Dieser Vorschlag ist nicht als Schnapsidee abzutun. *This proposal*
    shouldn't be dismissed as a hare-brained scheme.

---

die Schnapszahl — *multidigit number with all digits identical,*
numerical palindrome, fanciful number
  Sie heirateten am 8.8 2008, weil sie an die Numerologie glauben, und ihr
    Leben nach Schnapszahlen richten. *They got married on August 8, 2008*
    because they believe in numerology and live their lives according to
    fanciful numbers.

---

der Schneider — *tailor*
  aus dem Schneider/vom Schneider sein — *to be in the clear/off the*
    hook/out of the woods.
  Gegen den Senator wird noch ermittelt; er ist noch nicht vom Schneider.
    The senator's still being investigated; he's not off the hook yet.

---

schneien — *to snow*
  ins Haus schneien — *to snow into the house; to descend unannounced on*
    someone.
  Wir müssen es ihm abgewöhnen, uns ins Haus zu schneien. *We'll have to*
    get him to break the habit of descending unannounced on us.

---

der Schock — *shock*
  unter Schock stehen — *to be in shock.*
  Die Passagiere stehen noch unter Schock. *The passengers are still in a*
    state of shock.

---

der Schönheitsfehler — *blemish; (minor) drawback*
Es gibt mehr als einen Schönheitsfehler in seinem Plan. *There's more than one drawback in his plan.*

der Schrei — *cry; scream*
der letzte Schrei — *the latest fashion.*
In den sechziger Jahren war der Minirock der letzte Schrei. *In the sixties the mini skirt was the latest fashion.*

der Schrecken — *horror*
mit dem Schrecken davonkommen — *to have had a close call but be safe.*
Beim Zugunfall gab es zwei leicht Verletzte, aber die meisten Passagiere kamen mit dem Schrecken davon. *Two were slightly injured in the train accident, but most passengers were scared but safe.*

der Schritt — *step*
Schritt halten — *to keep up with.*
Seiner Firma fällt es schwer, auf dem internationalen Markt Schritt zu halten. *It's difficult for his firm to keep pace with the international market.*

die Schuld — *guilt; debt*
Schulden machen — *to go into debt.*
Wir wollen keine Schulden machen. *We don't want to go into debt.*

die Schule — *school*
Schule machen — *to find imitators; be taken up.*
Diese Idee macht jetzt überall Schule. *This idea is being taken up everywhere now.*
schulmeistern — *to lecture in a prescriptive way.*
Ich will mich nicht weiter von ihm schulmeistern lassen. *I won't be lectured to anymore by him.*

die Schulter — *shoulder*
auf die Schulter klopfen — *to give a pat on the back.*

Der Chef klopfte mir auf die Schulter, gab mir aber keine
Gehaltserhöhung. *The boss gave me a pat on the back but no salary
raise.*

auf die leichte Schulter nehmen — *to underestimate.*
Nehmen Sie seine Drohungen nicht auf die leichte Schulter! *Don't
underestimate his threats.*

der Schulterschluss — *act of solidarity.*
Das Abkommen wurde als Schulterschluss bezeichnet. *The agreement was
called an act of solidarity.*

---

der Schuss — *shot*
  ein Schuss in den Ofen — *a total waste of effort.*
Der Oppositionschef behauptete, das Regierungsprogramm sei ein Schuss
in den Ofen. *The head of the opposition said the government's program
was a total waste of effort.*

  in Schuss — *in working order.*
Die Straßenbeleuchtung ist nicht immer in Schuss. *The street lights aren't
always in working order.*

---

der Schwamm — *sponge*
Schwamm drüber! Ich will nichts mehr davon hören. *Drop it! I don't want
to hear anymore about it.*

---

schwarz — *black*
  schwarzarbeiten — *to do work not reported for taxes.*
Er bezieht Arbeitslosengeld und arbeitet auch ein bisschen schwarz.
*He collects unemployment and also does a little unreported work on
the side.*

  schwarzbrennen — *to distill illegally; make moonshine.*
Sie las Burns' Gedichte über das Schwarzbrennen von Scotch vor. *She
recited Burns' poems about the illegal distilling of scotch.*

  schwarzfahren — *to ride without having paid.*
Man hat uns erwischt, als wir in Wien mit der Straßenbahn
schwarzgefahren sind. *They caught us in Vienna when we rode the
streetcar without paying.*

schwarzsehen — *to be pessimistic*.
Was die Wirtschaft betrifft, sehen die meisten Experten noch schwarz.
   Most experts are still pessimistic about the economy.

---

die Schwebe — *state of suspension*
   in der Schwebe liegen — *to be uncertain, open*.
   Die Entscheidung liegt noch in der Schwebe. *The decision is still open.*

---

das Schwein — *pig*
   Schwein haben — *to be (very) lucky*.
   Das ist das erste Mal, das wir beim Lotto Schwein haben. *That's the first
   time we've been lucky in the lottery.*

---

schwer — *heavy*
   schwer fallen — *to find difficult*.
   Am Golf von Biskaya fiel es der hübschen Brünette schwer, sich von
   ihrem blonden Matrosen zu trennen. *The pretty brunette found it hard to
   part from her blond sailor by the Bay of Biscay.*

   schweres Geld kosten — *to cost a lot of money, a bundle*.
   So ein Wagen muss schweres Geld gekostet haben. *A car like that must
   have cost a lot of money.*

   der Schwerpunkt — *center of gravity; focus*.
   Der Schwerpunkt unserer heutigen Berichterstattung ist der
   Regierungswechsel. *The focus of our reporting today is the change in
   government.*

   sich schwertun mit — *to have trouble with*.
   Viele Wähler in einigen Ländern tun sich schwer mit der Idee einer
   Europäischen Union. *Many voters in some countries have trouble with
   the idea of a European union.*

   der Schwerverbrecher — *serious offender*.
   Die Polizei verfolgte die Schwerverbrecher. *The police pursued the
   serious offenders.*

---

schwimmen — *to swim*
   ins Schwimmen kommen — *to be all at sea*.

Er verhaspelte sich und kam bald ins Schwimmen. *He stumbled on his words and was soon all at sea.*

---

die See — *sea, ocean*
zur See fahren — *to go to sea, be a sailor.*
Ich bin mehrere Jahre zur See gefahren. *I was a sailor for many years.*

---

die Seele — *soul*
die Seele baumeln lassen — *to relax, drift and dream.*
Am Strand haben wir die Seele baumeln lassen. *We relaxed on the beach.*

---

das Seil — *rope*
in den Seilen hängen — *to be on the ropes (boxing); be exhausted.*
Tag und Nacht hab ich geastet; kein Wunder, dass ich jetzt in den Seilen hänge. *I slaved away night and day; no wonder I'm knocked out now.*

die Seilschaft — *mountain climbers joined by ropes; coterie, clique.*
Gegen den alten Parteichef und seine Seilschaft kommst du nicht an. *You can't buck the old party boss and his coterie.*

---

sehen — *to see*
sich sehen lassen — *to be impressive.*
Trotz des Rückgangs lässt sich die Handelsbilanz noch sehen. *Despite the decline, the balance of trade is still impressive.*

---

seinesgleichen — *similar to oneself*
wie seinesgleichen behandeln — *to treat as an equal.*
Die Königin hat mich wie ihresgleichen behandelt. *The queen treated me as an equal.*

seinesgleichen suchen — *to be unequaled.*
Ihre Skulpturen suchen auf der Welt ihresgleichen. *Her sculptures are unequaled anywhere.*

---

selig — *blessed*
nach seiner Fasson selig werden — *to pursue happiness in one's own way.*

"Jeder soll nach seiner Fasson selig werden," sagte Friedrich der Große. *"Let everyone turn on to religion in his/her/their own way," said Frederick the Great.*

der Senkel — *shoelace; plumbline*
　jmdm. auf den Senkel gehen — *to get on s.o.'s nerves.*
　Du gehst mir echt auf den Senkel mit deiner Nörgelei. *Your nagging is really getting on my nerves.*

　jmdn. in den Senkel stellen — *to put s.o. in his/her place; lay down the law to s.o.*
　Diesen Aufmüpfigen werden wir bald in den Senkel stellen. *We'll soon put that uppity guy in his place.*

senkrecht — *vertical*
　Immer schön senkrecht bleiben! *Keep your spirits up/don't let things get you down.*

　das einzig Senkrechte — *the only good choice, only thing that stands up to comparison.*
　In der ganzen Stadt ist dieses Restaurant das einzig Senkrechte. *This restaurant's the only good choice in the whole town.*

die Serie — *series*
　serienreif — *ready for mass production.*
　Dieses Modell ist noch nicht serienreif. *This model isn't ready for mass production yet.*

　serienweise — *in series; in great quantities.*
　Serienweise schrieb Dumas Romane. *Dumas cranked out quantities of novels.*

setzen — *to put; to set*
　auf etwas setzen — *to bet on, count on.*
　Wir setzen auf einen Konjunkturaufschwung. *We're counting on an economic upturn.*

　eins/einen drauf setzen — *to go one better/one step further; add insult to injury.*

Seiner bisherigen Leistung will er noch eins draufsetzen. *He wants to go beyond his previous record.*

Signale/Zeichen setzen — *to send a message; indicate a trend.*

Mit dieser Äußerung wollte der Kanzler Zeichen setzen. *With that statement the chancellor wanted to indicate a trend.*

---

sieben — *seven*

die Siebensachen — *belongings.*

Vor Einbruch der Soldaten packten die Einwohner ihre Siebensachen zusammen und flohen. *Before the soldiers broke through, the inhabitants packed up their belongings and fled.*

---

sitzen — *to sit*

auf sich sitzen lassen — *to take lying down.*

Diesen Vorwurf will der Senator nicht auf sich sitzen lassen. *The senator won't take that accusation lying down.*

sitzenbleiben — *to lag behind; be left back in school.*

Auf technischem Bereich läuft unsere Firma Gefahr, sitzenzubleiben. *In technical areas our firm is in danger of lagging behind.*

In der Schule ist er oft sitzengeblieben; später ließ ihn seine Verlobte sitzen. *He often got left back in school; later his fiancée jilted him.*

sitzenlassen — *to jilt.*

Er hatte Angst, dass sie ihn sitzenlassen würde. *He was afraid that she would jilt him.*

---

die Socke — *sock*

sich auf die Socken machen — *to get a move on; get going.*

Mach dich auf die Socken! *Get a move on!*

---

spanisch — *Spanish*

Das kommt mir spanisch vor. *That seems odd to me (that's Greek to me).*

spanische Reiter — *barbed-wire barricades.*

Wir konnten nicht durch, weil die Polizei spanische Reiter aufgestellt hatte. *We couldn't get through because the police had set up barbed-wire barricades.*

---

der Sparren — *rafter*

  einen Sparren (zu viel/zu wenig) haben — *to be off the beam*.

  Ja, sie hat einen Sparren, aber lustig und nett ist sie doch. *Yes, she's got bats in the belfry but still, she's jolly and kind*.

---

der Spaß — *fun*

  an etwas Spaß haben — *to enjoy*.

  Sie hat viel Spaß an ihrem Beruf. *She enjoys her profession very much*.

  nur zum Spaß machen — *to do just for fun*.

  Er behauptet, er hätte es nur zum Spaß getan. *He alleges that he did it just for fun*.

  keinen Spaß verstehen — *to have no sense of humor*.

  Der versteht keinen Spaß. *He has no sense of humor*.

  Spaß machen — *to kid*.

  Ach, ich hab nur Spaß gemacht. *Oh, I was only kidding*.

  der Spaßverderber — *killjoy; spoilsport*.

  Sei doch kein Spaßverderber! *Don't be a spoilsport*.

---

der Speck — *bacon*

  abspecken — *to lose weight*.

  Ihr seid zu dick und musst abspecken. Ran an den Speck! *You're overweight and have to get the lard off. Tackle that fat!*

  leben wie die Made im Speck — *to live off the fat of the land*.

  Er wurde reich und lebt jetzt wie die Made im Speck. *He got rich and lives off the fat of the land*.

  Mit Speck fängt man Mäuse. *You need a sprat to catch a mackerel*.

  Ran an den Speck! — *Let's get going/let's tackle the goal/job. It's time for action!*

---

spendieren — *to treat, make a present of*

  die Spendierhosen anhaben — *to be in a generous mood*.

  Damals hatte ich oft die Spendierhosen an, aber ich wurde arbeitslos und musste sie auszuziehen. *In those days I often gave treats to everybody, but I lost my job and I've had to tighten my belt*.

die Spesen — *expenses*

's war wieder 'n Flop. Außer Spesen nichts gewesen; die Firma hat zu viele Spesenrittter. *Another flop. Money spent with nothing to show for it; the firm's got too many expense account jockeys.*

auf Spesen — *on an expense account.*

Weil er auf Spesen ist, sucht er sich die besten Restaurants aus. *Because he's on an expense account, he seeks out the best restaurants.*

das Spiel — *game*

auf dem Spiel stehen — *to be at stake.*

Seine Glaubwürdigkeit steht auf dem Spiel. *His credibility is at stake.*

ein abgekartetes Spiel — *a rigged, put-up job.*

Das Ganze war nur ein abgekartetes Spiel. *The whole thing was just a put-up job.*

spielen — *to play*

die Muskeln spielen lassen — *to make a show of force.*

Die neue Regierung will in der Außenpolitik die Muskeln spielen lassen. *The new government wants to make a show of force in its foreign policy.*

spinnen — *to spin; to be daft; to plot an intrigue*

Es ist nichts so fein gesponnen, es kommt doch ans Licht der Sonnen.
Truth will out, however elaborate the intrigues that conceal it.

etwas spinnen — *to make up, spin out of whole cloth.*

Das hast du wohl gesponnen. *You probably made that up.*

Ich hätt's getan? Ach, du spinnst, du Spinner! *I did it? You're making that up, you screwball!*

die Spitze — *point*

auf die Spitze treiben — *to carry things too far.*

Immer muss er alles auf die Spitze treiben. *He always has to carry things too far.*

---

die Sprechstunde — *office hours*
  Außerhalb ihrer Sprechstunden kann sie Sie nicht sprechen. *She can't see you outside of her office hours.*

---

der Sprung — *leap; crack in crockery*
  auf die Sprünge helfen — *to help get started; give hints.*
  Nachdem sie ihm auf die Sprünge geholfen hatte, konnte er das Rätsel lösen. *After she helped him get started, he solved the riddle.*

  den Sprung schaffen — *to succeed in making a transition.*
  Er hat den Sprung zum Tonfilm nicht geschafft. *He didn't succeed in making the transition to talking pictures.*

  einen Sprung in der Schüssel haben — *to be cracked; to be off one's rocker.*
  Der hat einen Sprung in der Schüssel. *He's cracked.*

  keine großen Sprünge machen können — *to be unable to spend much money.*
  Im Augenblick können wir keine großen Sprünge machen. *At the moment we can't afford to spend much money.*

---

die Spucke — *spit*
  die Spucke bleibt weg — *left speechless/breathless/flabbergasted.*
  Mir blieb die Spucke weg, als ich sie nach 20 Jahren wieder sah. *I was flabbergasted when I saw her again after 20 years.*

---

stampfen — *to stamp (feet); mash (potatoes, etc.)*
  etwas aus dem Boden stampfen — *to create from nothing; to put up a building, etc., rapidly.*
  Die Fabrik wurde in kürzester Zeit aus dem Boden gestampft. *The factory was put up in the shortest possible time.*

---

die Stange — *pole*
  bei der Stange bleiben — *to keep at it.*
  Bleibt noch bei der Stange; wir sind bald am Ziel. *Keep at it; we'll soon reach the goal.*

  die Stange halten — *to stick up for.*
  Die Kollegen hielten mir die Stange. *My colleagues stuck up for me.*

---

der Staub — *dust*

sich aus dem Staub machen — *to clear off (out).*

Statt Rede und Antwort zu stehen, machte er sich aus dem Staub. *Instead of explaining his actions he cleared off.*

staubsaugen — *to vacuum.*

Ich habe aber gestern gestaubsaugt. *But I vacuumed yesterday.*

---

der Stegreif — *stirrup*

aus dem Stegreif — *extemporaneously; without a prepared text.*

Wenn der Professor aus dem Stegreif spricht, ist er interessanter. *When the professor talks without a prepared text, he's more interesting.*

---

stehen — *to stand; to be*

gut/schlecht um etwas stehen — *to do/go well/badly.*

In einigen Ländern steht es nicht gut um die Pressefreiheit. *In some countries freedom of the press is not doing well.*

stehen auf — *to point to.*

Die Zeichen stehen auf Streik. *The indicators point to a strike.*

stehen — *to suit.*

Kleider und Röcke stehen mir besser als Hosen. *Dresses and skirts suit me better (look better on me) than pants.*

das Stehaufmännchen — *tumbler, acrobat.*

Hans ist ein richtiges Stehaufmännchen. *Nothing can keep Hans down.*

---

steil — *steep*

eine steile Karriere machen — *to have a meteoric career.*

Trotz aller Hindernisse hat sie eine steile Karriere gemacht. *Despite all obstacles, she's had a meteoric career.*

---

der Stein — *stone*

bei jemandem einen Stein im Brett haben — *to be in someone's good graces.*

Es gelang ihm, beim Chef einen Stein im Brett zu haben. *He succeeded in getting into the boss's good graces.*

den Stein ins Rollen bringen — *to set things in motion.*

Ein Brief seiner Exehefrau brachte den Stein ins Rollen; jetzt wird gegen
  ihn ermittelt. *A letter from his ex-wife got things started; now he's being
  investigated.*

Stein des Anstoßes — *bone of contention.*

Seit Jahrhunderten ist diese Provinz ein Stein des Anstoßes zwischen
  beiden Ländern. *For centuries this province has been a bone of
  contention between the two countries.*

---

der Stern — *star*

in den Sternen stehen — *to be in the lap of the gods.*

Das Ergebnis steht noch in den Sternen. *The outcome is still in the lap of
  the gods.*

nach den Sternen greifen — *to reach for the moon.*

Auch mit zunehmendem Alter griff sie noch nach immer höheren Sternen.
  Even in advancing years she still reached for the moon and beyond.

die Sternstunde — *great moment, memorable experience.*

Mit diesem sehr alten Wein können Sie eine Sternstunde erleben, oder
  sehr enttäuscht werden. *With this very old wine you might have a
  memorable experience or be very disappointed.*

---

still — *quiet, silent*

im Stillen — *privately, secretly.*

Sie hatte sich im Stillen etwas Schöneres gehofft. *Secretly she'd hoped for
  something nicer.*

---

die Stimme — *voice*

seine Stimme abgeben — *to vote.*

Ich habe meine Stimme für die Senatorin abgegeben. *I voted for the
  senator.*

stimmen — *to tune an instrument; to be correct.*

Alles, was sie berichtet hat, stimmt. *Everything she reported is correct.*

---

die Stirn — *forehead*

die Stirn bieten — *to defy.*

Mutig bot sie dem Diktator die Stirn. *She courageously defied the dictator.*

jmdm. hinter die Stirn sehen — *to read s.o.'s mind.*
Wieso hätte ich's wissen sollen? Ich konnte ihm nicht hinter die Stirn sehen. *How am I supposed to have known? I couldn't read his mind.*

stoßen — *to push, shove*
vor den Kopf stoßen — *to insult, offend.*
Hüte dich, diesen Milliardär vor den Kopf zu stoßen. *Be careful not to offend that billionaire.*

der Strich — *line*
auf den Strich gehen — *to be a streetwalker, practice prostitution.*
Die Armut zwang sie, auf den Strich zu gehen. *Poverty compelled her to be a streetwalker.*

einen Strich unter etwas machen/ziehen — *to make a clean break.*
Jetzt versucht sie, einen Strich unter die Vergangenheit zu ziehen. *Now she's trying to make a clean break with the past.*

unterm Strich — *all things considered.*
Unterm Strich ist ihr Leben interessant und positiv zu bewerten. *All things considered, her life must be rated as interesting and positive.*

unterm Strich sein — *to be feeling under the weather, not to be up to snuff/scratch.*
Onkel Otto ist heute wieder unterm Strich. *Uncle Otto's feeling a bit under the weather again today.*

das Stück — *piece*
aus freien Stücken — *of one's own free will.*
Sie behaupteten, sie hätten ihr Grundstück in der DDR nicht aus freien Stücken verkauft. *They claimed they didn't sell their property in the GDR of their own free will.*

ein ganzes/gutes Stück — *quite a bit.*
Das Kind ist wieder ein ganzes Stück gewachsen. *The child has grown quite a bit.*

große Stücke halten auf — *to have a high opinion of.*

Ihre Lehrer halten große Stücke auf sie. *Her teachers have a high opinion of her.*

die Stunde — *hour*

zur vollen Stunde — *on the hour.*

Mehr berichten wir darüber in den Nachrichten zur vollen Stunde. *We'll have more to say about that in the news on the hour.*

der Sturm — *storm*

ein Sturm im Wasserglas — *a tempest in a teapot.*

Weil es dich nicht betrifft, tust du's als Sturm im Wasserglas ab. *Because it doesn't affect you, you dismiss it as a tempest in a teapot.*

Sturm laufen — *to be up in arms.*

Umweltschützer laufen Sturm gegen die geplante Talsperre. *Environmentalists are up in arms about the planned dam.*

stürzen — *to plunge*

sich in Unkosten stürzen — *to go to great expense.*

Ja, das Haus ist schön, aber jetzt will ich mich nicht in Unkosten stürzen. *Yes, the house is beautiful, but I don't want to incur great expense now.*

die Suche — *search*

sich auf die Suche machen — *to start looking for.*

Hänsel und Gretels Eltern machten sich auf die Suche nach den Kindern. *Hänsel and Gretel's parents started to look for the children.*

suchen — *to look for*

zu suchen haben — *to have business; be pertinent.*

Sie haben hier nichts zu suchen. *You have no business here.*

Was haben solche komplizierten Bücher in unserem Lehrplan zu suchen? *What place is there for complicated books like that in our curriculum?*

die Suppe — *soup*

jemandem die Suppe versalzen — *to put a spoke in someone's wheel, rain on someone's parade, spoil someone's plans.*

Du versuchst wieder, mir die Suppe zu versalzen. *You're trying to rain on my parade again.*

seine eigene Suppe/sein eigenes Süppchen kochen — *to pursue a private agenda.*

Bei den Verhandlungen wollte jeder nur sein eigenes Süppchen kochen. *During the negotiations everyone just wanted to pursue a private agenda.*

---

die Szene — *scene*

sich in Szene setzen — *to get noticed.*

Der Senator weiß, sich in Szene zu setzen und benutzt die Medien zu seinen Zwecken. *The senator knows how to get media attention and exploits it.*

T

Tacheles reden — *to do some straight talking*

Wann wird er endlich mit uns Tacheles reden? *When will he finally talk straight to us?*

---

der Tag — *day*

alle Tage — *every day.*

Alle Tage sieht man dergleichen nicht. *One doesn't see things like that every day.*

an den Tag legen — *to display.*

Er hat eine neue Hilfsbereitschaft an den Tag gelegt. *He displayed a new readiness to help.*

den Tag vor dem Abend loben — *to count one's chickens before they're hatched.*

Man soll den Tag nicht vor dem Abend loben. *One shouldn't count one's chickens before they're hatched.*

dieser Tage — *recently.*

Dieser Tage stand etwas darüber in der Zeitung. *There was something about it recently in the newspaper.*

in den Tag hineinleben/von Tag zu Tag leben — *to live day by day with
no thought for the future.*

Sie sind verliebt und wollen von Luft und Liebe in den Tag hineinleben.
They're in love and want to live day by day on love and air.

über Tage — *above ground (mining);* **unter Tage** — *below ground.*

Jahrelang arbeitete er unter Tage aber er wurde krank und kann jetzt nur
über Tage arbeiten. *For years he worked in an underground mine, but
he got sick and now can only work above ground.*

unter Tags — *during the day.*

Schon unter Tags sitzt er in der Kneipe. *Even during the day he's in
the bar.*

---

die Talfahrt — *descent into the valley; decline*

Durch Kostensenkungen versuchte sie, die Talfahrt der Firma aufzuhalten.
By reducing costs she tried to stop the firm's decline.

sich auf Talfahrt befinden — *to be on a downhill course.*

Er behauptete, die Wirtschaft befinde sich auf stetiger Talfahrt. *He alleged
that the economy was on a steady downhill course.*

---

das Tamtam — *tomtom; noise; ballyhoo*

Die neue Entfettungspille wird mit viel Tamtam vermarktet. *The new
weight-reducing pill is being marketed with much ballyhoo.*

---

die Tapete — *wallpaper*

die Tapeten wechseln — *to have a change of scenery.*

Der Hausmann (die Hausfrau) sehnte sich danach, die Tapeten zu
wechseln. *The houseman/housewife longed for a change of scenery.*

---

die Taufe — *baptism*

aus der Taufe heben — *to launch, start.*

Die Salzburger Festspiele wurden 1920 aus der Taufe gehoben. *The
Salzburg Festival was started in 1920.*

---

tausend — *thousand*

Tausende und Abertausende — *thousands upon thousands.*

Tausende und Abertausende besuchen jetzt die einst abgelegene Insel.
Thousands upon thousands now visit that once remote island.

das Techtelmechtel — *amorous dalliance; hanky-panky*
Die so fromm geglaubte Helene wurde beim Techtelmechtel erwischt.
Helene, thought so pious, was caught in amorous dalliance.

der Teich — *pond*
  der große Teich — *the Atlantic Ocean.*
  Oma will wieder über den großen Teich, um unsere Verwandten in
  Amerika zu besuchen. *Grandma wants to cross the Atlantic again to
  visit our relatives in America.*

der Teufel — *devil*
  auf Teufel komm raus — *to beat the band; like all get-out.*
  Er und seine ganze Familie lügen auf Teufel komm raus. *He and his
  whole family lie like all get-out.*

  den Teufel an die Wand malen — *to imagine the worst; tempt fate.*
  Brauchst nicht gleich den Teufel an die Wand zu malen. *You don't have to
  imagine the worst-case scenario right away.*

  in Teufels Küche kommen — *to get into deep trouble.*
  Seine beiden Söhne waren Fixer und kamen in Teufels Küche. *His two
  sons were drug addicts and got into deep trouble.*

  der Teufelskreis — *vicious circle.*
  Die Ärztin will ihnen helfen, den Teufelskreis von Sucht und Kriminalität
  zu sprengen. *The doctor wants to help them to break the vicious cycle of
  addiction and criminality.*

ticken — *to tick*
  Bei dem tickt's nicht richtig. *That guy's off his rocker.*

  anders ticken — *to be of a different mentality.*
  In Bayern ticken die Uhren anders. *Bavaria's in its own (political) time-
  zone/Bavaria marches to a different drummer.*

das Tier — *animal*

　ein hohes/großes Tier — *a big shot*.

　Sie will sich mit den großen Tieren des Betriebs zusammentreffen. *She wants to meet with the big shots in the company.*

　Jedem Tierchen sein Pläsierchen. *To each his/her own/Whatever turns you on.*

　tierischer Ernst — *deadly seriousness*.

　Er betreibt alles mit tierischem Ernst. *He does everything with deadly seriousness.*

　das Tierkreiszeichen — *sign of the zodiac*.

　Welches Tierkreiszeichen bist du? *Under what sign were you born?*

---

die Tinte — *ink*

　in der Tinte sitzen — *to be in a mess*.

　Das ganze Land saß in der Tinte. *The whole country was in a mess.*

　Tinte gesoffen haben — *to be out of one's mind*.

　Du musst wohl Tinte gesoffen haben, wenn du das wieder versuchen willst. *You must be out of your mind if you want to try that again.*

---

der Tisch — *table*

　am grünen Tisch (vom grünen Tisch aus) — *entirely theoretical*.

　Das, was sie am grünen Tisch geplant und beschlossen haben, ist völlig wirklichkeitsfremd. *What they planned and decided is entirely theoretical and totally unrealistic.*

　über den Tisch ziehen — *to outmaneuver, cheat*.

　Lassen Sie sich von ihm und seinem unehrlichen Anwalt nicht über den Tisch ziehen. *Don't let him and his unethical lawyer outmaneuver you.*

　vom Tisch sein — *to be settled; to no longer be an issue*.

　Die meisten Streitfragen sind jetzt vom Tisch. *Most of the issues have now been settled.*

Toi, toi, toi — *good luck*

Toi, toi, toi für dein Examen! *Good luck in your exam!*

　unberufen, toi, toi, toi — *knock on wood*.

Viele meiner Kumpel in der Fabrik sind entlassen; mich haben sie noch
nicht gefeuert — unberufen, toi, toi, toi. *Many of my buddies in the
factory were let go; they haven't fired me yet, knock on wood.*

---

der Ton — *tone*

Der Ton macht die Musik. *It's not what you say, but how you say it.*

den Ton angeben — *say what goes.*

Warum soll immer nur der den Ton angeben? *Why should it always be just
he who says what goes?*

Jede Bohn' hat ihren Ton. *Each bean has its own tone.*

Der Kellner riet uns davon ab, Bohnen zu essen, denn jede Bohn' hat
ihren Ton. *The waiter recommended we not eat beans, for each bean
has its own tone.*

große/dicke Töne reden/spucken — *to talk big.*

Du spuckst wieder große Töne, aber wann folgen Taten den Tönen?
You're talking big again, but will you when we see action?

---

der Topf — *pot*

alles in einen Topf werfen — *to lump everything together.*

So etwas Kompliziertes kannst du doch nicht in einen Topf werfen. *You
really can't lump together such complicated things.*

Leere Töpfe klappern und leere Köpfe plappern am meisten. *Empty
pots and empty heads make the most noise/Among walnuts only the
empty one speaks.*

Hurrapatrioten schreien am lautesten—ohne zu wissen warum, meinte
Mark Twain. Ja, leere Töpfe klappern und leere Köpfe plappern am
meisten. *Super-patriots yell the loudest—without knowing why, declared
Mark Twain. Yes, empty pots and empty heads make the most noise.*

der Topfgucker — *a busybody.*

Unser Nachbar ist nett, aber leider ein alter Topfgucker. *Our neighbor is
nice but, unfortunately, a busybody.*

Jeder Topf findet seinen Deckel. *No matter how ugly you are there's
somebody for you/Every Jack has his Jill/There's a cover to fit
every pot.*

---

das Tor — *gate*

    die Torschlusspanik — *last minute panic; fear of being left out.*
    Ihn erwischte Torschlusspanik, sonst hätte er mich nicht geheiratet. *He*
      wouldn't have married me if he hadn't been afraid of being left on
      the shelf.

    kurz vor Torschluss — *at the last minute, 11th hour.*
    Kurz vor Torschluss besann er sich anders. *He had a change of heart at*
      the last minute.

tot — *dead*

    sich totlachen — *to die laughing.*
    Wir haben uns über ihre Witze fast totgelacht. *We almost died laughing at*
      her jokes.

    totschlagen — *to beat to death.*
    Du kannst mich totschlagen, aber ich kann mich nicht mehr daran
      erinnern. *For the life of me I can't remember it any more.*

die Tour — *tour*

    auf vollen Touren laufen — *to operate at full capacity/speed/volume.*
    Die Klimaanlage läuft schon auf vollen Touren. *The air conditioner is*
      already operating at full capacity.

    in einer Tour — *all the time.*
    Er hatte große Lust, ihr in einer Tour noch mehr Schmuckstücke und
      Pelzmäntel zu schenken. *He longed to give her even more jewels and*
      fur coats all the time.

der Trab — *trot*

    auf Trab — *on the go.*
    Oma ist immer auf Trab. *Granny's always on the go.*

treiben — *to drive*

    Kurzweil treiben — *to have fun.*
    Er will immer nur Kurzweil treiben, statt an den Ernst des Lebens zu
      denken. Vielleicht hat er recht. *All he wants is to have fun, instead of*
      thinking of the serious side of life. Maybe he's right.

trinken — *to drink*

Brüderschaft trinken — *to pledge close friendship (by intertwining arms, drinking, and using the du form).*

Sie betranken sich und tranken Brüderschaft. *They got drunk and pledged close friendship.*

einen trinken gehen — *to go for a drink (or two).*

Nach der Arbeit gingen sie einen trinken. *After work they went for a drink.*

trinkfest — *able to hold one's liquor.*

Sie will nur trinkfeste Männer um sich. *She wants only men who are able to hold their liquor around her.*

---

trocken — *dry*

auf dem Trockenen sein/sitzen — *to be bankrupt, economically stranded/high and dry; to be without anything to drink.*

Der Vorstand hat das Unternehmen heruntergewirtschaftet und es ist jetzt auf dem Trockenen. *The executive board ran the company into the ground and now it's in a tight spot.*

Hier sitzen wir, arbeitslos und auf dem Trockenen; schenk uns doch endlich ein! *We're sitting here unemployed and without a drink; set us up, will you!*

sein Schäfchen ins Trockene bringen — *to look out for one's own interests.*

Mit seiner großzügigen Abfindung wusste der alte Firmenchef sein Schäfchen ins Trockene zu bringen; die neue Chefin versucht das Unternehmen wieder flottzubekommen. *With his golden parachute the old CEO looked out for number one; the new boss is trying to get the company on its feet again.*

---

der Tropf — *intravenous feeding apparatus, drip feeder*

am Tropf hängen — *to be extremely weak.*

Die Wirtschaft der ehemaligen Kolonie hängt noch am Tropf. *The former colony's economy is still entirely dependent on outside aid.*

---

der Tropfen — *drop*
  ein Tropfen auf den heißen Stein — *a drop in the bucket*.
  Danke fürs Geld; es ist aber nur ein Tropfen auf den heißen Stein. Ich
    brauche noch viel mehr. *Thanks for the money, but it's just a drop in the*
    bucket. I need lots more.
  Steter Tropfen höhlt den Stein. *Constant dripping erodes the stone*
    (sustained effort will eventually pay off).

---

der Trost — *consolation, comfort*
  nicht bei Trost sein — *not to be all there*.
  Im Krieg hat er viel Schweres erlitten und ist nicht mehr ganz bei Trost.
    He suffered much in the war and isn't quite all there any more.

  Trost spenden — *to comfort*.
  Sie hat den Armen Trost gespendet. *She comforted the poor*.

das Trostpflaster — *consolation prize*
  Als Trostpflaster bekam sie einen Plüschbären. *As a consolation prize she*
    got a teddy bear.

---

trüb — *dreary*
  im Trüben fischen — *to fish in troubled waters*.
  Das liegt mir nicht, im Trüben zu fischen, um Profit zu schlagen. *Fishing*
    in troubled waters to make a profit doesn't appeal to me.

---

das Tuch — *cloth; towel*
  das Handtuch werfen — *to throw in the towel*.
  Endlich musste sie das Handtuch werfen. *She finally had to throw in the*
    towel.

  in trockene Tücher bringen — *to accomplish, wrap up*.
  Sie will ihre Doktorarbeit in trockene Tücher bringen, bevor sie an ihrem
    Roman weiterschreibt. *She wants to complete her doctoral dissertation*
    before continuing her novel.

---

die Tür — *door*
  mit der Tür ins Haus fallen — *to come right out and say what one*
    wants.

Ich muss leider gleich mit der Tür ins Haus fallen, denn ich brauche das Geld sofort. *Unfortunately, I've got to come right out and say so, for I need the money right away.*

Tür und Tor öffnen — *to open wide the door.*
In den zwanziger Jahren öffnete die Prohibition der Kriminalität Tür und Tor. *In the twenties Prohibition opened the door wide for criminal behavior.*

vor die Tür setzen — *to throw out.*
Der Wirt musste den Betrunkenen vor die Tür setzen. *The tavern owner had to throw the drunk out.*

vor seiner eigenen Tür kehren — *to set one's own house in order.*
Er sollte zuerst vor seiner eigenen Tür kehren, statt andere zu beschuldigen. *He should set his own house in order before accusing others.*

U

übel — *bad*
einem übel werden — *to feel sick.*
Es wurde mir übel. *I felt sick.*

zu allem Übel — *on top of everything else.*
Zu allem Übel sprang der Wagen nicht an. *On top of everything else, the car didn't start.*

über — *over*
über sein — *to be superior.*
Liesl ist mir in Mathe über. *Liesl is superior to me in math.*

über und über — *completely.*
Der U-Bahnhof war über und über mit Graffiti besprüht. *The subway station was completely sprayed with graffiti.*

zu allem Überfluss — *on top of it all.*
Zu allem Überfluss fing es zu schneien an. *On top of it all, it began to snow.*

übertrumpfen — *to trump; to surpass, best*.
In allem übertrumpfte ihn seine Schwester. *His sister bested him in everything*.

übrig — *remaining*
   ein Übriges tun — *to contribute*.
   Das unsympatische Personal tat noch ein Übriges, uns den Aufenthalt zu verleiden. *The unpleasant staff contributed to spoiling our stay*.

   nichts übrig haben für — *not to care for*.
   Für moderne Malerei hat er nichts übrig. *He doesn't care for modern painting*.

   übrigbleiben — *to be left (over)*.
   Es blieb uns nichts anderes übrig als auszuziehen. *We had no other choice but to move out*.

   übrigens — *by the way, incidentally*.
   Übrigens, gestern hab ich deine Freundin gesehen. *By the way, I saw your friend yesterday*.

---

das Ufer — *shore*
   ins Uferlose gehen — *to have no end; to know no boundaries*.
   Sie schreibt noch an ihrem Roman, der ins Uferlose geht. *She's still working on her novel that never ends*.

---

umbringen — *to kill*
   nicht umzubringen sein — *to be indestructible*.
   Columbos alter Regenmantel ist nicht umzubringen. *Columbo's old raincoat is indestructible*.

---

der Umgang — *contact; dealings*
   die Umgangssprache — *colloquial speech*.
   Die Lehrerin erklärte den Unterschied zwischen der gehobenen und der Umgangssprache. *The teacher explained the distinction between elevated and colloquial speech*.

---

umgehen — *to go round; to deal/work with*
Sie versteht es, mit Computern umzugehen. *She knows how to work with computers.*

   mit etwas nicht umgehen können — *to be unable to handle something.*
Ihr Vater kann nicht mit Geld umgehen. *Her father doesn't know how to handle money.*

---

ummünzen — *to convert into something else*
   eine Niederlage in einen Sieg ummünzen — *to turn defeat into victory.*
Sie wusste, ihre Niederlagen in Siege umzumünzen. *She knew how to turn her defeats into victories.*

---

umsonst — *free, gratis*
Umsonst ist nur der Tod, und der kostet das Leben. *Everything comes with a price; there's no free lunch.*

   nicht umsonst — *not for nothing, for good reason.*
Nicht umsonst hab ich euch vor ihm gewarnt. *I had good reason to warn you about him.*

---

der Umstand — *circumstance*
   den Umständen entsprechend — *as can be expected in the circumstances.*
Es geht dem Patienten den Umständen entsprechend gut. *The patient is doing as well as can be expected in the circumstances.*

   keine Umstände machen — *not to make a fuss.*
Valentin wusste, dass er sterben musste, und machte keine Umstände. *Valentin knew he had to die and didn't make a fuss.*

   unter Umständen — *perhaps; possibly.*
Unter Umständen wird sich das machen lassen. *Perhaps that can be done.*

---

ungefähr — *approximate*
   nicht von ungefähr sein — *not be unjustified.*
Sein schlechter Ruf ist nicht von ungefähr. *His bad reputation is not unjustified.*

   ungefähr können — *to know more or less how to do.*
Wenn man's kann ungefähr, ist's nicht schwer. *If you more or less know how to do it, it isn't difficult.*

wie von ungefähr — *as if by chance*.
Er kam ihr wie von ungefähr entgegen. *He came toward her as if by chance*.

der Unrat — *garbage*
Unrat wittern — *to smell a rat*.
Der Polizist witterte sofort Unrat. *The policeman smelled a rat right away*.

die Urne — *urn*
zur Urne gehen — *to vote*.
Nicht alle Wahlberechtigten gingen zur Urne. *Not all those eligible to vote did so*.

der Urnengang — *way to the polls; election*.
Nächstes Jahre finden viele Urnengänge statt. *Next year many elections will take place*.

der Urknall — *the big bang*
Die Wissenschaftler sprachen vom Urknall. *The scientists talked of the big bang*.

die Urzeit — *primeval times*
seit Urzeiten — *since time immemorial*.
Der Bauer behauptete, die Wiese hätte seit Urzeiten seiner Familie angehört. *The farmer maintained that the meadow had belonged to his family since time immemorial*.

die Verachtung — *contempt*
mit Verachtung strafen — *to treat with contempt*.
Die Malerin konnte seine Meinung nur mit Verachtung strafen. *The painter could treat his opinion only with contempt*.

verboten — *forbidden*
  verboten aussehen — *to look weird.*
  Als Fledermaus verkleidet, sah er verboten aus. *He looked weird dressed as a bat.*

der Verdacht — *suspicion*
  auf Verdacht — *just in case.*
  Auf Verdacht hab ich große Mengen gekauft. *Just in case, I bought large amounts.*

verhexen — *to bewitch*
  wie verhext — *jinxed.*
  Alles, was mit der Feier in Hornberg zu tun hatte, war wie verhext. *Everything that had to do with the celebration in Hornberg seemed jinxed.*

die Verlegenheit — *embarrassment*
  in Verlegenheit bringen — *to embarrass.*
  Im Restaurant brachte das Kind die Eltern in Verlegenheit. *In the restaurant the child embarrassed his parents.*

die Vernunft — *reason*
  Vernunft annehmen — *to be reasonable; come to one's senses.*
  Du kannst unmöglich diesen Kerl heiraten — nimm doch Vernunft an! *It's impossible for you to marry that fellow. Come to your senses!*

  zur Vernunft bringen — *to make someone listen to reason.*
  Sie versuchten vergebens, die Fanatiker zur Vernunft zu bringen. *They tried in vain to make the fanatics listen to reason.*

  zur Vernunft kommen — *to see reason; to come to one's senses.*
  Es wird Generationen dauern, bevor sie zur Vernunft kommen. *It will take generations before they see reason.*

das Vertrauen — *trust, confidence*
  ins Vertrauen ziehen — *to take into one's confidence.*
  Erst als es zu spät war, zogen sie uns ins Vertrauen. *Only when it was too late did they take us into their confidence.*

verwechseln — *to confuse*
   zum Verwechseln ähnlich sehen — *to be the spitting image of*.
   Er sieht seinem Vater zum Verwechseln ähnlich. *He is the spitting image
      of his father.*

---

das Vitamin — *vitamin*
   durch Vitamin B (Beziehungen) kriegen — *to get through connections*.
   Ohne Vitamin B hätte er es nicht gekriegt. *Without connections he never
      would have gotten it.*

---

der Vogel — *bird*
   einen Vogel haben — *to have bats in one's belfry, be nuts*.
   Er hat einen Vogel, ist aber sehr liebenswürdig. *He's nuts but very nice.*

   das Vögelchen — *little bird*.
   Woher ich's weiß? Das hat mir ein Vögelchen gesungen. *How do I know?
      A little bird told me.*

---

voll — *full*
   voll und ganz — *totally, 100 percent*.
   Wir stehen voll und ganz auf deiner Seite. *We're 100 percent behind you.*

   voll — *plastered*.
   Gib ihm nichts mehr; er ist schon voll. *Don't give him any more (to
      drink); he's already plastered.*

---

von — *of; from*
   ein von und zu sein — *to be an aristocrat, have a very aristocratic name*.
   Er ist ein richtiger von und zu, ist aber bettelarm. *He's a genuine aristo-
      crat, but poor as a church mouse.*

   mit einer/einem von verheiratet sein — *to be married to an aristocrat*.
   Sie glaubte, mit einem von verheiratet zu sein, aber alles an ihm war
      Schwindel. *She thought she was married to an aristocrat, but
      everything about him was fraudulent.*

   von vornherein — *from the (very) beginning*.
   Von vornherein hat er unehrlich gehandelt. *His behavior was unethical
      from the very beginning.*

von wegen — *By no means/Not at all/You must be joking/No way!*
Die Böttcherei ein veraltetes Handwerk? Von wegen! Holzfässer werden noch stark gefragt. *A cooper's trade old-fashioned? Not at all! Wooden barrels are still in great demand.*

---

vor — *in front of*
vor allem — *above all.*
Du musst vor allem danach streben, ein guter Mensch zu sein. *Above all, you must strive to be a good human being.*

im Voraus — *in advance.*
Wir hatten leider alles im Voraus bezahlt. *Unfortunately, we had paid for everything in advance.*

vorbei — *past, gone.*
Dicht vorbei ist auch daneben. *Close, but no cigar. (A miss is as good as a mile.)*

vorbestraft — *to have previous convictions, be an ex-con.*
Obwohl er vorbestraft ist, wird man ihn einstellen. *Although he's an ex-con, they're going to hire him.*

---

der Vordermann — *person in front*
auf Vordermann bringen — *to get/keep in good order.*
Sie weiß, Garten und Haushalt auf Vordermann zu bringen. *She knows how to keep the garden and the house in good order.*

---

der Vorsatz — *intention; resolution*
Der Weg zur Hölle ist mit guten Vorsätzen gepflastert. *The road to hell is paved with good intentions.*

Vorsätze fassen — *to make resolutions.*
Am Silvesterabend fasste er wieder große Vorsätze. *On New Year's Eve he made many ambitious resolutions again.*

---

die Vorsicht — *caution*
mit Vorsicht zu genießen sein — *to take with caution; to be wary of.*
Alles, was er behauptet, ist mit Vorsicht zu genießen. *You must be wary of everything he says.*

---

die Vorsorge — *precaution*
  Vorsorge treffen — *to take precautions.*
  Die Behörden behaupteten, Vorsorge gegen Terroristen getroffen zu
  haben. *The authorities claimed to have taken precautions against
  terrorists.*

---

der Vorwurf — *reproach*
  zum Vorwurf machen — *to reproach; to hold against.*
  Man soll ihm sein bisheriges Verhalten nicht zum Vorwurf machen. *One
  shouldn't hold his former behavior against him.*

die Waage — *scale*
  das Zünglein an der Waage sein — *to tip the scales; to hold the balance
  of power.*
  Im neuen Parlament könnte diese kleine Splitterpartei das Zünglein an der
  Waage sein. *In the new parliament this little splinter party could hold
  the balance of power.*

  sich die Waage halten — *to be equally divided.*
  In dem Wahlreformstreit halten sich Befürworter und Gegner die Waage.
  *In the electoral reform dispute, supporters and opponents are equally
  divided.*

---

wachsen — *to grow*
  etwas gewachsen sein — *to be able to handle.*
  Diese Straße ist dem immer stärkeren Verkehr nicht gewachsen. *This road
  can't handle the ever increasing traffic.*

  über den Kopf wachsen — *to become too much for.*
  Die Arbeit wuchs ihm über den Kopf. *The job became too much
  for him.*

die Waffel — *waffle*

    einen an der Waffel haben — *to be a bit crazy/cracked*.

    Die ganze Mannschaft hat einen an der Waffel. *The whole team is a
    bit cracked*.

---

wagen — *to dare*

    Wer nicht wagt, der nicht gewinnt. (Frisch gewagt ist halb gewonnen.)
    Nothing ventured, nothing gained.

---

wahr — *true*

    nicht wahr — *isn't that so*.

    Ihr seid müde, nicht wahr? *You're tired, aren't you?*

    Du hast es für mich getan, nicht wahr? *You did it for me, didn't you?*

    Er hat es gründlich überprüft, nicht wahr? *He's checked it thoroughly,
    hasn't he?*

---

der Wald — *forest*

    Wie man in den Wald hineinruft, so schallt es heraus. *As you sow, so
    shall you reap. (Others will treat you as you treat them.)*

    den Wald vor lauter Bäumen nicht sehen — *to not see the forest for
    the trees*.

    Er warf mir vor, den Wald vor lauter Bäumen nicht zu sehen. *He accused
    me of not seeing the forest for the trees*.

    einen vom Wald erzählen — *to tell a fib*.

    Erzähl mir nicht wieder einen vom Wald. *Don't tell me another fib*.

---

die Wand — *wall*

    dass die Wände wackeln — *so as to raise the roof*.

    Die Mannschaft feierte, dass die Wände wackelten. *The team was
    celebrating so as to raise the roof*.

    gegen eine Wand reden — *to talk to a wall*.

    Weitere Gespräche sind zwecklos — mit ihm reden heißt gegen eine Wand
    reden. *Further conversations serve no purpose. Talking to him is like
    talking to a wall*.

---

warm — *warm*

warm ums Herz werden — *to be touched*.

Mir wurde warm ums Herz, als ich ihre tröstenden Worte las. *I was touched when I read her comforting words*.

---

die Warte — *watchtower; observatory*

von höherer Warte aus — *from a loftier perspective*.

Seit seiner Reise nach Tibet glaubt er, alles von höherer Warte aus zu sehen. *Ever since his trip to Tibet, he thinks he sees everything from a loftier perspective*.

---

warten — *to wait; to service*

warten auf — *to wait for*.

Ich habe lange auf dich gewartet. *I waited for you for a long time*.

warten bis man schwarz wird — *to wait till one is blue in the face*.

Ihr könnt warten, bis ihr schwarz werdet — das tu ich nie. *You can wait till you're blue in the face. I'll never do that*.

die Wartung — *service*.

wartungsfreundlich — *easy to service; requiring little service*.

Dies ist ein wartungsfreundliches Gerät. *This is an easy-to-service appliance*.

---

was — *what*

Was Sie nicht sagen! *You don't say!*

Was man nicht weiß, macht man nicht heiß. *Ignorance is bliss. No news is good news*.

---

die Wäsche — *laundry*

schmutzige Wäsche waschen — *to wash one's dirty linen*.

Einige Kinder von Filmstars schrieben Bücher, in denen schmutzige Wäsche gewaschen wird. *Some children of movie stars wrote books in which dirty linen is washed in public*.

dumm aus der Wäsche gucken — *to look dumbfounded*.

Nachdem sie das hörte, guckte sie dumm aus der Wäsche. *After she heard that, she looked dumbfounded*.

waschecht — *dyed-in-the-wool.*

Der Verkäufer war ein waschechter Lügner. *The salesperson was a dyed-in-the-wool liar.*

---

waschen — *to wash*

wasch mir den Pelz, aber mach mich nicht nass. — *to want benefits without any drawbacks/expense/work.*

Oma meint, heute handeln zu viele nach dem Spruch: wasch mir den Pelz, aber mach mich nicht nass. *Grandma thinks that too many behave according to the saying, "I'd like the job done, but I don't want to get my hands dirty."*

---

das Wasser — *water*

einem das Wasser reichen — *to hold a candle to.*

Trotz Fusionen kann keine andere Börse Wall Street das Wasser reichen. *Despite mergers, no other stock exchange can hold a candle to Wall Street.*

ins Wasser fallen — *to fall through.*

Unsere Urlaubspläne sind ins Wasser gefallen. *Our vacation plans have fallen through.*

jemandem das Wasser abgraben — *to cut the ground from someone's feet.*

Durch die neue Technik wurde uns das Wasser abgegraben. *We were left high and dry/cut off at the pass because of the new technology.*

mit allen Wassern gewaschen sein — *to know all the tricks.*

Ihre Anwältin ist mit allen Wassern gewaschen. *Her lawyer knows all the tricks.*

Wasser auf die Mühle — *grist for the mill.*

Der letzte Skandal ist Wasser auf die Mühle der Opposition. *The latest scandal is grist for the mill of the opposition.*

---

der Wecker — *alarm clock*

auf den Wecker fallen/gehen — *to get on someone's nerves.*

Ich vermeide ihn, weil er mir auf den Wecker geht. *I avoid him because he gets on my nerves.*

---

weg — *away; gone*

in einem weg — *constantly.*

Beim Essen klingelte das Telefon in einem weg. *The telephone rang constantly while we were eating.*

über etwas weg sein — *to have gotten over something.*

Ihr Kind starb letztes Jahr und sie sind noch nicht darüber weg. *Their child died last year, and they haven't gotten over it yet.*

weg sein — *to be carried away.*

Lola tanzte, und alle Männer waren weg. *Lola danced, and all the men were carried away.*

---

der Weg — *way, path*

Hier trennen sich unsere Wege. *This is where we part company.*

an etwas geht kein Weg vorbei — *to be unavoidable.*

An den Haushaltskürzungen geht kein Weg vorbei. *There's no getting around having to make budget cuts.*

auf den Weg bringen — *to get started, initiate.*

Ein neues Drogenbekämpfungsgesetz wurde auf den Weg gebracht. *New anti-drug legislation was introduced.*

aus dem Weg räumen — *to get out of the way.*

Jetzt sind alle Hindernisse aus dem Weg geräumt. *All obstacles are now out of the way.*

den Weg des geringsten Widerstandes gehen — *to take the line of least resistance.*

Er ging den Weg es geringsten Widerstandes, und behauptete, er sei oft der beste Weg. *He took the line of least resistance and said it was often the best line to take.*

etwas in die Wege leiten — *to start s.t. on its way through channels.*

Ihren Antrag werden wir in die Wege leiten. *We'll start processing your request.*

sich auf den Weg machen — *to set out.*

Erst spät in der Nacht machten wir uns auf den Weg. *It wasn't till late at night that we set out.*

sich selbst im Weg stehen — *to be one's own worst enemy.*
Wenn sie sich selbst nicht im Weg stünde, könnte sie mehr erreichen.
   If she weren't her own worst enemy, she could achieve more.

---

wegdenken — *to imagine as not there*
nicht wegzudenken sein — *to be inconceivable without.*
Sie ist aus der jüngsten Geschichte ihres Landes nicht wegzudenken.
   The recent history of her country is inconceivable without her.

---

wegsehen — *to look away*
vom Wegsehen kennen — *to want nothing to do with.*
Seit er mich betrogen und belogen hat, kenn ich ihn nur vom Wegsehen.
   Ever since he cheated and lied to me, I want nothing to do with him.

---

das Weh — *woe*
das Fernweh — *longing for far-off places, wanderlust.*

das Heimweh — *nostalgia for one's home(land), homesickness.*
In der Heimat hab ich Fernweh; in der Ferne hab ich Heimweh. *At home
   I yearn for far-off places; when abroad I'm homesick.*

---

wehtun — *to hurt*
Wo tut's denn weh? *What's the problem?*

---

die Weiche — *switch*
die Weichen stellen — *to set a course.*
Durch Namenwechsel und ein neues Programm will die Partei die
   Weichen für die Zukunft stellen. *By changing its name and with a new
   program the party wants to set a course for the future.*

---

der Weihnachtsmann — *Santa Claus, Father Christmas*
noch an den Weihnachtsmann glauben — *to still believe in Santa
   Claus; be very naïve.*
Virginia glaubt noch an den Weihnachtsmann, und den Märchenprinzen
   auch. *Virginia still believes in Santa Claus, and in Prince Charming
   too.*

---

weinen — *to cry*
  zum Weinen bringen — *to make cry.*
  Der bloße Anblick der Trümmer brachte mich zum Weinen. *The mere sight of the ruins made me weep.*

---

weit — *far*
  weit entfernt sein — *to be a long way from.*
  Von einem Abkommen sind wir noch weit entfernt. *We're still a long way from an agreement.*

  bis auf weiteres — *for the present; until further notice.*
  Bis auf weiteres können Sie hier bleiben. *For the present you can stay here.*

---

die Welle — *wave*
  die weiche Welle — *the soft approach/line.*
  Zuerst versuchte er's mit der weichen Welle. *At first he took a soft line.*

  hohe Wellen schlagen — *to cause a commotion, make waves.*
  Die Enthüllungen der Journalistin schlugen hohe Wellen. *The journalist's revelations made waves.*

---

die Welt — *world*
  Davon geht die Welt nicht unter. *That's not the end of the world.*

  alle Welt — *everyone.*
  Das weiß schon alle Welt. *Everybody knows that already.*

  aus der Welt schaffen — *to get rid of, put an end to.*
  Der Senator verlangte eine Ermittlung, um die Gerüchte aus der Welt zu schaffen. *The senator demanded an investigation to put an end to the rumors.*

  bis ans Ende der Welt — *to the ends of the earth.*
  Er reist oft bis ans Ende der Welt, um seinen Gral zu suchen. *He often travels to the ends of the earth looking for his Grail.*

  die große Welt — *high society.*
  Er verließ die große Welt und wohnt jetzt im Himalaja. *He left high society and lives in the Himalayas now.*

  Die Welt ist ein Dorf. *It's a small world.*

Dich hier im Himalaja zu sehen — ach die Welt ist wahrhaftig ein Dorf!
To see you here in the Himalayas — it sure is a small world!

heile Welt — *ideal, picture-pefect, Norman Rockwell world.*
Wir schauten uns Omas Photoalbum an—das war noch eine heile Welt!
We looked at grandma's photo album—that was a saner age!

die Weltanschauung — *world view; philosophy of life.*
Nietzsches Weltanschauung ist noch viel umstritten. *Nietzsche's philosophy of life is still very controversial.*

---

der Wermut — *wormwood; vermouth*
    der Wermutstropfen (im Becher der Freude) — *the drop of bitterness (in the cup of joy).*
    Bei der Olympiade gewann sie Gold; einziger Wermutstropfen, sie hat sich dabei das Fußgelenk leicht verstaucht. *She won gold at the Olympics; the only little problem was a sprained ankle.*

---

der Wert — *value*
    Wert auf etwas legen — *to be a great believer in.*
    Mutter legte großen Wert auf eine gesunde Ernährung. *Mother was a great believer in a healthy diet.*

---

die Westentasche — *vest pocket*
    wie seine Westentasche kennen — *to know inside out.*
    Er kennt Wien wie seine Westentasche. *He knows Vienna inside out.*

    im Westentaschenformat — *pocket-sized; tin-pot.*
    Sie kaufte einen Rechner im Westentaschenformat. *She bought a pocket-sized calculator.*
    Der General, der über die kleine Insel herrscht, ist ein Diktator im Westentaschenformat. *The general who rules the little island is a tin-pot dictator.*

---

die Wette — *bet, wager*
    etwas um die Wette tun — *to compete; try to outdo.*
In Mozarts *Der Schauspieldirektor* singen die Sopranistinnen um die Wette. *In Mozart's "The Impresario" the sopranos try to outsing each other.*

---

der Wettergott — *god of the weather; the weather*
Wir hoffen, dass der Wettergott uns gnädig sein wird. *We hope the weather will be kind to us (cooperate).*

wichtig — *important*
sich wichtig machen/tun — *to behave pompously.*
Er machte sich wichtig und gab seinen Senf dazu. *He behaved pompously and put an oar in.*

wie — *how; as*
Wie du mir, so ich dir. *Tit for tat. I'll pay you back in kind.*

die Wiege — *cradle*
in die Wiege legen — *to bestow at birth.*
Die Muse hat ihm keine dichterischen Gaben in die Wiege gelegt, trotzdem hält er sich für einen großen Dichter. *The Muse didn't bestow any poetic gifts on him at birth; nevertheless he thinks he's a great poet.*

der Wind — *wind*
Wer Wind sät, wird Sturm ernten. *Sow the wind, and reap the whirlwind.*

im Ab-/Aufwind sein — *to be (on the way) down/up.*
Im gestrigen Kurs stand der Dollar im Auf- die Euro im Abwind. *At yesterday's rates the dollar was up, the euro down.*

in den Wind schlagen — *to disregard.*
Unsere Warnungen hat er in den Wind geschlagen. *He disregarded our warnings.*

in den Wind schreiben — *to give up as lost.*
Er denkt daran, seine Karriere als Rechtsanwalt in den Wind zu schreiben, weil er dreimal beim Examen durchgefallen ist. *He's thinking of giving up a career as a lawyer, because he failed the (bar) exam three times.*

Wind machen — *to brag.*
Das stimmt nicht; er hat nur Wind gemacht. *That's not true; he was just bragging.*

der Gegenwind — *headwind; opposition.*

der Rückenwind — *tail wind; support.*

Rückenwind haben wir von der Regierung nicht erwartet, aber mit Gegenwind haben wir nicht gerechnet. *We didn't expect the government's support, but we didn't count on their opposition.*

das Windei — *dud, non-starter, wind egg.*

Der vermeintlich geniale Plan stellte sich als Windei heraus. *The supposedly brilliant plan turned out to be a dud.*

---

der Wink — *sign; hint*

ein Wink mit dem Zaunpfahl — *a broad hint.*

Alle verstanden sofort den Wink mit dem Zaunpfahl. *Everyone immediately understood the broad hint.*

---

der Winterschlaf — *hibernation*

Winterschlaf halten — *to hibernate.*

Diese Tiere halten jetzt ihren Winterschlaf. *These animals are now hibernating.*

---

wissen — *to know*

Von ihm will ich nichts mehr wissen. *I don't want anything more to do with him.*

weder ein noch aus wissen — *not to have the remotest idea of what to do.*

In seiner Verzweiflung wußte er weder ein noch aus. *In his despair he didn't have the remotest idea of what to do.*

---

die Woge — *wave; surge*

die Wogen glätten — *to calm things down.*

Wenn sich die Wogen wieder geglättet haben, fangen wir wieder an. *When things have calmed down, we'll start again.*

---

der Wolf — *wolf; meat grinder*

wie durch den Wolf gedreht — *thoroughly exhausted.*

Während der Weinlese war ich jede Nacht wie durch den Wolf gedreht. *During the grapepicking season (vintage), I was thoroughly exhausted every night.*

---

die Wolke — *cloud*
  aus allen Wolken fallen — *to be dumbfounded*.
  Sie fiel aus allen Wolken, als sie erfuhr, dass er in Honolulu eine Frau hatte. *She was dumbfounded when she found out that he already had a wife in Honolulu.*

die Wolkenfelder — *cloud banks*
  Wolkenfelder schieben — *to drift and dream, deal in abstractions*.
  Statt Wolkenfelder zu schieben, hilf mir den Schnee schaufeln. *Instead of drifting and dreaming, help me shovel the snow.*

  das Wolkenkuckucksheim — *cloud-cuckoo-land, dream world*.
  Mein verträumter Bruder wohnt in einem Wolkenkratzer und lebt im Wolkenkukucksheim. *My absent-minded brother resides in a skyscraper and lives in cloud-cuckoo-land.*

die Wolle — *wool*
  sich in die Wolle geraten — *to get into a squabble*.
  Die Verbündeten gerieten sich in die Wolle. *The allies got into a squabble.*

wollen — *to want; claim*
  Sie will das Loch Ness-Ungeheur oft gesehen haben. *She claims to have seen the Loch Ness monster often.*

das Wort — *word*
  zu Wort kommen lassen — *to allow to speak*.
  Die Parteiführer ließen die neue Abgeordnete selten zu Wort kommen. *The party leaders rarely allowed the new congresswoman to speak.*

wund — *sore*
  sich die Hände wund arbeiten — *to work one's fingers to the bone*.
  Die Chefin ist ein richtiges Arbeitstier und arbeitet sich die Hände wund. *The boss is a real workaholic and works her fingers to the bone.*

  sich wund laufen — *to walk until one's feet are sore; walk one's feet off*.
  Auf der Suche nach Arbeit lief sie sich einst wund. *Once she walked her feet off looking for work.*

der Wurf — *throw*
 einen großen/glücklichen Wurf tun — *to score a great success.*
 Mit der Rolle tat sie einen glücklichen Wurf. *She scored a great success with that role.*

der Würfel — *cube; dice; die*
 die Würfel sind gefallen — *the die is cast.*
 Jetzt hast du dich anders besonnen aber es ist zu spät; die Würfel sind gefallen. *You've changed your mind now but it's too late—the die is cast.*

der Wurm — *worm*
 die Würmer aus der Nase ziehen — *to worm out; to get to spill the beans.*
 Durch List gelang es der Polizei, ihm die Würmer aus der Nase zu ziehen. *Through cunning the police succeeded in getting him to spill the beans.*

die Wurst — *sausage*
 Alles hat ein Ende, nur die Wurst hat zwei. *Everything must come to an end.*

um die Wurst gehen — *to be down to the nitty-gritty.*
 Das ist deine letzte Chance — es geht jetzt um die Wurst. *This is your last chance. Things are down to the nitty-gritty now.*

Wurst sein — *to be all the same.*
 Er kann machen, was er will — es ist mir Wurst. *He can do what he wants. It's all the same to me.*

wursteln — *to putter about; muddle through.*
 Ja, es geht alles schlecht, aber wir wollen doch weiter wursteln. *Yes, everything is going badly, but we'll continue to muddle through.*

X

X

ein X für ein U vormachen — *to pull a fast one.*
 Die Rechnung ist unverschämt; man will uns ein X für ein U vormachen. *The bill is outrageous; they're trying to pull a fast one on us.*

X-Beine — *knock-knees*

Seine Frau findet seine X-Beine schön. *His wife thinks his knock-knees are nice.*

X-Beine haben — *to be knock-kneed.*

Hat er X- oder O-Beine? *Is he knock-kneed or bowlegged?*

x-beliebig — *just any old (thing)*

In der Galerie werden nicht x-beliebige, sondern wohlbekannte Maler ausgestellt. *In that gallery they don't exhibit just any old painters, only well-known ones.*

das x-temal — *the umpteenth time*

zum x-tenmal — *for the umpteenth time.*

Zum x-tenmal, wir wollen es nicht kaufen. *For the umpteenth time, we don't want to buy it.*

Z

die Zahl — *number*

rote/schwarze Zahlen schreiben — *to be in the red/black.*

Unser Theater schreibt noch rote Zahlen, aber nächstes Jahr hoffen wir schwarze Zahlen schreiben zu können. *Our theater is still in the red this year, but next year we hope to be in the black.*

zahlen — *to pay*

Herr Ober! Wir möchten bitte zahlen. *Waiter! We'd like the check please.*

der Zahn — *tooth*

Ihm tut kein Zahn mehr weh. *He has no toothache anymore. (He's dead, out of it.)*

auf den Zahn fühlen — *to sound out/check out.*

Bevor wir ihn akzeptieren, müssen wir ihm auf den Zahn fühlen. *We'll have to check him out before accepting him.*

die Zähne zusammenbeißen — *to grit one's teeth.*

Sie musste die Zähne zusammenbeißen, um nicht zu heulen. *She had to grit her teeth to keep from screaming*.

dritte Zähne — *false teeth*.
Opa trägt nur ungern seine dritten Zähne. *Grandpa doesn't like to wear his false teeth*.

einen Zahn zulegen — *to hurry it up, get a move on*.
Legt doch einen Zahn zu, sonst werden wir nicht fertig. *Hurry it up, or we won't get done*.

---

zappeln — *to wriggle; fidget*
zappeln lassen — *to let dangle; to keep guessing*.
Sie ließ ihn zappeln. *She kept him guessing*.

---

zart — *tender*
zartbesaitet — *high-strung, oversensitive*.
Der Film ist nichts für zartbesaitete Naturen. *The movie isn't for oversensitive sorts*.

---

der Zauber — *magic*
einen großen Zauber ausüben — *to fascinate*.
Mozarts Werke üben großen Zauber auf viele aus. *Mozart's works fascinate many*.

fauler Zauber — *fraud*.
Mach uns keinen faulen Zauber vor! *Don't try to defraud us!*

---

der Zaum — *bridle*
im Zaum halten — *to keep under control, in check*.
Der Tiger konnte seinen Instinkt nicht im Zaume halten und fraß seine Dompteuse auf. *The tiger couldn't keep his instinct under control and devoured his trainer*.

---

der Zaun — *fence*
einen Streit vom Zaun brechen — *to start a quarrel suddenly*.
Ohne Grund brach er einen Streit vom Zaun. *For no reason he suddenly picked a fight*.

---

das Zeichen — *sign*

im Zeichen eines Tierkreises geboren sein — *to be born under an
astrological sign.*

Sie ist im Zeichen des Wassermans geboren. *She was born under the sign
of Aquarius.*

im Zeichen von etwas stehen — *to be influenced/determined/
characterized by.*

Ihr letztes Schuljahr stand ganz im Zeichen der bevorstehenden
Abschlussprüfung. *Her last year in school was entirely influenced by
the finals she had to take.*

---

die Zeit — *time*

Kommt Zeit, kommt Rat. *If you give it time, the solution will come.*

auf Zeit — *temporarily.*

Ihm wurde der Führerschein auf Zeit entzogen. *His driver's license was
temporarily suspended.*

Das waren noch Zeiten! *Those were the days!*

Einst waren wir jung, reich und verliebt — das waren noch Zeiten! *Once
we were young, rich, and in love. Those were the days!*

es wird (höchste/allerhöchste) Zeit — *it's about time (it's high time).*

Einige im Publikum meinten, es wird Zeit, dass sie nicht mehr Rollen wie
Julia spielt. *Some in the audience thought it was about time that she
stopped playing roles like Juliet.*

---

das Zeug — *stuff*

sich ins Zeug legen — *to work very hard.*

Sie hat sich ins Zeug gelegt und den ersten Preis gewonnen. *She knuckled
down and won the first prize.*

was das Zeug hält — *like all get out, to beat the band.*

Man muss den Werbetrommel rühren, was das Zeug hält. *We'll have to go
all out on an advertising campaign.*

---

die Zicke — *she goat*

Zicken machen — *to act up.*

Der alte Wagen macht wieder Zicken und muss repariert werden. *The old
car is acting up again and needs repair.*

---

ziehen — *to pull*

  Es zieht wie Hechtsuppe hier! *There's a terrible draft here.*

  die Augen aller auf sich ziehen — *to attract everyone's attention.*
  In ihrem roten Ballkleid zog sie die Augen aller auf sich. *In her red ball gown she attracted everyone's attention.*

---

zittern — *to tremble; to shiver*

  mit Zittern und Zagen — *with fear and trembling.*
  Mit Zittern und Zagen erinnerte er sich an die Vergangenheit. *With fear and trembling he remembered the past.*

  wie Espenlaub zittern — *to shake like a leaf.*
  Als er das Gespenst erblickte, zitterte er wie Espenlaub. *When he saw the ghost, he shook like a leaf.*

  die Zitterpartie — *cliff-hanger; nail-biter.*
  Bis zum Ende war die Wahl eine Zitterpartie. *Till the very end the election was a cliff-hanger.*

---

der Zoll — *inch*

  jeder Zoll; Zoll für Zoll — *every inch.*
  Auch im Elend war sie noch jeder Zoll eine Dame. *Even in wretched circumstances she was still every inch a lady.*

---

das Zubrot — *supplementary income*

  Mit ihrem Singen in Kirchen und Kneipen verdient sie sich ein schönes Zubrot. *Singing in churches and bars brings her in a nice bit of extra cash.*

---

der Zucker — *sugar*

  Zuckerbrot und Peitsche — *carrot and stick.*
  Die Politik von Zuckerbrot und Peitsche ging nicht auf. *The politics of carrot and stick didn't work out.*

---

der Zug — *train; draught*

  In einem Zug leern — *to empty in one go.*
  Er leerte den Maßkrug in einem Zug. *He emptied his beermug in one go.*

Im Zug von etwas sein — *in the course/process of.*

Im Zuge der Sparmaßnahmen hat die Stadt die Subventionen an unser Theater gestrichen. *In the course of economy measures, the city cut subsidies to our theater.*

---

zugrunde gehen — *to die; to be destroyed, ruined*

In Mozarts Lied hofft Luise, dass ihr untreuer Liebhaber zugrunde gehen wird. *In Mozart's song, Luise hopes that her unfaithful lover will drop dead.*

---

zum einen . . . zum ander(e)n — *for one thing . . . for another*

Zum einen haben wir das dafür nötige Geld nicht, zum andern, wenn wir's hätten, würden wir's für etwas anderes ausgeben. *For one thing, we haven't got the money needed for it, for another, if we had it, we'd spend it on something else.*

---

zumute sein — *to feel*

Ihr war traurig zumute. *She felt sad.*

zumuten — *to ask/expect something unreasonable.*

Willst du mir noch zumuten, dass ich nach der Arbeit noch die Hausarbeit mache? *Do you expect me to do the housework after getting home from work?*

---

zuschieben — *to push shut*
    den schwarzen Peter zuschieben — *to pass the buck; to blame someone else.*

Der Senator versuchte, seinem Sekretär den schwarzen Peter zuzuschieben. *The senator tried to pass the buck to his secretary.*

---

der Zweig — *branch*
    auf (k)einen grünen Zweig kommen — *(not) to amount to something.*

Trotz seiner reichen Familie kam er auf keinen grünen Zweig. *Despite his wealthy family, he never amounted to anything.*

---

zwicken — *to pinch*
    zwicken und zwacken — *to suffer aches and pains.*

Ihn zwickt's und zwackt's öfters, aber trotz seines hohen Alters ist seine Gesundheit verhältnismäßig gut. *He's often plagued by aches and pains, but despite his age his health is relatively good.*

---

das Zwielicht — *twilight*

ins Zwielicht geraten — *to come under suspicion.*

Der Vorsitzende ist ins Zwielicht geraten. *The chairman has come under suspicion.*

zwielichtig — *shady.*

Seine Frau hat nichts von seinen zwielichtigen Geschäften gewusst. *His wife knew nothing of his shady dealings.*

---

zwischen — *between*

zwischen Tod und Teufel/zwischen Baum und Borke sein — *to be between the devil and the deep blue sea/between a rock and a hard place.*

Beide Lösungen gingen mir gegen den Strich; ich war zwischen Tod und Teufel. *Both solutions went against my grain; I was between the devil and the deep blue sea.*

zwischen Tür und Angel — *hurriedly; haphazardly.*

Mittags esse ich nur zwischen Tür und Angel. *I always have lunch on the run.*

---

zwitschern — *to chirp*

einen zwitschern — *to tipple.*

Nach dem Essen wollten sie noch einen zwitschern. *After eating they wanted to tipple some more.*

Abkürzungen—Deutsch-Englisch
(Abbreviations—German-English)

Abkürzung	Bedeutung	Englisches Aquivalent	Englische Abkürzung

A

Abkürzung	Bedeutung	Englisches Aquivalent	Englische Abkürzung
a.a.O.	am angegebenen (*od.* angeführten) Ort	in the place cited	loc. cit.
Abb.	Abbildung	figure	fig.
Abg.	Abgeordnete(r)	Representative	Rep.
Abs.	Absatz	paragraph	par.
Abt.	Abteilung	department	dept.
a.D.	außer Dienst	retired	ret., (R)
ADAC	Allgemeiner Deutscher Automobil-Club	German Automobile Club	
AEG	Allgemeine Elektrizitäts-Gesellschaft	General Electric Company	
AKW	Atomkraftwerk	nuclear energy plant	
a.M.	am Main	on the Main (river)	
Anm.	Anmerkung	note	
App.	Appartment	apartment	apt.
App.	Apparat	extension	ext.
a.O.	an der Oder	on the Oder (river)	
a.Rh.	am Rhein	on the Rhine	
ARD	Arbeitsgemeinschaft der öffentlich-rechtlichen Rundfunkanstalten der Bundesrepublik Deutschland	German public radio and television network	

Abkürzung	Bedeutung	Englisches Aquivalent	Englische Abkürzung

B

Bd.	Band	volume	vol.
bes.	besonders	especially	esp.
betr.	betreffs	re	
BH	Büstenhalter	brassiere	bra
BKA	Bundeskriminalamt	Federal Bureau of Investigation	F.B.I.
BMW	Bayerische Motorenwerke	Bavarian Motor Works	BMW
BND	Bundesnachrichten-dienst	Central Intelligence Agency	C.I.A.
BRD	Bundesrepublik Deutschland	Federal Republic of Germany	F.R.G.
b.w.	bitte wenden	please turn over	P.T.O.
Bz.	Bezirk	district	dist.

C

C	Celsius	Celsius, Centigrade	C
cbm	kubikmeter	cubic meter	cu. m.
CDU	Christlich-Demokratische Union	Christian Democratic Union	C.D.U.
cm	Zentimeter	centimeter	cm.
CSU	Christlich-Soziale Union	Chirstian Social Union	C.S.U.
Co.	Compagnie	Company	Co.

D

D	Deutschland	Germany	Ger.
DAAD	Deutscher Akademischer Austauschdienst	German Academic Exchange Service	
DAX	Deutscher Aktienindex	Index of leading German stocks	

Abkürzung	Bedeutung	*Englisches* *Aquivalent*	*Englische* *Abkürzung*
DB	Deutsche Bundesbahn	German Federal Railroad	
DBP	Deutsche Bundespost	German Federal Postal Service	
DDR	Deutsche Demokratische Republik	German Democratic Republic	G.D.R.
d.h.	das heißt	*id est* (that is)	i.e.
DIN	Deutsche Industrie Norm(en)	German Standard Specificiation(s)	
dm	Dezimeter	decimeter	dm.
DM	Deutsche Mark	German mark	DM
DNS	Desoxyribonu-kleinsäure	deoxyribonucleic acid	DNA
do.	dito	ditto	do.
dpa	Deutsche Presse-Agentur	German Press Agency	
Dr. jur.	Doktor der Rechte	Doctor of Law	LL.D.
Dr. med.	Doktor der Medizin	Doctor of Medicine	M.D.
Dr. phil.	Doktor der Philosophie	Doctor of Philosophy	Ph.D.
Dr. theol.	Doktor der Theologie	Doctor of Theology	D.D.
dt.	deutsch	German	Ger.
DW	Deutsche Welle	international German radio and television service	
DZT	Deutsche Zentrale für Tourismus	German National Tourist Office	

E

EDV	Elektronische Datenverarbeitung	electronic data processing	EDP
einz.	einzeln	separate	sep.
engl.	englisch	English	Eng.

Abkürzung	Bedeutung	Englisches Aquivalent	Englische Abkürzung
EU	Europäische Union	European Union	EU
e.V.	eingetragener Verein	registered association	
Ew.	Euer, Eure	your	
Expl.	Exemplar	copy	

F

F	Fahrenheit	Fahrenheit	F
Fa	Firma	firm, company	
FDP	Freie Demokratische Partei	Free Democratic Party	
ff	sehr fein	extra fine	EF
ff.	folgende (Seiten)	following	fol.
FKK	Freikörperkultur	Free Physical Culture (nudism)	
Fr.	Frau	woman	Mrs., Ms.
Frl.	Fräulein	girl	Miss, Ms.

G

g	Gramm	gram	g.
geb.	geboren	born	
Gebr.	Gebrüder	Brothers	Bros.
geg.	gegen	versus	vs.
Gew.	Gewicht	weight	wt.
GFM.	Generalfeldmarschall	field marshal	F.M.
GmbH	Gesellschaft mit beschränkter Haftung	corporation with limited liability	Corp.
GUS	Gemeinschaft Unabhängiger Staaten	Community of Independent States	CIS

Abkürzung	Bedeutung	*Englisches Aquivalent*	*Englische Abkürzung*

H

H., Hr.	Herr	man, Sir	Mr.
Hbf.	Hauptbahnof	main railroad station	
Hptst.	Hauptstadt	capital city	
hrsg.	herausgegeben	edited; published	ed.; pub.
Hs.	Handschrift	manuscript	ms.

I

i. allg.	im Allgemeinen	in general	
i.A.	im Auftrag	for, by order of	
i.J.	im Jahre	in the year	
Ing.	Ingenieur	engineer	
Inh.	Inhaber	proprietor	propr.
inkl.	inklusive	including	
i.R.	im Ruhestand	retired	retd.
i.V.	in Vertretung	by proxy	

J

J.	Jahr	year	yr.
Jh., Jahrh.	Jahrhundert	century	cen.
JH	Jugendherberge	youth hostel	
JHV	Jahreshauptvers-ammlung	annual general meeting	AGM

K

kfm.	kaufmännisch	commercial	
kg	Kilogramm	kilogram	kg.
Kfz.	Kraftfahrzeug	motor vehicle	
Kgr.	Königreich	kingdom	
km	Kilometer	kilometer	km.
kW	Kilowatt	kilowatt	kw.

Abkürzung	Bedeutung	Englisches Aquivalent	Englische Abkürzung

L

l	Liter	liter	l,
lfd.	laufend	current	
Lfg.	Lieferung	delivery	delvy.
LKW	Lastkraftwagen	truck	
Lt.	Leutnant	lieutenant	Lieut., Lt.

M

m	Meter	meter	m.
m.b.H.	mit beschränkter Haftung	with limited liability	ltd.
m.E.	meines Erachtens	in my opinion	
mg	Milligramm	milligram	mg.
mm	Millimeter	millimeter	mm.
m.W.	meines Wissens	so far as I know	
Mz.	Mehrzahl	plural	pl., plu.

N

N	Nord, Norden	North	N.
Nachf.	Nachfolger	successor	
nachm.	nachmittags	in the afternoon	p.m.
n. Chr.	nach Christus	Anno Domini	A.D.
Nr.	Nummer	number	no.
NS	Nachschrift	postscript	P.S.
NZ	Normalzeit	standard time	

O

O	Osten	East	E.
ö., österr.	österreichisch	Austrian	Aust.
ÖBB	Österreichische Budesbahnen	Austrian Railroad	
o.J.	ohne Jahr	no date/year	n.d.

Abkürzung	Bedeutung	*Englisches Aquivalent*	*Englische Abkürzung*
od.	oder	or	
o.O.u.J.	Ohne Ort und Jahr	without place or date	n.p., n.d.
o.V.	ohne Verzögerung	without delay	

P

p.A., p.Adr.	per Adresse	in care of	c/o
Pf., Pfg.	Pfennig	pfennig (coin)	
Pfd.	Pfund	pound	lb.
PKW	Personenkraftwagen	passenger car, automobile	
PLZ	Postleitzahl	zip code	
PS	Pferdestärke	horsepower	h.p.

Q

q	Quadrat	square	sq.
qcm	Quadratzentimeter	square centimeter	sq. cm.
qkm	Quadratkilometer	square kilometer	sq. km.

R

r.	rechts	right	rt.
RB	Reichsbahn	pre-1945 and former G.D.R. railroad	
Reg.	Regierung	government	govt.
Rh.	Rhein	Rhine	
RIAS	Radio im amerikanischen Sektor	Radio in the American Sector (of Berlin)	RIAS

S

S	Süden	South	S., So.
S.	Seite	page	p.
S-Bahn	Stadtbahn	urban-suburban railway	
SBB	Schweizerische	Swiss Federal Railroad	

Abkürzung	Bedeutung	Englisches Aquivalent	Englische Abkürzung
	Bundesbahnen		
s.o.	siehe oben	see above	
sog.	sogenannte	so-called	
SPD	Sozialdemokratische Partei Deutschlands	Social Democratic Party of Germany	
Str.	Straße	street	St.
s.u.	siehe unten	see below	

T

tägl.	täglich	daily	
Tb	Tuberkulose	tuberculosis	T.B.
teilw.	teilweise	partly	
Th.	Thema	subject	

U

u.	und, unter, unten	and, under, below	
U.A.w.g.	um Antwort wird gebeten	répondez s'il vous plaît (an answer is requested)	R.S.V.P.
U-Bahn	Untergrundbahn	subway	
Uffz.	Unteroffizier	noncommissioned officer	NCO
usw.	und so weiter	and so forth	etc.
u.Z.	unserer Zeitrechnung	Common Era	C.E.

V

v.	von, vom	of	
v.Chr.	vor Christus	before Chirst	B.C.
v.u.Z.	vor unserer Zeitrechnung	Before the Common Era	B.C.E.
Ver. St.v.A	Vereinigte Staaten von Amerika	United States of America	U.S.A.

Abkürzung	Bedeutung	Englisches Aquivalent	Englische Abkürzung

W

W	Westen	West	W.
Wwe.	Witwe	widow	

Z

z.B	zum Beispiel	*exempli gratia* (for example)	e.g.
ZDF	Zweites Deutsches Fernsehen	Second German Television Channel	
z.T	zum Teil	in part	
Ztg.	Zeitung	newspaper	
z.Z.	zur Zeit	at the present time	

Abbreviations—English-German
(Abkürzungen—Englisch-Deutsch)

Please note that many German abbreviations are written with a period, but not all of them. In English, abbreviations for centimeter, kilometer, etc., are written with a period—cm., km. The same abbreviations are written without a period in German—cm, km, etc. Please do not add periods to those German abbreviations listed without one.

Abbreviation	Meaning	German Equivalent	German Abbreviation

A

Abbreviation	Meaning	German Equivalent	German Abbreviation
A.A.	Alcoholics Anonymous	Anonyme Alkoholiker	A.A.
A.A.A.	American Automobile Association	Amerikanischer Automobil-Club	
A.B.	*Artium Baccalaureus* (Bachelor of Arts)	Bakkalaureus der philosophischen Fakultät	
abbr.	abbreviation	Abkürzung	Abk.
a.c.	alternating current	Wechselstrom	WS
A.D.	Anno Domini	nach Christus	n. Chr.
ADC	aide-de-camp	Adjutant	
Adm.	Admiral	Admiral	Adm.
alt.	altitude	Höhe	H
amt.	amount	Betrag	Betr.
a.m.	ante meridiem	vormittags	vorm.
A.M.	*Artium Magister* (Master of Arts)	*Magister Artium*	M.A.
anon.	anonymous	anonym	anon.
Apr.	April	April	Apr.
apt.	apartment	Appartement	App.
appt.	appointment	Termin	T.
ASCII	American Standard Code for Information Interchange	amerikanischer Standard-code für Datentausch	ASCII

Abbreviation	Meaning	German Equivalent	German Abbreviation
assn.	association	Verband	Vb.
asst.	assistant	Assistent	Asst.
att(n).	(to the) attention (of)	zu Händen (von)	z.Hd. (v.)
atty.	attorney	Anwalt	Anw.
at. wt.	atomic weight	Atomgewicht	At.-Gew.
Aug.	August	August	Aug.
AWOL	absent without official leave	ohne Urlaub entfernt	

B

b.	born	geboren	geb.
B.A.	Bachelor of Arts	Bakkalaureus der philosophischen Fakultät	
B.C.	before Christ	vor Christus	v. Chr.
B.D.	Bachelor of Divinity	Bakkalaureus der Theologie	
bl.	barrel	Fass	F.
bldg.	building	Gebäude	Gbd., Geb.
Br.	British	britisch	brit.
Bros.	brothers	Gebrüder	Gebr.
B.S.	Bachelor of Science	Bakkalaureus der Naturwissenschaften	

C

C.	Celsius	Celsius	C
Can.	Canada	Kanada	Kan.
capt.	captain	Hauptmann	Hptm.
C.E.	Common Era	unserer Zeitrechnung	u.Z.
cent.	century	Jahrhundert	Jahrh., Jh.
CEO	chief executive officer	Vorstandsvorsitzende(r)	
cf.	compare	vergleiche	vgl.
CFC	chlorofluorocarbon	Fluorchlorkohlen-wasserstoff	FCKW

Abbreviation	Meaning	German Equivalent	German Abbreviation
chap.	chapter	Kapitel	Kap.
CIS	Community of Independent States	Gemeinschaft Unabhängiger Staaten	GUS
cm.	centimeter	Zentimeter	cm
c/o	in care of	bei, per Adresse	p.Adr.
Co.	Company	Compagnie	Co.
C.O.D.	cash on delivery	per Nachnahme	p. Nachn.
Col.	Colonel	Oberst	O., Obst.
Comdr.	Commander	Kommandeur	Kdr.
corp.	corporation	Gesellschaft mit beschränkter Haftung	GmbH
C.P.O.	Certified Public Accountant	staatlich anerkannter Wirtschaftsprüfer	
cr.	credit	Kredit	Kr.
cu.	cubic	kubisch	kub.

D

Abbreviation	Meaning	German Equivalent	German Abbreviation
D.A.	District Attorney	Staatsanwalt	St.-Anw.
d.c.	direct current	Gleichstrom	GS, Gs
D.D.	Doctor of Divinity	Doktor der Theologie	Dr. theol.
dec.	deceased	verstorben	verst.
Dec.	December	Dezember	Dez.
dept.	department	Abteilung	Abt.
dist.	district	Bezirk	Bez.
D.N.A.	deoxyribonucleic acid	Desoxyribonukleinsäure	DNS
do.	ditto	dito	dto.
doz.	dozen	Dutzend	Dtzd.
Dr.	doctor	Doktor	Dr.
D.S.T.	Daylight Saving Time	Sommerzeit	SZ

Abbreviation	Meaning	German Equivalent	German Abbreviation

E

Abbreviation	Meaning	German Equivalent	German Abbreviation
E.	East	Ost	O
E.	Eastern	östlich	ö
ea.	each	je	
ed.	editor	Herausgeber	Hrsg.
E.D.P.	electronic data processing	elektronische Datenverarbeitung	EDV
e.g.	for example	zum Beispiel	z.B.
encl.	enclosure	Anlage	Anl.
Eng.	English	englisch	engl.
ENG	electronic news gathering	elektronische Berichterstattung	EB
Esq.	Esquire	Herr	Hr.
esp.	especially	besonders	bes.
E.S.P.	extra sensory perception	außersinnliche Wahrnehmung	ASW
et al.	and others	und andere	u.a.
etc.	et cetera	und so weiter	usw.
E.U.	European Union	Europäische Union	EU
ext.	extension	Apparat	App.

F

Abbreviation	Meaning	German Equivalent	German Abbreviation
F.	Fahrenheit	Fahrenheit	F
F.B.I.	Federal Bureau of Investigation	Bundeskriminalamt	BKA
Feb.	February	Februar	Febr.
Fed.	Federal	Bundes-	B
fem.	Feminine	weiblich	w.
fig.	figure	Abbildung	Abb.
fl.	fluid	flüssig	fl.
f.o.b.	free on board	frei Schiff	
for.	foreign	ausländisch	ausl.

Abbreviation	Meaning	German Equivalent	German Abbreviation
Fr.	France	Frankreich	Fr.
Fr.	French	französisch	franz.
F.R.G.	Federal Republic of Germany	Bundesrepublik Deutschland	BRD
Fri.	Friday	Freitag	Fr.
ft.	foot	Fuß	
fwd.	forward	weiterleiten	

G

g.	gram	Gramm	g
G.D.P.	gross domestic product	Bruttoinlandsproduct	BIP
G.D.R.	German Democratic Republic	Deutsche Demokratische Republik	DDR
gen.	gender	Geschlecht	
gen.	general	allgemein	allg.
Gen.	General	General	Gen.
Ger.	Germany	Deutschland	Dtld., D
Ger.	German	deutsch	dt.
G.O.P.	Grand Old Party	amerikanische republikanische Partei	
govt.	Government	Regierung	Reg.
Gr. Brit.	Great Britain	Großbritannien	GB
gr. wt.	gross weight	Bruttogewicht	Br.-Gew.

H

HQ	headquarters	Hauptquartier	HQ, H.-Qu.
H.M.S.	Her/His Majesty's Ship	britisches Königschiff	
Hon.	(The) Honorable	ehrenwert	
h.p.	horsepower	Pferdestärke	PS
hr.	hour	Stunde	Std.

Abbreviation	Meaning	German Equivalent	German Abbreviation

I

id.	the same	dasselbe	dass.
I.D.	identity (papers)	Personalausweis	P.-Ausw.
i.e.	that is	das heißt	d.h.
I.M.F.	International Monetary Fund	Internationaler Währungsfonds	IWF
in.	inch(es)	Zoll	
Inc.	incorporated	eingetragene Gesellschaft	e.G.
I.O.U.	I owe you	Schuldschein	
I.Q.	intelligence quotient	Intelligenzquotient	I.Q.
It.	Italy	Italien	Ital.
It.	Italian	italienisch	ital.
ital.	italics	kursiv	kurs.

J

Jan.	January	Januar	Jan.
Jap.	Japanese	japanisch	jap.
J.C.	Jesus Christ	Jesus Christus	J.C.
J.C.	Julius Caesar	Julius Cäsar	J.C.
J.P.	Justice of the Peace	Friedensrichter	
Jr.	junior	Junior	jun.
jt.	joint	gemeinsam	gem.
Jul.	July	Juli	
Jun.	June	Juni	

K

kg.	kilogram	Kilogramm	kg
km.	kilometer	Kilometer	km
kw.	kilowatt	Kilowatt	kW

L

lab.	laboratory	Labor	
lat.	latitude	Breite	Br.

Abbreviation	Meaning	German Equivalent	German Abbreviation
Lat.	Latin	lateinisch	lat.
lb.	pound	Pfund	Pfd.
l.c.	lower case	Kleinbuchstaben	
L.C.	Library of Congress	Kongressbibliothek	
Lieut., Lt.	lieutenant	Leutnant	Lt.
Lit. D.	*Litterarum Doctor* (Doctor of Letters)	literarum humaniorum doctor	Dr. lit. hum.
LL.D.	*Legum Doctor* (Doctor of Laws)	Doktor der Rechte	Dr. jur.
loc. cit.	in the place cited	am angegebenen Ort	a.a.O.
long.	longitude	Länge	Lg.
Ltd.	limited	Gesellschaft mit beschränkter Haftung	GmbH

M

m.	meter	Meter	m
M.A.	Master of Arts	Magister Artium	MA
Maj.	Major	Major	Maj.
Mar.	March	März	Mrz.
masc.	masculine	männlich	m., m
M.C.	master of ceremonies	Zeremonienmeister	
M.D.	Doctor of Medicine	Doktor der Medizin	Dr. med.
Messrs.	plural of Mr.	Herren	HH
mfg.	manufacturing	Herstellung	Herst.
mfr.	manufacturer	Hersteller	Herst.
mg.	milligram	Milligramm	mg
min.	minute	Minute	Min.
misc.	miscellaneous	verschieden	versch.
mm.	millimeter	Millimeter	mm
mo.	month	Monat	Mo.
Mon.	Monday	Montag	Mo.
M.P.	Military Police	Militärpolizei	MP
M.P.	Member of Parliament	Parlamentsabgeordneter	
m.p.h.	miles per hour	Meilen pro Stunde	

Abbreviation	Meaning	German Equivalent	German Abbreviation
Mr.	Mister	Herr	Hr.
Mrs.	Mistress	Frau	Fr.
Ms.	Miss, Mrs.	Frau	Fr.
ms.	manuscript	Manuskript, Handschrift	Ms., Hs.
M.S.	Master of Science	Magister der Naturwissenschaften	Mag. rer. nat.
Mt.	Mount	Berg	Bg.
mthly.	monthly	monatlich	mtl.

N

Abbreviation	Meaning	German Equivalent	German Abbreviation
n.	noun	Hauptwort	Hptw.
N./No.	North	Nord	N
N.C.O.	noncommissioned officer	Unteroffizier	Uffz.
n.d.	no date	ohne Datum	o.D.
neut.	neuter	sächlich	s.
no.	number	Nummer	Nr.
Nov.	November	November	Nov.
N.T.	New Testament	Neues Testament	N.T.
nt.	net weight	Nettogewicht	Nettogew.

O

Abbreviation	Meaning	German Equivalent	German Abbreviation
OAU	Organization of African Unity	Organisation der afrikanischen Einheit	OAE
Oct.	October	Oktober	Okt.
O.T.	Old Testament	Altes Testament	A.T.
O.K.	all right	in Ordnung	
oz.	ounce	Unze	

P

Abbreviation	Meaning	German Equivalent	German Abbreviation
p.	page	Seite	S.
P.A.	public address system	Lautsprecheranlage	LS-Anlage
Pac.	Pacific	Pazifik	
par.	paragraph	Absatz	Abs.
p.c.	percent	vom Hundert	v.H.

258

Abbreviation	Meaning	German Equivalent	German Abbreviation
pd.	paid	bezahlt	bez.
Pfc.	Private First Class	Obergefreiter	Ogefr.
Ph.D.	*Philosophical Doctor* (Doctor of Philosophy)	Doktor der Philosophie	Dr. phil,
p.m.	post meridian	nachmittags	nachm.
P.M.	Prime Minister	Bundeskanzler, Premier	
P.M.	Postmaster	Postamtvorsteher	PAV
P.O.	post office	Postamt	PA
p.p.	parcel post	Paketpost	
pr.	pair	Paar	P.
Pres.	President	Präsident	Präs.
pres.	present	Gegenwart	Gegenw., Ggw.
Prof.	Professor	Professor	Prof.
pron.	pronoun	Fürwort	Fürw.
P.S.	postscript	Nachschrift	NS
P.T.A.	Parent-Teacher Association	Eltern-Lehrer-Vertretung	ELV
P.T.O.	please turn over	bitte wenden	b.w.
P.(O.)W.	prisoner of war	Kriegsgefangener	KrGf, Kr.-Gf.
P.X.	post exchange	Kaufhaus fürs Militär	
publ.	publisher	Verlag	Verl.

Q

Q.E.D.	*quod erat demonstrandum* (which was to be demonstrated)	was zu beweisen war	w.z.b.w.
qt.	quart	Quart	qt
q.v.	which see	siehe dies	s.d.

R

R.A.F.	Royal Air Force	Königliche Britische Luftwaffe	
R.C.	Roman Catholic	römisch-katholisch	rk.

Abbreviation	Meaning	German Equivalent	German Abbreviation
Rd.	road	Straße	Str.
ref.	reference	Verweis, Bezug	Verw., Bez.
reg.	registered	eingetragen	eingetr., e.
regt.	regiment	Regiment	Rgt.
Rep.	Representative	Abgeordneter	Abg.
Rep.	Republic	Republik	Rep.
retd.	retired	im Ruhestand	i.R., a.D.
Rev.	Reverend	Ehrwürden	Ehrw.
R.F.D.	Rural Free Delivery	ländliche Postzustellung	
riv.	river	Fluß	
R.N.	Registered Nurse	staatlich geprüfte Krankenschwester	
RNA	ribonucleic acid	Ribonukleinsäure	RNS
r.p.m.	revolutions per minute	Umdrehungen pro Minute	U.p.M., UpM
R.R.	railroad	Eisenbahn	
R.S.V.P.	please answer	um Antwort wird gebeten	U.A.w.g.

S

Abbreviation	Meaning	German Equivalent	German Abbreviation
S., So.	South	Süd(en)	S
S.A.	South America	Südamerika	Südamer.
Sat.	Saturday	Samstag	Sa.
sec.	second	Sekunde	Sek.
secy.	secretary	Sekretär	Sekr.
Sen.	Senator	Senator	Sen.
Sept.	September	September	Sept.
Sgt.	Sergeant	Feldwebel	Fdw.
sing.	singular	Einzahl	Ez.
Soc.	Society	Gesellschaft	G., Ges.
Sp.	Spanish	spanisch	span.
sq.	square	Quadrat	q
Sr.	Sister	Schwester	Sr.
S.S.	steamship	Dampfer	D
St.	Saint	Sankt	St.
St.	street	Straße	Str.
STD	sexually transmitted disease	Geschlechtskrank	
sub.	substitute	Ersatz	

Abbreviation	Meaning	German Equivalent	German Abbreviation
subj.	subject	Subjekt, Thema	Subj., Th.
subj.	subjunctive	Konjunktiv	Konj
Sun.	Sunday	Sonntag	So.
supp.	supplement	Zuschlag	
supt.	superintendent	Leiter	
S.W.	short wave	Kurzwelle	KW

T

Abbreviation	Meaning	German Equivalent	German Abbreviation
T.B.	tuberculosis	Tuberkulose	Tb, Tbc
tbs.	tablespoon	Esslöffel	
T.D.	Treasury Department	Finanzministerium	
tel.	telephone	Telefon	Tel.
Thurs.	Thursday	Donnerstag	Do.
T.N.T.	trinitrotoluene	Trinitrotoluol	TNT
trans.	transitive	transitiv	trans.
trans.	transportation	Transport	
tsp.	teaspoon	Teelöffel	
Tues.	Tuesday	Dienstag	Di.
T.V.	television	Fernsehen	tv

U

Abbreviation	Meaning	German Equivalent	German Abbreviation
U., Univ.	university	Universität	Univ., Uni
U.A.E.	United Arab Emirates	Vereinigte Arabische Emirate	VAE
u.c.	upper case	Großbuchstaben	
U.F.O.	unidentified flying object	unbekanntes Flugobjekt	UFO
U.K.	United Kingdom	Vereinigtes Königreich	VK
U.N.	United Nations	Vereinte Nationen	UNO
U.S.A.	United States of America	Vereinigte Staaten von Amerika	Ver.St.v.A., USA
U.S.A.	United States Army	Heer der Vereinigten Staaten von Amerika	
U.S.A.F.	United States Air Force	Luftwaffe der Vereinigten Staaten	
U.S.M.C.	United States Marine Corps	Marineinfanterie der Vereinigten Staaten	

Abbreviation	Meaning	German Equivalent	German Abbreviation
U.S.N.	United States Navy	Marine der Vereinigten Staaten	
U.S.S.R.	Union of Soviet Socialist Republics	Union der Sozialistischen Sowjetrepubliken	UdSSR

V

v.	verb	Zeitwort	Ztw.
v.	volt	Volt	V
V.A.T.	value added tax	Mehrwertsteuer	MwSt.
V.D.	venereal disease	Geschlechtskrankheit	
V.I.P.	very important person	prominente Person	
viz.	namely	nämlich	
vol.	volume	Band	Bd.
V.P.	Vice President	Vizepräsident	
vs.	versus	gegen	gg.

W

W.	west	West(en)	W
w.	watt	Watt	W
W.C.	water closet	Toilette	WC
Wed.	Wednesday	Mittwoch	Mi.
W.H.O.	World Health Organization	Weltgesundheitsorganisation	
wk.	Week	Woche	Wo.
wt.	weight	Gewicht	Gew.

Y

yd.	yard	Yard	Yd.
yr.	year	Jahr	J.

Z

Z.	Zone	Zone	Z.

262

Maße und Gewichte
(Weights and Measures)

Metrische Maße		Metric Measures	

Gewichte
Weights

Tonne	2204,6 Pfd.	ton	2204.6 lbs
Kilogramm	2,2046 Pfd.	kilogram	2.2046 lbs.
Gramm	15,532 Gran	gram	15.432 grains
Zentigramm	0,1543 Gran	centigram	0.1543 grains

Längenmaße
Linear Measures

Kilometer	0,62137 Meilen	kilometer	0.62137 miles
Meter	39,37 Zoll	meter	39.37 inches
Dezimeter	3,937 Zoll	decimeter	3.937 inches
Zentimeter	0,3937 Zoll	centimeter	0.3937 inches
Millimeter	0,03937 Zoll	millimeter	0.03937 inches

Hohlmaße
Measures of Capacity

Hektoliter	2,838 Scheffel	hectoliter	2.838 bushels
	26,418 Gallone		26.418 gallons
Liter	0,9081 Quart (trocken)	liter	0.9081 dry qt.
	1,0567 Quart (flüssig)		1.0567 liq. qt.

Raummaße
Cubic Measures

Kubikmeter	1,308 Kubikyard	cubic meter	1.308 cu. yards
Kubikdezimeter	61,023 Zoll^3	cubic decimeter	61.023 cu. inches
Kubikzentimeter	0,610 Zoll^3	cubic centimeter	0.610 cu. inches

Flächenmaße
Surface Measures

Quadratkilometer	247,104 Morgen	sq. kilometer	247.104 acres
Hektar	2,471 Morgen	hectare	2.471 acres
Quadratmeter	1550 Zoll²	sq. meter	1550 sq. inches
Quadratdezimeter	15,50 Zoll²	sq. decimeter	15.50 sq. inches
Quadratzentimeter	0,155 Zoll²	sq. centimeter	0.155 sq. inches

Weights and Measures
(Maße und Gewichte)

U.S. Measures		Maße U.S.	

Weights
Gewichte

ounce	28.35 grams	Unze	28,35 Gramm
pound	0.4536 kilograms	Pfund	0,4536 kg
ton (short)	907.18 kilograms	Tonne	907,18 kg
grain 0.648	grams	Gran	0,648 Gramm

Linear Measures
Längenmaße

mile	1.609 kilometers	Meile	1,609 km
knot	1.853 kilometers	Knoten	1,853 km
yard	0.914 meters	Yard	0,914 Meter
foot	0.3048 meters	Fuß	0,3048 Meter
inch	2.54 centimeters	Zoll	2,54 Zentimeter

Measures of Capacity
Hohlmaße

quart (liquid)	0.9463 liters	Quart (flüssig)	0,9463 Liter
quart (dry)	1.1 liters	Quart (trocken)	1,1 Liter
gallon	3.785 liters	Gallone	3,785 Liter
bushel	35.24 liters	Scheffel	35,24 Liter

Cubic Measures
Raummaße

cubic inch	16.387 cu. cm.	Kubikzoll	$16,387$ Zentimeter^3
cubic foot	0.0283 cu. ms.	Kubikfuß	$0,0283$ Meter^3
cubic yard	0.765 cu. ms.	Kubikyard	$0,765$ Meter^3

Surface Measures
Flächenmaße

acre	0.4047 hectare	Morgen	0,4047 Hektar
square mile	259.0 hectares	Quadratmeile	259,0 Hektar
square yard	0.836 sq. meters	Quadratyard	0,836 Meter^2
square foot	929.03 sq. cms.	Quadratfuß	929,03 cm^2
square inch	6.4516 sq. cms.	Quadratzoll	6,4516 cm^2

Common English Idioms

The German words in parentheses indicate the entry word under which you will find the English idiom.

A

a done deal. 166 (*perfekt*)
above ground. 210 (*der Tag*)
according to my arithmetic. 153 (*nach*)
acid test, the. 66 (*die Feuerprobe*)
act of God. 81 (*die Gewalt*)
act the fat cat, to. 44 (*dick*)
act up, to. 238 (*die Zicke*)
add fuel to the flames, to. 163 (*das Öl*)
advanced age. 102 (*hoch*)
after a fashion. 192 (*schlecht*)
after all's said and done. 56 (*das Ende*)
after all. 57 (*das Ende*)
after the event. 153 (*nach*)
airtight alibi, an. 101 (*der Hieb*)
all along the line. 139 (*die Linie*)
all at once. 182 (*der Ritt*)
all at sea. 198 (*schwimmen*)
all of a sudden. 144 (*das Mal*)
all over the place. 50 (*die Ecke*)
all spruced up. 39 (*bügeln*)
all that glitters is not gold. 83 (*das Gold*)
all things considered. 207 (*der Strich*)
all's well that ends well. 57 (*das Ende*)
amount to much, to. 38 (*bringen*)
amount to something, to. 240 (*der Zweig*)
anybody who is anybody. 176 (*der Rang*)

appearances are deceptive. 190 (*der Schein*)
arm in arm. 54 (*einhaken*)
armchair revolutionary. 186 (*der Salon*)
arouse interest, to. 103 (*der Hocker*)
as alike as two peas in a pod. 52 (*das Ei*)
as can be expected in the circumstances. 219 (*der Umstand*)
as if by magic. 77 (*der Geist*)
as if with one voice. 151 (*der Mund*)
astound s.o., to. 103 (*der Hocker*)
as you sow, so shall you reap. 225 (*der Wald*)
at a moment's notice. 101 (*heute*)
at any moment. 150 (*der Moment*)
at first go. 13 (*der Anhieb*)
at great length. 130 (*lang*)
at one's own risk. 177 (*die Rechnung*)
at the crack of dawn. 99 (*der Herr*)
at the outside. 9 (*allenfalls*)
avant-gardist, pioneer. 180 (*der Reiter*)
awful blunder, an. 90 (*der Hammer*)

B

back out, to. 5 (*der Abstand*)
back the wrong horse, to. 112 (*die Karte*)

267

backbreaking job. 122 *(der Knochen)*

bag and baggage. 116 *(das Kind)*

barefaced lie, a. 62 *(die Faust)*

be a cinch, to. 117 *(der Klacks)*

be a great believer in, to. 231 *(der Wert)*

be a killjoy, to. 202 *(der Spaß)*

be a little cracked/crazy, to. 43 *(dicht)*

be a live wire, to. 46 *(der Draht)*

be a matter of, to. 92 *(handeln)*

be a social climber, to. 162 *(oben)*

be a spoilsport, to. 202 *(der Spaß)*

be a stickler for detail, to. 107 *(der I-Tüpfel Reiter)*

be able to handle, to. 224 *(wachsen)*

be able to hold one's liquor, to. 215 *(trinken)*

be able to size up/gauge situations, to. 21 *(das Auge)*

be able to tell a thing or two about, to. 138 *(das Lied)*

be about to, to. 79 *(gerade)*

be about, to. 92 *(handeln)*

be about to do something, to. 26 *(der Begriff)*

be afraid, to. 12 *(die Angst)*

be afraid, to. 145 *(die Manschette)*

be all ears, to. 163 *(das Ohr)*

be all Greek, to. 23 *(der Bahnhof)*

be all the same, to. 235 *(die Wurst)*

be an out-and-out liar, to. 142 *(lügen)*

be around the bend, to. 90 *(der Hammer)*

be as plain as the nose on your face, to. 118 *(klar)*

be at cross purposes, to. 126 *(das Kreuz)*

be at issue, to. 77 *(gehen um)*

be at rock bottom, to. 115 *(der Keller)*

be at stake, to. 203 *(das Spiel)*

be attached to s.t., to. 93 *(hängen)*

be bankrupt, to. 215 *(trocken)*

be barking up the wrong tree, to. 41 *(der Dampfer)*

be between the devil and the deep blue sea, to. 241 *(zwischen)*

be boiling mad, to. 81 *(das Gift)*

be born yesterday, to. 48 *(dumm)*

be breathing down someone's neck, to. 154 *(der Nacken)*

be brewing, to. 40 *(der Busch)*

be caught dead, to. 3 *(abmalen)*

be conspicuous by one's absence, to. 6 *(die Abwesenheit)*

be cracked, to. 204 *(der Sprung)*

be cracked, to. 225 *(die Waffel)*

be cuckoo, to. 175 *(das Rädchen)*

be deeply felt, to. 122 *(der Knochen)*

be dim-witted, soft in the head, to. 32 *(die Birne)*

be dim-witted, to. 117 *(die Kirche)*

be double Dutch, to. 23 *(der Bahnhof)*

be down the drain, to. 52 *(der Eimer)*

be dumbfounded, to. 234 *(die Wolke)*

be dying to do something, to. 39 *(brennen)*

be evasive, to. 89 *(der Haken)*

be facing ruin, to. 159 *(das Nichts)*

be fed up with, to. 157 *(die Nase)*

be feeling fit again, to. 41 *(der Damm)*

be feeling under the weather, to. 207 *(der Strich)*

be fighting for a lost cause, to. 170 *(der Posten)*

be filthy rich, to. 78 *(das Geld)*

be first-rate, to. 118 *(die Klasse)*

be fishy, to. 94 *(der Hase)*

be flabbergasted, to. 25 *(der Bauklotz)*

be flat-tasting, to. 194 *(schmecken)*

be fond of, to. 80 *(gern)*; 87 *(gut)*

be gainfully employed, to. 141 *(das Loch)*

be game for anything, to. 168 *(das Pferd)*

be game for, to. 88 *(haben)*

be going smoothly, to. 40 *(die Butter)*

be good at figures, to. 177 *(rechnen)*

be halfway home, to. 148 *(die Miete)*

be henpecked, to. 165 *(der Pantoffel)*

be high time, to. 102 *(hoch)*

be history, be passé, to. 44 *(dienen)*

be hungry, to. 106 *(der Hunger)*

be in a bind/fix, to. 120 *(die Klemme)*

be in a fine fix, to. 186 *(der Salat)*

be in a generous mood, to. 202 *(spendieren)*

be in a good mood, to. 132 *(die Laune)*

be in a mess, to. 212 *(die Tinte)*

be in a sorry state, to. 35 *(der Boden)*

be in control, to. 183 *(das Ruder)*

be in good hands, to. 20 *(aufheben)*

be in great shape, to. 103 *(die Höhe)*

be in one's prime, to. 30 *(best)*

be in shock, to. 195 *(der Shock)*

be in someone's good graces, to. 205 *(der Stein)*

be in someone's good/bad books, to. 14 *(anschreiben)*

be in store for, to. 95 *(das Haus)*

be in the clear, to. 195 *(der Schneider)*

be in the lap of the gods, to. 206 *(der Stern)*

be in the limelight, to. 176 *(das Rampenlicht)*

be in the red/black, to. 236 *(die Zahl)*

be in the same boat, to. 36 *(das Boot)*

be indestructible, to. 218 *(umbringen)*

be just what's needed, to. 79 *(gerade)*

be keen on, to. 189 *(scharf)*

be last, to. 183 *(rot)*

be loaded/drunk, to. 129 *(laden)*

be lucky, to. 198 *(das Schwein)*

be no bed of roses, to. 104 *(der Honig)*

be no great shakes, to. 98 *(der Held)*

be no picnic, to. 104 *(der Honig)*

be not quite right upstairs, to. 161 *(oben)*

be nuts about, to. 7 *(der Affe)*

be nuts, to. 222 *(der Vogel)*

be of great concern, to. 155 *(der Nagel)*

be off one's rocker, to. 8 *(der Affe)*

be off one's rocker, to. 117 *(der Klaps)*

be off one's rocker, to. 204 *(der Sprung)*

be off the beam, to. 202 *(der Sparren)*

be on a diet, to. 43 *(die Diät)*

be on an expense account, to. 203 *(die Spesen)*

be on one's last legs, to. 141 *(das Loch)*

be on the ball, to. 23 *(der Ball)*

be on the horns of a dilemma, to. 26 *(der Baum)*

be on the move, to. 6 *(die Achse)*

be on the road to recovery, to. 30 *(die Besserung)*

be on the ropes, to. 199 *(das Seil)*

be on the way up/down, to. 232 *(der Wind)*

be on the wrong track, to. 104 *(das Holz)*

be one's own worst enemy, to. 229 *(der Weg)*

be one's sort of thing, to. 88 *(haben)*

be out for, to. 4 *(absehen)*

be out of joint, to. 12 *(die Angel)*

be out of one's mind, to. 212 *(die Tinte)*

be out of order, to. 30 *(der Betrieb)*

be out of the question, to. 169 *(die Platte)*; 70 *(die Frage)*

be out of the woods, to. 28 *(der Berg)*

be plastered, to. 111 *(der Kanal)*

be plastered, to. 33 *(blau)*

be prepared to pay good money for, to. 125 *(kosten)*

be pushy, to. 56 *(der Ellbogen)*

be right, to. 178 *(recht)*

be rooted to the spot, to. 16 *(anwurzeln)*

be short of funds, to. 113 *(die Kasse)*

be slow on the uptake, to. 38 *(das Brett)*

be slow on the uptake, to. 137 *(die Leitung)*

be slow on the uptake, to. 26 *(der Begriff)*

be smart, to. 162 *(das Ohr)*

be soaked to the skin, to. 60 *(der Faden)*

be soft in the head, to. 115 *(der Keks)*

be someone's business, to. 31 *(das Bier)*

be someone's cup of tea, to. 125 *(der Kragen)*

be someone's turn, to. 179 *(die Reihe)*

be sorry, to. 135 *(leid)*

be speechless, to. 146 *(das Maul)*

be spirited, to. 65 *(das Feuer)*

be successful, to. 57 *(der Erfolg)*

be sunk, to. 138 *(liefern)*

be taken in, to. 135 *(der Leim)*

be taken with, to. 15 *(antun)*

be the last straw, to. 125 *(der Kragen)*

be the last straw, to. 62 *(das Fass)*

be the latest thing, to. 123 *(kommen)*

be the spitting image of, to. 222 *(verwechseln)*

be thirsty, to. 50 *(der Durst)*

be tired of, to. 135 *(leid)*

be too much for anybody, to. 59 *(der Eskimo)*

be touch and go, to. 116 *(die Kippe)*

be touch and go, to. 148 *(das Messer)*

be tough, to. 94 *(hart)*

be unable to make head or tail of, to. 121 *(klug)*

be unable to stand, to. 135 *(leiden)*

be unavoidable, to. 228 *(der Weg)*

be under control, to. 86 *(grün)*

be up in arms, to. 208 *(der Sturm)*

be up to no good, to. 191 *(der Schild)*

be up to, to. 139 *(liegen)*

be urgent, to. 155 *(der Nagel)*

be wary of, to. 223 *(die Vorsicht)*

be well in with, have a connection with/line to, to. 46 *(der Draht)*

be well off, to. 44 *(dick)*

be with it, to. 185 *(die Sache)*

be yes man (person), to. 151 *(der Mund)*

be/become too much for, to. 224 *(wachsen)*

beat about the bush, to. 37 *(der Brei)*

beat to a pulp, to. 37 *(der Brei)*

beat out, to. 63 *(das Feld)*

beat the band, to. 211 *(der Teufel)*

below ground. 210 *(der Tag)*

belt down, to. 194 *(schmettern)*

belt down, to. 81 *(gießen)*

best of the best, the. 62 *(fein)*

bet one's life on, to. 81 *(das Gift)*

between you and me. 186 *(sagen)*

beyond all praise. 140 *(das Lob)*

big bang, the. 220 *(der Urknall)*

big cheese, the. 170 *(der Platz)*

big fish in a small pond, a. 97 *(der Hecht)*

big shot, a. 212 *(das Tier)*

bite the bullet, to. 16 *(der Apfel)*

bite the dust, to. 84 *(das Gras)*

bleed white, to. 145 *(das Mark)*

bloom is off the rose, the. 129 *(der Lack)*

blow one's own trumpet, to. 166 *(die Pauke)*

blow one's top, to. 61 *(fahren)*

blow one's top, to. 103 *(die Höhe)*

blow up, to. 142 *(die Luft)*

bone of contention. 205 *(der Stein)*

bottomless pit, a. 62 *(das Fass)*

brand new. 72 *(funkel)*

break a leg. 39 *(der Bruch)*

bring into being, to. 132 *(das Leben)*

bring oneself to do something, to. 28 *(bekommen)*

broad hint, a. 233 *(der Wink)*

buckle down and study, to. 156 *(die Nase)*

bull in a china shop, a. 55 *(der Elefant)*

bump off, rub out, kill, to. 51 *(die Ecke)*

burn one's bridges behind one, to. 39 *(die Brücke)*

burn the candle at both ends. 1 *(aasen)*

burn the midnight oil, to. 154 *(die Nacht)*

bury oneself in a book, to. 194 *(schmockern)*

bury the hatchet, to. 126 *(das Kriegsbeil)*

busybody, a. 213 *(der Topfgucker)*

butter up, to. 104 *(der Honig)*

buy a pig in a poke, to. 114 *(die Katze)*

buzz off, scram, to. 68 *(die Fliege)*

by a hair. 87 *(das Haar)*

by hook or by crook, one way or another. 31 *(biegen)*

by no means. 223 *(von)*

by the skin of one's teeth. 6 *(ach)*

by the way. 218 *(übrigens)*

C

call a spade a spade, to. 115 *(das Kind)*

call the tune, to. 77 *(die Geige)*

calm things down, to. 233 *(die Woge)*

carrot and stick. 239 *(der Zucker)*

carry coals to Newcastle, to. 59 *(die Eule)*

carry coals to Newcastle, to. 103 *(das Holz)*

carry on a conversation, to. 71 *(führen)*

carry things too far, to. 203 *(die Spitze)*

cast doubt on, to. 69 *(die Frage)*

cast pearls before swine, to. 187 *(die Sau)*

catch off guard, unprepared, to. 111 *(kalt)*

catch red-handed, to. 71 *(frisch)*

catch someone's eye, to. 20 *(das Auge)*

cave in to, to. 121 *(das Knie)*

character assassination. 183 *(der Rufmord)*

charity begins at home. 99 *(das Hemd)*

chatter on and on, to. 174 *(quasseln)*

clear off, to. 7 *(der Acker)*

clear off, to. 136 *(die Leine)*

clear off, to. 205 *(der Staub)*

clear out, to. 150 *(die Mücke)*

cliff-hanger, a. 239 *(die Zitterpartie)*

clip joint, a. 158 *(das Nepplokal)*

close, but no cigar. 223 *(vorbei)*

clothes make the man/persons. 119 *(die Kleider)*

coast is clear, the. 142 *(die Luft)*

cock of the walk. 88 *(der Hahn)*

cog in the machinery, a. 176 *(das Rädchen)*

come down in the world, to. 5 *(absteigen)*

come down to the crunch, to. 94 *(hart)*

come to one's senses, to. 221 *(die Vernunft)*

come to terms with, to. 118 *(klar)*

come true, to. 31 *(sich bewahrheiten)*

come unglued, to. 135 *(der Leim)*

come up with just like that, to. 18 *(der Ärmel)*

come up with right away, to. 106 *(der Hut)*

compliments to the chef. 140 *(das Lob)*

consolation prize. 216 *(das Trostpflaster)*

cook up a surprise, to. 148 *(die Mine)*

cope with a difficult problem, to. 38 *(das Brett)*

cost a bundle, to. 198 *(schwer)*

count for little, to. 120 *(kleinschreiben)*

count one's chickens before they're hatched, to. 209 *(der Tag)* crack up, to. 49 *(durchdrehen)*

creature comforts. 134 *(leiblich)*

cross swords with, to. 120 *(die Klinge)*

crying shame, a. 8 *(die Affenschande)*

cut across, to. 174 *(quer)*

cut off one's nose to spite one's face, to. 67 *(das Fleisch)*

cut the ground from someone's feet, to. 227 *(das Wasser)*

D

dance to someone's tune, to. 77 *(die Geige)*

dangerous spot, a. 168 *(das Pflaster)*

deadly serious. 31 *(das Bier)*; 58 *(der Ernst)*

deadly seriousness. 212 *(das Tier)*

death blow. 83 *(die Gnade)*

die is cast, the. 235 *(der Würfel)*

die laughing, to. 214 *(tot)*

discretion is the better part of valor. 121 *(klug)*

do everything by the book, to. 10 *(der Amtsschimmel)*

do in, to. 111 *(kaltmachen)*

do just for fun, to. 202 *(der Spaß)*

do/exercise a profession, to. 29 *(der Beruf)*

don't make me laugh! 129 *(lachen)*

double over with laughter, to. 129 *(lachen)*

down to the last cent/detail. 167 *(der Pfennig)*

down to the nitty-gritty. 235 *(die Wurst)*

down to the smallest detail. 107 *(das I-Tüpfelchen)*

draw to a close, to. 157 *(die Neige)*

dream world. 234 *(die Wolkenfelder)*

drift and dream, to. 234 *(die Wolkenfelder)*

drink like a fish, to. 187 *(saufen)*

drink to the dregs, to. 157 *(die Neige)*

drive up the wall, to. 158 *(der Nerv)*

drive up the wall, to. 164 *(die Palme)*

drop anchor, to. 13 *(der Anker)*

drop drastically, to. 115 *(der Keller)*

drop in the bucket, a. 216 *(der Tropfen)*

dyed-in-the-wool. 226/7 *(die Wäsche)*

E

easy come, easy go. 81 *(gewinnen)*

eat humble pie, to. 73 *(der Gang)*

eat humble pie, to. 126 *(das Kreuz)*

eat one's hat, to. 29 *(der Besen)*

eat out of house and home, to. 87 *(das Haar)*

ego-trip. 152 *(der Nabel)*

eleventh hour, the. 72 *(fünf)*

empty in one go, to. 239 *(der Zug)*

ends of the earth, to the. 230 *(die Welt)*

engage in idle chatter, talk aimlessly, to. 33 *(das Blaue)*

enough is enough. 145 *(das Maß)*

every day. 209 *(der Tag)*

every inch. 239 *(der Zoll)*

every other day. 9 *(all)*

everyone looks out for number one. 153 *(nächst)*

exercise moderation, to. 145 *(das Maß)*

expensive district, an. 169 *(das Pflaster)*

experience is the best teacher. 188 *(der Schaden)*

F

fall apart at the seams, to. 12 *(die Angel)*

fall flat on one's face, to. 25 *(der Bauch)*

fall on deaf ears, to. 133 *(leer)*

fall through, to. 227 *(das Wasser)*

fan the flames, to. 156 *(die Nahrung)*

fall to pieces, to. 65 *(der Fetzen)*

feel fit, to. 125 *(die Kraft)*

feel great, to. 103 *(die Höhe)*

feel like, to. 143 *(die Lust)*

feel on top of the world, to. 172 *(der Pudel)*

few and far between. 185 *(säen)*

fight a losing battle against s.t., to. 13 *(ankommen)*

fight battles already won, to. 162 *(offen)*

fight fire with fire, to. 121 *(der Klotz)*

fight to the finish, to. 132 *(das Leben)*

find acceptance, to. 75 *(das Gefallen)*

find out what fear really is, to. 72 *(das Fürchten)*

finishing touch, the. 192 *(der Schliff)*

fire a shot in the dark, fire at random, to. 33 *(das Blaue)*

first it's "do this," then it's "do that." 113 *(die Kartoffel)*

fish in troubled waters, to. 216 *(trüb)*

fly off the handle, to. 16 *(der Anzug)*

fool's errand. 73 *(der Gang)*

for a song. 165 *(der Pappenstiel)*

for the life of me. 214 *(tot)*

for the present. 58 *(erst)*

form an impression, to. 31 *(das Bild)*

free and easy. 103 *(der Hocker)*

freelance professional, a. 70 *(frei)*

from all over. 99 *(der Herr)*

from far and wide. 155 *(nah)*

from one source/supplier. 91 *(die Hand)*

from the frying pan into the fire. 178 *(der Regen)*

front-runner; top seller; number-one hit. 180 *(der Reiter)*

G

gain a foothold, to. 72 *(der Fuß)*

get a bad reputation, to. 79 *(das Gerede)*

get a bargain, to. 195 *(das Schnäppchen)*

get a chewing out, to. 106 *(der Hut)*

get a move on, to. 201 *(die Socke)*

get a move on, to. 236 *(der Zahn)*

get a word in edgewise, to. 234 *(das Wort)*

get along in years, to. 109 *(das Jahr)*

get angry, to. 17 *(sich ärgern)*

get around by word of mouth, to. 100 *(sich herumsprechen)*

get back on one's feet, to. 179 *(die Reihe)*

get back on one's feet, to. 27 (das Bein)

get bogged down, to. 79 (geraten)

get by on, to. 21 (auskommen)

get caught in the crossfire, to. 65 (das Feuer)

get drunk, to. 8 (der Affe)

get fat, to. 37 (breit)

get going, to. 201 (die Socke)

get going, to. 69 (der Fluss)

get going, to. 73 (der Gang)

get into a squabble, to. 234 (die Wolle)

get into deep trouble, to. 211 (der Teufel)

get into hot water, to. 158 (die Nessel)

get into shape, to. 46 (der Draht)

get married, to. 108 (Ja)

get noticed, to. 209 (die Szene)

get nowhere at all, to. 161 (die Null)

get off easy, to. 21 (das Auge)

get on one's nerves, to. 158 (nerven)

get on one's nerves, to. 77 (der Geist)

get on someone's nerves, to. 115 (der Keks)

get on someone's nerves, to. 227 (der Wecker)

get on s.o.'s nerves, to. 200 (der Senkel)

get one's hands on, to. 68 (die Flinte)

get one's money's worth, to. 125 (kosten)

get one's money's worth, to. 177 (die Rechnung)

get one's second wind, to. 172 (der Punkt)

get out of a tight spot, to. 49 (sich durchbeißen)

get out of/clean up a mess, to. 46 (der Dreck)

get rich, to. 123 (kommen)

get rid of, to. 230 (die Welt)

get roaring drunk, to. 156 (die Nase)

get something out of one's head, to. 4 (abschminken)

get somewhere, to. 13 (ankommen)

get started, to. 228 (der Weg)

get stuck, to. 64 (fest)

get the hang of, to. 85 (der Griff)

get the worst of, to. 128 (kurz)

get things sorted out, to. 115 (das Kind)

get through connections/pull, to. 222 (das Vitamin)

get to be too much for, to. 40 (bunt)

get to spill the beans, to. 235 (der Wurm)

get to the bottom of, to. 86 (der Grund)

get to the heart of the matter, to. 158 (der Nerv)

get to the point, to. 171 (der Pott)

get to the point, to. 185 (die Sache)

get under control, to. 85 (der Griff)

get under control, to. 99 (der Herr)

give a good going over to, to. 100 (das Herz)

give a good talking to, to. 75 (das Gebet)

give a hoot, to. 88 (der Hahn)

give a pat on the back, to. 196 (die Schulter)

give an inch./take a mile, to. 66 (der Finger)

275

give fresh impetus to, to. 15 *(der Antrieb)*

give moral support to, to. 154 *(der Nacken)*

give offense, to. 155 *(nah)*

give proof of, to. 31 *(der Beweis)*

give s.o. a good talking to, to. 163 *(das Ohr)*

give someone a bawling out, to. 32 *(blasen)*

give the lie to, to. 142 *(die Lüge)*

give up as lost, to. 232 *(der Wind)*

give vent to one's feelings, to. 100 *(das Herz)*

go about in the wrong/right way, to. 56 *(das Ende)*

go all out, to. 118 *(kleckern)*

go all out, to. 148 *(die Mine)*

go barhopping, to. 188 *(die Sause)*

go down in history, to. 53 *(eingehen)*

go down the drain, to. 22 *(der Bach)*

go down the drain, to. 32 *(die Binse)*

go down the drain, to. 69 *(flöten)*

go down with all on board, to. 145 *(der Mann)*

go Dutch, to. 113 *(die Kasse)*

go for a drink, to. 215 *(trinken)*

go for a spin, to. 31 *(die Biege)*

go for broke, to. 112 *(die Karte)*

go it alone, to. 9 *(der Alleingang)*

go off well, to. 117 *(klappen)*

go off without a hitch, to. 40 *(die Bühne)*

go on and on, to. 130 *(die Länge)*

go one better, to. 200 *(setzen)*

go out of one's way to avoid, to. 35 *(der Bogen)*

go steady, to. 64 *(fest)*

Go take a walk/hike. 115 *(der Keks)*

go to bat for, stand up for, to. 37 *(die Bresche)*

go to bat for, to. 130 *(die Lanze)*

go to great expense, to. 208 *(stürzen)*

go to hell, to. 167 *(der Pfeffer)*

go to rack and ruin, to. 175 *(das Rad)*

go to sea, to. 199 *(die See)*

go to the dogs, to. 105 *(der Hund)*

go to the dogs, to. 175 *(das Rad)*

go too far, to. 35 *(der Bogen)*

go too far, to. 40 *(bunt)*

go wild with excitement, to. 95 *(das Haus)*

God helps those who help themselves. 98 *(helfen)*

good luck! 212 *(toi, toi, toi)*

good measure, a. 145 *(das Maß)*

grin like a Cheshire cat, to. 104 *(der Honig)*

grist for the mill. 227 *(das Wasser)*

grit one's teeth, to. 236 *(der Zahn)*

H

hale and hearty. 81 *(gesund)*

hands up! 91 *(die Hand)*

hang around, to. 100 *(herum)*

hang on every word, to. 140 *(die Lippe)*

hanky-panky. 211 *(das Techtelmechtel)*

hard cash. 152 *(die Münze)*

hard-sell methods. 103 *(das Holz)*

hare-brained scheme. 195 *(die Schnapsidee)*

hats off! 106 *(der Hut)*

have a blast, to. 127 *(die Kuh)*

have a blast, to. 166 *(die Pauke)*

have a bone to pick, to. 104 *(das Huhn)*

have a burden to bear, to. 126 *(das Kreuz)*

have a chip on one's shoulder, to. 133 *(die Leberwurst)*

have a command of a language, to. 143 *(mächtig)*

have a cushy job, to. 127 *(die Krippe)*; 184 *(die Runde)*

have a few drinks, to. 156 *(die Nase)*

have a few too many, to. 81 *(das Glas)*

have a golden voice, to. 83 *(das Gold)*

have a green thumb, to. 91 *(die Hand)*

have a hangover, to. 124 *(der Kopf)*; 114 *(der Kater)*

have a knack for, to. 91 *(die Hand)*

have a light, to. 65 *(das Feuer)*

have a shady past/skeletons in the closet, to. 46 *(der Dreck)*

have a skeleton in the closet, to. 134 *(die Leiche)*

have ants in one's pants, to. 174 *(das Quecksilber)*

have bats in the belfry, to. 147 *(die Meise)*

have bats in the belfry, to. 222 *(der Vogel)*

have big ideas/ambitions, to. 102 *(hoch)*

have come to the right/wrong place, to. 7 *(die Adresse)*

have gotten over something, to. 228 *(weg)*

have gotten the hang of it, to. 35 *(der Bogen)*

have had a close call but be safe, to. 196 *(der Schrecken)*

have had as much as one can take, to. 111 *(der Kanal)*

have had it, to. 138 *(liefern)*

have in reserve, to. 91 *(die Hand)*

have in the bag, to. 185 *(der Sack)*

have it in for, to. 4 *(absehen)*

have on one's mind, to. 100 *(das Herz)*

have one's cross to bear, to. 164 *(das Päckchen)*

have one's heart in the right place, to. 100 *(das Herz)*

have one's moods, to. 151 *(die Mucken)*

have repercussions, to. 126 *(der Kreis)*

have rough edges, to. 50 *(die Ecke)*

have taken leave of one's senses, to. 77 *(der Geist)*

have to give/grant, to. 131 *(lassen)*

have up one's sleeve, to. 18 *(der Ärmel)*

have used up one's ammunition, to. 172 *(das Pulver)*

head over heels in love. 90 *(der Hals)*; 162 *(das Ohr)*

heal by faith, to. 81 *(gesund)*

healthy respect for, a. 97 *(der Heide)*

hear a pin drop, to. 154 *(die Nadel)*

hear confession, to. 3 *(abnehmen)*

here today, gone tomorrow. 182 *(rot)*

high society. 230 *(die Welt)*

high time, to be. 55 *(die Eisenbahn)*

high-strung. 237 *(zartbesaitet)*

hit the ceiling, to. 42 *(die Decke)*

hit the jackpot, to. 141 *(das Los)*

hit the nail on the head, to. 155 *(der Nagel)*

hold a candle to, to. 227 *(das Wasser)*

hold a gun to someone's head, to. 169 *(die Pistole)*

hold against, to. 224 *(der Vorwurf)*

hold the balance of power, to. 224 *(die Waage)*

homebody, a. 97 *(das Heimchen)*

hot potato, a. 55 *(das Eisen)*

hub of the universe, the. 152 *(der Nabel)*

humdrum. 161 *(nullachtfünfzehn)*

hunger is the best sauce. 106 *(der Hunger)*

hurry it up, to. 236 *(der Zahn)*

I

if the shoe fits, wear it. 108 *(die Jacke)*

Ignorance is bliss. 226 *(was)*

imagine the worst, to. 211 *(der Teufel)*

in advance. 223 *(vor)*

in broad daylight. 98 *(hell)*

in every respect. 139 *(die Linie)*

in no time at all. 161 *(die Null)*

in no time at all. 93 *(im Handumdrehen)*

in one's heart of hearts. 100 *(das Herz)*

in plain language. 117 *(klar)*

in the last analysis. 137 *(letzt)*

in working order. 197 *(der Schuss)*

iron out a difficult problem, to. 126 *(der Kreis)*

it's a small world. 230 *(die Welt)*

it's about time! 238 *(die Zeit)*

it's not what you say, but how you say it. 213 *(der Ton)*

J

Jack of all trades. 93 *(Hans)*

jockey for position, to. 127 *(die Krippe)*

John Hancock (signature). 71 *(Friedrich Wilhelm)*

John Q. Public. 164 *(Otto Normalverbraucher)*

just any old. 236 *(x-beliebig)*

just in case. 221 *(der Verdacht)*

just like that. 149 *(mir)*

K

keep a foot in both camps, to. 165 *(die Partei)*

keep a tight rein on, to. 60 *(der Faden)*

keep a tight rein, to. 136 *(die Leine)*

keep at it, to. 204 *(die Stange)*

keep at it, to. 23 *(der Ball)*

keep away, to. 34 *(bleiben)*

keep down, to. 119 *(kleinkriegen)*

keep going round in circles, to. 192 *(die Schlange)*

keep guessing, to. 237 *(zappeln)*

keep hands off, to. 66 *(der Finger)*

keep in good order, to. 223 *(der Vordermann)*

keep one's chin up, to. 154 *(der Nacken)*

keep one's cool, to. 84 *(der Gott)*

keep one's fingers crossed for, to. 42 *(der Daumen)*

keep under control, to. 237 *(der Zaum)*

keep up appearances, to. 190 *(der Schein)*

keep up with, to. 196 *(der Schritt)*

kick up a fuss, to. 173 *(die Puppe)*

kill the goose that lays the golden eggs, to. 104 *(das Huhn)*

kill two birds with one stone, to. 68 *(die Fliege)*

knock for a loop, to. 94 *(hauen)*

knock off from work, to. 63 *(der Feierabend)*

knock on wood. 212 *(unberufen, toi, toi, toi)*

know all the tricks, to. 105 *(der Hund)*

know all the tricks, to. 227 *(das Wasser)*

know inside out, to. 108 *(inwendig)*

know it all before it happens, to. 68 *(der Floh)*

know one's way around, to. 29 *(der Bescheid)*

know the reason behind s.t., to. 105 *(der Hund)*

know what's in store for, to. 82 *(die Glocke)*

know which way the wind is blowing, to. 94 *(der Hase)*

L

lag behind, to. 153 *(nachstehen)*

lag behind, to. 201 *(sitzen)*

last minute, at the. 214 *(das Tor)*

last resort. 160 *(der Notnagel)*

laugh up one's sleeve, to. 62 *(die Faust)*

lay down the law, to. 144 *(das Machtwort)*

lay the groundwork for, to. 86 *(der Grund)*

laze away the day, to. 84 *(der Gott)*

lead by the nose, to. 156 *(die Nase)*

learn a thing or two, to. 190 *(die Scheibe)*

leave in the lurch, to. 178 *(der Regen)*

leave it at that, to. 87 *(gut)*

leopard can't change its spots, a. 114 *(die Katze)*

leopard can't change its spots, a. 189 *(der Schatten)*

let it all hang out, to. 173 *(die Puppe)*

let it all hang out, to. 187 *(die Sau)*

let pass, to. 131 *(lassen)*

let the cat out of the bag, to. 114 *(die Katze)*

let the dust settle, to. 84 *(das Gras)*

lie like mad, to. 142 *(lügen)*

lie through one's teeth, to. 33 *(das Blaue)*

lies come back to haunt the liar. 142 *(die Lüge)*

like all get-out. 211 *(der Teufel)*

like clockwork. 163 *(ölen)*

like crazy. 23 *(der Balken)*

limit operations, downsize, to. 39 *(das Brötschen)*

little by little. 153 *(nach)*

live and let live. 133 *(leben)*

live day by day with no thought for the future, to. 210 *(der Tag)*

279

live in great style, to. 72 (der
   Fuß)
live in the lap of luxury, to. 84
   (der Gott)
live in the sticks, to. 71 (Fuchs)
live off the fat of the land, to.
   133 (leben)
live off the fat of the land, to.
   202 (der Speck)
live the life of Riley, to. 84 (der
   Gott)
live the life of Riley, to. 188 (in
   Saus und Braus leben)
live wire, a. 174 (der Quirl)
loads of. 147 (die Menge)
look down on, to. 7 (die Achsel)
look dumbfounded, to. 226 (die
   Wäsche)
look for, to. 208 (suchen)
look for a needle in a haystack,
   to. 154 (die Nadel)
look for a too simple solution, to.
   37 (das Brett)
look good enough to eat, to. 11
   (anbeißen)
look out for one's own interests,
   to. 215 (trocken)
lord it over others, to. 182 (das
   Ross)
lucid intervals. 150 (das Moment)
lucky devil, a. 93 (Hans)
lump everything together, to. 213
   (der Topf)
lump together, to. 111 (der
   Kamm)
lump together, to. 136 (der
   Leisten)

M

maid of all work. 144 (das
   Mädchen)

maintain morale, to. 162 (das
   Ohr)
make a blunder, to. 35 (der
   Bock)
make a bundle, to. 113
   (kassieren)
make a clean break, to. 207 (der
   Strich)
make a fool of, to. 90 (halten)
make a fresh start, to. 159 (neu)
make a fuss, to. 19 (aufheben)
make a good job of, to. 155 (der
   Nagel)
make a monkey out of, to. 7 (der
   Affe)
make a mountain out of a mole-
   hill, to. 150 (die Mücke)
make a move to do something, to.
   15 (die Anstalt)
make a show of force, to. 203
   (spielen)
make a show of, to. 190 (die
   Schau)
make amends, to. 1 (die Abbitte)
make cry, to. 230 (weinen)
make do with what's available,
   to. 42 (die Decke)
make ends meet, to. 184 (die
   Runde)
make fun of, to. 143 (die Lust)
make haste slowly, to. 52 (eilen)
make hay while the sun shines,
   to. 63 (die Feier)
make it one's business, to. 13
   (anlegen)
make it, to. 82 (das Glück)
make moonshine, to. 197
   (schwarz)
make off with, to. 155 (der
   Nagel)
make one's mark, to. 171 (das
   Profil)

make oneself scarce, to. 170 *(die Platte)*

make resolutions, to. 223 *(der Vorsatz)*

make short work of, to. 172 *(der Prozess)*

make s.o. part of a group, firm, etc., to. 36 *(das Boot)*

make someone laugh, to. 129 *(lachen)*

make s.o./s.t. get going/get a move on, to. 27 *(das Bein)*

make s.t. up, to. 187 *(saugen)*

make the rounds, to. 184 *(die Runde)*

make trouble, raise objections, to. 174 *(quer)*

make up one's mind, to. 171 *(der Pott)*

make up one's mind, to. 194 *(schlüssig)*

make up, to. 203 *(spinnen)*

make waves, to. 230 *(die Welle)*

man (girl) Friday. 144 *(das Mädchen)*

mess up, to. 95 *(der Haufen)*

mind someone else's business, to. 93 *(das Handwerk)*

miss is as good as a mile, a. 223 *(vorbei)*

miss the boat, to. 2 *(abfahren)*

Mom and Pop store. 130 *(der Laden)*

money makes the world go round. 78 *(das Geld)*

moral and practical support. 177 *(der Rat)*

mouth trite phrases, to. 47 *(dreschen)*

much ado about nothing. 131 *(der Lärm)*

muddle through, to. 235 *(wursteln)*

N

name names, to. 182 *(das Ross)*

neat as a pin. 52 *(das Ei)*

Necessity is the mother of invention. 160 *(die Not)*

neck and neck. 124 *(der Kopf)*

new broom sweps clean, A. 29 *(der Besen)*

no holds barred. 89 *(der Halbstarke)*

no kidding. 186 *(sagen)*

no sooner said than done. 43 *(denken)*

not at a loss for words. 151 *(der Mund)*

not be all there, to. 216 *(der Trost)*

not be very bright, to. 138 *(das Licht)*

not for nothing. 219 *(umsonst)*

not get one's share, to. 129 *(kurz)*

not give someone the time of day, to. 186 *(das Salz)*

not go overboard, to. 116 *(die Kirche)*

not have the faintest idea, to. 191 *(der Schimmer)*

not have the heart to, to. 100 *(das Herz)*

not hurt a hair on someone's head, to. 87 *(das Haar)*

not know at all what to do, to. 233 *(das Wissen)*

not know what to make of, to. 11 *(anfangen)*

not make a fuss, to. 219 *(der Umstand)*

not matter either way, to. 106 *(hüpfen)*

not see the forest for the trees, to. 225 *(der Wald)*

not to be able to stand, to. 181
(*riechen*)

not to be all there, to. 179 *(die
Reihe)*

not to care a damn about, to. 167
(*pfeifen*)

not to have all one's marbles, to.
160 *(die Niete)*

not turn a hair, to. 148 *(die
Miene)*

not want to be in someone's
shoes, to. 96 *(die Haut)*

not want to get one's hands dirty,
to. 227 *(waschen)*

nothing ventured, nothing gained.
225 *(wagen)*

O

of one's own accord. 15 *(der
Antrieb)*

of one's own free will. 207 *(das
Stück)*

off the cuff. 92 *(das Handgelenk)*

old hand, an. 94 *(der Hase)*

old hat. 108 *(die Jacke)*; 110 *(der
Kaffee)*

on a trial basis. 171 *(die Probe)*

on one's own hook/initiative. 62
(die Faust)

on short notice. 101 *(heute)*

on the go. 214 *(der Trab)*

on the hour. 208 *(die Stunde)*

on the whole. 73 *(ganz)*

on top of everything else. 217
(übel); 217 *(über)*

once again. 2 *(abermals)*

once and for all. 144 *(das Mal)*

once and for all. 53 *(ein)*

once bitten, twice shy. 37
(brennen)

open wide the door to, to. 217
(die Tür)

operate at full speed, to. 214 *(die
Tour)*

operate on a small scale, to. 38
(das Brötschen)

Out of sight out of mind. 21 *(das
Auge)*

outmaneuver, to. 212 *(der Tisch)*

over my dead body! 134 *(die
Leiche)*

overkill, to. 111 *(die Kanone)*

P

pass one's lips, to. 140 *(die
Lippe)*

pass the buck, to. 240
(zuschieben)

pay back in kind, to. 152 *(die
Münze)*

pay off, to. 177 *(rechnen)*

people who live in glass houses
shouldn't throw stones. 82
(das Glashaus)

pester/ply with questions, to. 141
(das Loch)

pick a quarrel, to. 11 *(anbinden)*

picture-perfect. 231 *(die Welt)*

pile of money, a. 97 *(das
Heidengeld)*

pinch everything one can lay
one's hands on, to. 175 *(der
Rabe)*

pitch in, to. 91 *(die Hand)*

play deaf, to. 35 *(die Bohne)*

play down, to. 100
(herunterfahren)

play into someone's hands, to.
147 *(das Messer)*

play it safe, to. 161 *(die
Nummer)*

pour oil on troubled waters, to.
163 *(das Öl)*

practice makes perfect. 147 (der Meister)

praise to the skies, to. 119 (der Klee)

proclaim one's ignorance, inadequacy, to. 18 (die Armut)

promise the moon, to. 28 (der Berg)

pull a fast one, to. 235 (ein X für ein U)

pull a long face, to. 146 (das Maul)

pull no punches, to. 24 (die Bandage)

pull oneself together, to. 181 (der Riemen)

pull out all the stops, to. 179 (das Register)

pull out of a hat, to. 106 (der Hut)

pull someone's leg, to. 24 (der Bär)

pull s.o.'s leg/put on, to. 17 (der Arm)

pull the rug out from under, to. 35 (der Boden)

pull to pieces, to. 87 (das Haar)

pursue a private agenda, to. 208 (die Suppe)

push up daisies, to. 176 (das Radieschen)

put (money) by, to. 112 (die Kante)

put a bee in someone's bonnet, to. 68 (der Floh)

put a good face on it, to. 148 (die Miene)

put a lid on it, to. 197 (der Schwamm)

put a spoke in someone's wheel, to. 208 (die Suppe)

put all one's eggs in one basket, to. 112 (die Karte)

put an end to, to. 57 (das Ende)

put down roots, to. 192 (schlagen)

put in a nutshell, to. 172 (der Punkt)

put on the same broken record, to. 169 (die Platte)

put on trial, to. 80 (das Gericht)

put one over on, to. 30 (best)

put one over on, to. 48 (dumm)

put one's foot down, to. 144 (das Machtwort)

put one's foot in it, to. 22 (ausrutschen)

put one's foot in it, to. 65 (das Fett)

put one's nose to the grindstone, to. 181 (der Riemen)

put out of work, to. 38 (das Brot)

put s.o. down, to. 173 (putzen)

put s.o. in his/her place, to. 200 (der Senkel)

put the fear of God into s.o., to. 72 (das Fürchten)

put the screws on, to. 42 (der Daumen)

put to the test, to. 171 (die Probe)

put up with, to. 76 (das Gefallen)

put wise, to. 138 (das Licht)

put-up job, a. 203 (das Spiel)

Q

quarrel about trifles, to. 25 (der Bart)

queer fish, a. 97 (der Heilige)

R

rain cats and dogs, to. 105 (der Hund)

rain cats and dogs, to. 110 (jung)

raise the roof, to. 225 (die Wand)

reach for the moon, to. 206 *(der Stern)*

read s.o.'s mind, to. 207 *(die Stirn)*

real gift, a. 71 *(das Fressen)*

red tape. 10 *(der Amtsschimmel)*

reject out of hand, to. 91 *(die Hand)*

revenge is sweet. 175 *(die Rache)*

right a course; reverse a trend, to. 183 *(das Ruder)*

right and proper thing, the. 109 *(Jakob)*

rip off, to. 158 *(neppen)*

roll out the red carpet, to. 23 *(der Bahnhof)*

rope into, to. 112 *(kapern)*

round-the-clock. 184 *(rund)*

rub salt into the wound, to. 187 *(das Salz)*

run like clockwork, to. 132 *(laufen)*

run low on, to. 157 *(die Neige)*

run off and leave, to. 49 *(durchgehen)*

run-of-the-mill. 161 *(nullachtfünfzehn)*

S

save face, to. 80 *(das Gesicht)*

say what goes, to. 186 *(sagen)*

say what goes, to. 213 *(der Ton)*

scandal sheets. 178 *(der Regenbogen)*

scare tactics. 12 *(die Angstmacherei)*

score a great success, to. 235 *(der Wurf)*

see no further than the end of one's nose, to. 156 *(die Nase)*

see one's chance, to. 150 *(die Morgenluft)*

see pink elephants, to. 146 *(die Maus)*

see reason, to. 221 *(die Vernunft)*

sell like hotcakes, to. 117 *(die Kirsche)*

send packing, to. 3 *(ablaufen)*

serve a prison sentence, to. 55 *(einsetzen)*

set against, to. 19 *(aufbringen)*

set foot out of the house, to. 76 *(gehen)*

set one's own house in order, to. 217 *(die Tür)*

set things in motion, to. 206 *(der Stein)*

set out, to. 228 *(der Weg)*

shady character. 49 *(der Dunkelmann)*

shady horse trading. 128 *(die Kuh)*

shake like a leaf, to. 239 *(zittern)*

shoot one's mouth off, to. 146 *(das Maul)*

show one's colors, to. 61 *(Farbe)*

show one's true colors, take a stand, to. 67 *(die Flagge)*

show one's true colors, to. 80 *(das Gesicht)*

shrug one's shoulders, to. 6 *(die Achsel)*

shut one's trap, to. 146 *(das Maul)*

shut up shop, to. 43 *(dicht)*

sick and tired. 89 *(der Hals)*

since time immemorial. 220 *(die Urzeit)*

sing the blues, to. 32 *(blasen)*

sing the praises of, to. 140 *(das Lob)*

sing the same tune, to. 104 *(das Horn)*

skim off the cream, to. 64 *(das Fett)*

skip school/work, to. 33 *(blau)*

sleep the day away, to. 141 *(das Loch)*

slip through one's fingers, to. 131 *(die Lappen)*

smell a rat, to. 220 *(der Unrat)*

smell a rat, to. 36 *(der Braten)*

smoke like a chimney, to. 193 *(der Schlot)*

socially acceptable, presentable. 186 *(der Salon)*

soft line, the. 230 *(die Welle)*

some extent, to. 89 *(halb)*

sooner or later. 129 *(kurz)*

sort out, to. 179 *(rein)*

sort things out, to. 24 *(der Ball)*

sound an alarm, to. 8 *(der Alarm)*

sound out, to. 40 *(der Busch)*

sound out, to. 236 *(der Zahn)*

sow one's wild oats, to. 104 *(das Horn)*

sow the wind, reap the whirlwind. 232 *(der Wind)*

speak of the devil. 59 *(der Esel)*

spew venom, to. 81 *(das Gift)*

spill the beans, to. 156 *(das Nähkästchen)*

spin out of whole cloth, to. 203 *(spinnen)*

split one's sides laughing, to. 25 *(der Bauch)*

start at the bottom, to. 169 *(die Pike)*

state of flux, a. 69 *(der Fluss)*

stay down, to. 139 *(liegen)*

stay the same as before, to. 10 *(alt)*

step on someone's toes, to. 105 *(das Hühnerauge)*

stew in one's own juices, to. 185 *(der Saft)*

stick one's nose in everywhere, to. 173 *(der Quark)*

stick to one's trade, to. 136 *(der Leisten)*

stick to, to. 34 *(bleiben)*

stick to, to. 90 *(halten mit)*

stick up for, to. 204 *(die Stange)*

stone's throw away, a. 114 *(die Katze)*

stuck-up. 102 *(hochnäsig)*

stuff oneself, to. 25 *(der Bauch)*

swallow the bait, to. 12 *(die Angel)*

T

take a break for lunch, to. 149 *(der Mittag)*

take a chance on s.t., to. 13 *(ankommen)*

take a close look at, to. 142 *(die Lupe)*

take a different approach, to. 179 *(das Register)*

take a stand, to. 165 *(die Partei)*

take a strong line, to. 111 *(die Kandare)*

take a trip, to. 180 *(die Reise)*

take at face value, to. 152 *(die Münze)*

take credit for another's work, to. 62 *(die Feder)*

take drastic measures, to. 49 *(durchgreifen)*

take into one's confidence, to. 221 *(das Vertrauen)*

take lying down, to. 201 *(sitzen)*

take off fast, to. 27 *(das Bein)*

take root, to. 72 *(der Fuß)*

take sides, to. 165 *(die Partei)*

take something personally, to. 108 *(die Jacke)*

take the cake, to. 127 *(die Krone)*

take the cake, to. 62 *(das Fass)*

take the consequences, to. 21 *(auslöffeln)*

take the dog for a walk, to. 74 *(die Gasse)*

take the line of least resistance, to. 228 *(der Weg)*

take the minutes, to. 171 *(das Protokoll)*

take the rap for, to. 21 *(ausbaden)*

take the same line, to. 104 *(das Horn)*

take things as they come, to. 84 *(der Gott)*

take things easier, to. 73 *(der Gang)*

take to task, to. 80 *(das Gericht)*

take/run the risk, to. 53 *(eingehen)*

talk about this, that, and everything, to. 84 *(der Gott)*

talk big, to. 151 *(der Mund)*

talk big, to. 190 *(der Schaum)*

talk big, to. 213 *(der Ton)*

talk nonsense, to. 34 *(das Blech)*

talk nonstop, to. 173 *(der Punkt)*

talk one's head off, to. 141 *(das Loch)*

talk shop, to. 60 *(fachsimpeln)*

talk straight, to. 209 *(Tacheles reden)*

talk to a wall, to. 225 *(die Wand)*

talk to death, to. 112 *(kaputt)*

tan someone's hide, to. 166 *(der Pelz)*

tangle with, to. 117 *(die Kirsche)*

taste like more, to. 194 *(schmecken)*

teach someone a thing or two, to. 69 *(flöten)*

tell a fib, to. 225 *(der Wald)*

tell off, to. 29 *(der Bescheid)*

tell off, to. 101 *(das Herz)*

tell someone what they want to hear, to. 151 *(der Mund)*

tell the whole world, to. 82 *(die Glocke)*

tempest in a teapot, a. 208 *(der Sturm)*

that's life. 133 *(das Leben)*

that's not the end of the world. 230 *(die Welt)*

there's nothing to it! 128 *(die Kunst)*

think highly of, to. 90 *(halten auf)*

this is where we part company. 228 *(der Weg)*

those were the days! 238 *(die Zeit)*

thousands upon thousands. 210 *(tausend)*

throw in the towel, to. 68 *(die Flinte)*

throw in the towel, to. 216 *(das Tuch)*

throw money around, to. 1 *(aasen)*

throw out the baby with the bathwater, to. 115 *(das kind)*

ticked-off. 187 *(sauer)*

tighten one's belt, to. 181 *(der Riemen)*

till all hours. 173 *(die Puppe)*

tin-pot. 231 *(die Westentasche)*

to each his/her own. 212 *(das Tier)*

to my way of thinking. 26 *(der Begriff)*

to the attention of. 91 *(die Hand)*

to the quick. 145 *(das Mark)*

to the utmost. 137 *(letzt)*

tomfoolery. 59 *(die Eulenspiegelei)*

too many cooks spoil the broth. 122 *(der Koch)*

top secret. 76 *(geheim)*

topsy-turvy. 48 *(drunter)*

touch with a ten-foot pole, to. 121
  (die Kneifzange)

tough customer, a. 87
  (das Haar)

treat oneself to, to. 136 *(leisten)*

treat with contempt, to. 220
  (verachten)

trigger, to. 150 *(das Moment)*

trip up, to. 27 *(das Bein)*

true to life. 133 *(das Leben)*

trust to luck, to. 82 *(das Glück)*

turn a blind eye, to. 72 *(fünf)*

turn defeat into victory, to. 219
  (ummünzen)

turn down, to. 136 *(leise)*

turn in, to. 163 *(das Ohr)*

turn on one's heels, to. 3 *(der
  Absatz)*

turn out, to. 79 *(geraten)*

turn to one's advantage, to. 192
  (schlagen)

turn up one's nose, to. 156 *(die
  Nase)*

turn upside down, to. 12 *(die
  Angel)*

twiddle one's thumbs, to. 42 *(der
  Daumen)*

U

umpteenth time, the. 236
  (das x-temal)

under discussion. 80 *(das
  Gespräch)*

under lock and key. 193 *(das
  Schloss)*

under the weather. 103 *(die
  Höhe)*

Unlucky at cards, lucky in love.
  166 *(das Pech)*

unlucky person. 166 *(der
  Pechvogel)*

untill further notice. 230 *(weit)*

up close. 96 *(hautnah)*

up to one's neck in debt. 162
  (das Ohr)

upper crust, the. 162 *(ober)*

use it or lose it. 176 *(rasten)*

V

vicious circle. 211 *(der Teufel)*

W

wait and see, to. 6 *(abwarten)*

wait for, to. 226 *(warten)*

wait on hand and foot, to. 26
  (bedienen)

wait till one is blue in the face,
  to. 226 *(warten)*

walk all over, to. 157 *(die Nase)*

walk one's feet off, to. 234
  (wund)

wander like a ghost, to. 77 *(der
  Geist)*

wash dirty linen in public, to.
  226 *(die Wäsche)*

washout, a. 191 *(der Schlag)*

way off, a. 50 *(die Ecke)*

way to a man's heart is through
  his stomach, the. 138 *(die
  Liebe)*

wear out one's welcome, to. 2
  (abessen)

well-grounded. 91 *(die Hand)*

wellheeled. 31 *(betucht)*

wet one's whistle, to. 130 *(die
  Lampe)*

what will be will be. 123
  (kommen)

what's in a name? 156 *(der Name)*

when the cat's away the mice will
  play. 114 *(die Katze)*

white elephant. 130 *(der
  Ladenhüter)*

who laughs last, laughs best. 129 *(lachen)*

wild horses. 168 *(das Pferd)*

win big, to. 141 *(das Los)*

win hands down, to. 96 *(haushoch)*

windfall, a. 178 *(der Regen)*

wipe out, to. 181 *(der Rest)*

with all the trimmings. 48 *(drum)*

with bag and baggage. 185 *(der Sack)*

with hindsight. 153 *(nach)*

with mixed emotions. 21 *(das Auge)*

with no holds barred. 148 *(das Messer)*

without benefit of clergy. 51 *(die Ehe)*

work one's finger to the bone, to. 234 *(wund)*

work out all right, to. 66 *(sich finden)*

work out well, to. 117 *(klappen)*

work out, to. 19 *(aufgehen)*

worm out, to. 235 *(der Wurm)*

worry in advance, to. 52 *(das Ei)*

worth one's weight in gold. 83 *(das Gold)*

write off as too old, to. 55 *(das Eisen)*

Y

you can't make an omelette without breaking eggs. 102 *(hobeln)*

you can't take it with you. 182 *(der Rock)*

You don't look a gift horse in the mouth. 74 *(der Gaul)*

Index

A

A, 1
aasen, 1
Abbitte, 1
Abbitte leisten, 1
abbrechen, 1
Abbruch, 2
Abbruch tun, 2
Abend, 2
aber, 2
abermals, 2
abessen, 2
abfahren, 2
Abfuhr, 2
abgegessen haben, 2
abgetan sein, 5
abhanden kommen, 123
abhören, 3
ablaufen, 3
ablaufen lassen, 3
abmalen, 3
abnehmen, 3
abnehmend, 3
abreißen, 3
Absatz, 3
Abschluss, 4
abschminken, 4
abschnallen, 4
absehen, 4
Absicht, 4
Absicht merken und verstimmt
    werden, 147
absitzen, 4
abspecken, 202
abspielen, 5
Abstand, 5
Abstand nehmen, 5
absteigen, 5
abtun, 5

abwarten, 6
abwarten und Tee trinken, 6
Abwesenheit, 6
abwinken, 6
ach, 6
Ach, da liegt der Hund begraben!,
    105
Ach, du grüne Neune!, 159
Ach du lieber Gott!, 84
Achse, 6
Achsel, 6
Achsel zucken, 6
Achterbahn, 7
Achterbahn fahren, 7
Achtung, 7
Acker, 7
Adresse, 7
Affe, 7
Affenschande, 8
Affenzahn, 8
Aktie, 8
Akzent, 8
Akzente setzen, 8
Alarm, 8
Alarm schlagen, 8
Alibi, 8
All, 9
all, 9
Alle Achtung!, 7
alle Brücken hinter sich abbrechen,
    39
alle Fäden fest in der Hand halten,
    60
alle Hebel in Bewegung setzen, 96
Alleinerziehende, 9
Alleingang, 9
Alleinherrschaft, 9
Alleinstehende, 9
allemal, 9
allem die Krone aufsetzen, 127

Index

alle Minen springen lassen, 148

allenfalls, 9–10

alle Register ziehen/alle Register spielen lassen, 179

Aller guten Dinge sind drei!, 45

alles, was nicht niet-und nagelfest ist, 159

alles, was Rang und Namen hat, 176

alles auf eine Karte setzen, 112

alle seine Pfeil verschossen haben, 167

alles grau in grau sehen, 85

Alles hat seine Grenzen, 85

alles in einen Topf werfen, 213

alles über einen Leisten schlagen, 136

alle Tage, 209

alle Welt, 230

alle zwei Tage, 9

Alltag, 10

alltäglich, 10

alt, 10

alte Platte laufen lassen, 169

am Apparat bleiben, 16

am Ball bleiben, 23

am Ball sein, 23

am Boden liegen, 35

am eigenen Leib, 134

am Ende, 56

am Ende sein, 56

am falschen/richtigen Ende anfassen, 56

am grünen Tisch (vom grünen Tisch) aus, 212

am hellichten Tag, 98

am Herzen liegen, 100

am Hungertuch nagen, 155

am längeren Hebel sitzen, 96

am Leben sein, 132

am Platz sein, 170

am Ruder sein, 183

Amt, 10

am Tropf hängen, 215

Amtsschimmel, 10

Amtsschimmel wiehert, 10

an, 11

an allen Ecken und Enden, 50

anbeißen, 11

anbinden, 11

anbringen, 11

an den Kragen gehen, 125

an den Lippen hängen, 140

an den Mann bringen, 145

an den Nagel hängen, 155

an den Nerv der Sache rühren, 158

an den Pranger stellen, 171

an den Tag legen, 209

andere Register ziehen, 179

an der Krippe sitzen, 127

an der Leine halten, 136

an der Nase herumführen, 156

an der Reihe kommen, 179

an der Reihe sein, 179

an der richtigen/falschen Adresse sein, 7

anders ticken, 211

an die Decke gehen, 42

an die Kandare nehmen, 111

an die Nieren gehen, 159

an etwas geht kein Weg vorbei, 228

an etwas hängen, 93

an etwas/jemandem liegen, 139

an etwas Spaß haben, 202

Anfang, 11

anfangen, 11

anfangen mit, 11

Angel, 12

Angenehmes Flohbeißen!, 68

Angst, 12

Angst haben, 12
Angstmacherei, 12
Angst und Bange haben, 12
anhaben, 12
Anhieb, 13
Anker, 13
ankommen, 13
anlegen, 13
anmachen, 14
Anmarsch, 14
an Niveau einbüßen, 160
Anschluss, 14
anschreiben, 14
ans Herz drücken, 47
an sich, 11
ans Messer liefern, 147
Anspruch, 14
Anspruch erheben, 14
Ansprüche stellen, 14
Anstalt, 15
Anstalten treffen, 15
Anstand, 15
Anstand nehmen, 15
Anteil, 15
Anteil nehmen, 15
Antrieb, 15
antun, 15
Antwort, 15
an (und für) sich, 11
anwurzeln, 16
Anzug, 16
Apfel, 16
Apparat, 16
April, 16
Arbeiterdenkmal, 16
Arbeitgeber, 17
Arbeitnehmer, 17
arg, 17
Arm, 17
arm, 18

arm dran sein, 18
Ärmel, 18
Ärmel aufkrempeln, 18
Armut, 18
As, 18
Auch der beste Gaul strauchelt
    einmal., 74
auch nur mit Wasser kochen, 122
aud freien Fuß setzen, 72
außen vor bleiben, 34
außer Betrieb sein, 30
außer Frage stehen, 69
auf Abstand gehen, 5
auf Anhieb, 13
auf Biegen oder Brechen, 31
aufbringen, 18–19
Aufbruch, 19
Aufbruchstimmung, 19
auf dem Absatz kehrtmachen, 3
auf dem falschen Dampfer sitzen,
    41
auf dem hohen Ross sitzen, 182
auf dem Holzweg sein, 104
auf dem Laufenden halten, 132
auf dem letzten Loch pfeifen, 140
auf dem Spiel stehen, 203
auf dem Trockenen sein/sitzen, 215
auf dem Wedge der Besserung sein,
    30
auf den Beinen sein, 27
auf den Busch klopfen, 40
auf den Geist gehen, 77
auf den Hund kommen, 105
auf den Keks gehen, 115
auf den Leim gehen, 135
auf den Mann dressiert, 145
auf den Nägeln brennen, 155
auf den Nägeln brennend liegen,
    155
auf den Pfennig genau, 167

Index

auf den Punkt bringen, 172
auf den Schild haben, 191
auf den Strich gehen, 207
auf den Wecker fallen/gehen, 227
auf den Weg bringen, 228
auf den Zahn fühlen, 236
auf (der) Achse sein, 6
auf der Bärenhaut liegen, 24
auf der ganzen Linie, 139
auf der Höhe sein, 103
auf der Hut sein, 107
auf der Kippe stehen, 116
auf der Nase herumtanzen, 157
auf der roten Liste stehen, 182
auf des Messers Schneide stehen,
    148
auf die Beine bringen, 27
auf die falsche Karte setzen, 112
auf die Goldwaage legen, 84
auf die hohe Kante legen, 112
auf die kalte Tour, 110
auf die Knochen gehen, 122
auf die lange Bank schieben, 24
auf die leichte Achsel nehmen, 6
auf die leichte Schulter nehmen,
    196
auf die Palme bringen, 164
auf die Pauke hauen, 166
auf die Pelle rücken, 166
auf die Probe stellen, 171
auf die schiefe Bahn geraten, 23
auf die Schulter klopfen, 196
auf die Spitze treiben, 203
auf die Sprünge helfen, 204
auf Draht bringen, 46
auf Draht sein, 46
auf du und du sein, 48
auf eigene Faust, 62
auf eigene Rechnung, 177

auf einen groben Klotz gehört ein
    grober Keil, 121
auf einen Ritt, 182
auf einen Schlag, 191
auf ein Konto gehen, 76
auf einmal, 54
auf etwas ankommen, 13
auf etwas Gift nehmen können, 81
auf etwas pfeifen, 167
auf etwas setzen, 200
auf etwas zu Hause sein, 95
auffliegen, 19
auf frischer Tat ertappen, 71
aufgeben, 19
aufgeben in, 19
aufgehen, 19
auf großen Fuß leben, 72
auf Grund, 86
auf gut Glück, 82
aufheben, 19–20
auf Heller und Pfennig, 167
auf Herz und Nieren prüfen, 100
auf jemands Konto gehen, 124
auf kaltem Wege, 110
auf keine Kuhhaut gehen, 128
auf (k)einen grünen Zweig
    kommen, 240
auf Kriegsfuß stehen, 72
auf Leben und Tod kämpfen, 133
auf Nimmerwiedersehen
    verschwinden, 160
auf Nummer Sicher gehen, 161
auf Probe, 171
aufreißen, 20
aufs Auge drücken, 20
aufschieben, 20
auf seine Kosten kommen, 125
auf seine Rechnung kommen, 177
auf sich sitzen lassen, 201
aufs Neue, 158

auf Spesen, 203
auf Teufel komm raus, 211
auf Trab, 214
auftreiben, 20
auf Verdacht, 221
auf verlorenem Posten stehen, 170
auf vollen Touren laufen, 214
auf Vordermann bringen, 223
auf Zeit, 238
Auge, 20
Augen aller auf sich ziehen, 239
Augenmaß, 21
Augenmaß haben, 21
das A und O sein, 1
aus allen Wolken fallen, 234
aus aller Herren Länder(n), 99
ausbaden, 21
Ausbleiben, 21
aus dem Anzug fallen, 16
aus dem Anzug hauen, 94
aus dem Anzug springen, 16
aus dem ärmel schütteln, 18
aus dem Feld schlagen, 63
aus dem Handgelenk, 92
aus dem Häuschen geraten, 95
aus dem hohlen Bauch, 25
aus dem Hut machen, 106
aus dem Leben gegriffen, 133
aus dem Leim gehen, 135
aus dem Mund riechen, 151
aus dem Nähkästchen plaudern,
    156
aus dem Nichts, 159
aus dem Schneider/vom Schneider
    sein, 195
aus dem Stegreif, 205
aus dem Weg räumen, 228
aus den Angeln gehen, 12
aus den Angeln heben, 12
aus den Angeln sein, 12

Aus den Augen aus dem Sinn., 21
aus der Haut fahren, 61
aus der Reihe tanzen, 179
aus der Rolle fallen, 182
aus der Ruhe bringen, 184
aus der Taufe heben, 210
aus der Welt schaffen, 230
aus Dummsdorf sein, 48
aus eigenem Antrieb, 15
aus einer Hand, 91
aus einer Mücke einen Elefanten
    machen, 150
aus etwas nicht klug werden
    können, 121
aus freien Stücken, 207
ausgedient haben, 44
ausgehen, 21
ausgehen wie das Hornberger
    Schießen, 190
auskommen, 21–22
Ausland, 22
auslasten, 22
auslernen, 22
aus Liebe, 138
auslöffeln, 22
das auslösende Moment sein, 150
aus nah und fern, 155
ausrutschen, 22
ausschildern, 22
aus seinem Dornröschenschlaf
    erwachen, 46

B

Bach, 22
Bahn, 23
Bahn frei!, 23
Bahnhof, 23
Bahnhof verstehen, 23
Balken, 23
Ball, 23

Index

Bandage, 24
Bank, 24
Bär, 24
bärbeißig, 24
Bart, 25
Bauch, 25
bauen, 25
bauen auf, 25
Bauklotz, 25
Bauklötze staunen, 25
Baum, 25
Bäume ausreißen können, 25
baumeln, 25
Bäume wachsen nicht in den
    Himmel—in der Beschränkung
    zeigt sich der Meister., 26
bedienen, 26
Begriff, 26
bei, 27
bei aller Liebe, 138
Bei (an) ihm ist Hopfen und Malz
    verloren., 104
Beichte abnehmen, 3
Bei dem tickt's nicht richtig., 211
bei den Frauen Glück haben, 82
bei der Stange bleiben, 204
Bei dir piept's wohl! Du hast einen
    Vogel!, 169
Beifall klatschen, 118
bei jemandem einen Stein im Brett
    haben, 205
bei klarem Verstand sein, 117
bei Kräften sein, 125
(nicht) bei Laune sein, 132
bei lebendigem Leibe verbrennen,
    134
beilegen, 27
beim Alten bleiben, 10
Bein, 27
bei Nacht und Nebel, 154

Beine in den Bauch stehen, 25
bei seinem Leisten bleiben, 136
bekannt wie ein bunter Hund, 105
bekommen, 28
beleidigte Leberwurst spielen, 133
ben Ecken verwandt sein, 51
bereiten, 28
Berg, 28
bergab, 29
bergauf, 29
Beruf, 29
Bescheid, 29
Bescheid geben/sagen, 29
Bescheid stoßen, 29
Bescheid wissen, 29
Besen, 29
bessere Ende haben, 56
Besserung, 30
best, 30
Betreuer, 30
Betreuung, 30
Betrieb, 30
Betrieb herrschen, 30
betucht, 31
Beweis, 31
Biege, 31
biegen, 31
Bier, 31
bierernst, 31
Bild, 31
Bildung, 32
Bildungsroman, 32
billige Jakob, 109
binnen Kurzem, 128
Binse, 32
Binsenwahrheit, 32
Birne, 32
bis ans Ende der Welt, 230
bis auf das letzte I-Tüpfelchen, 107
bis auf den I-Punkt, 107

bis auf den letzten Pfennig, 168
bis auf die Knochen, 122
bis aufs Hemd ausziehen, 99
bis aufs Letzte, 137
bis aufs Messer, 148
bis auf weiteres, 230
bis in die Puppen, 173
bis ins Letzte, 137
bis ins Mark, 145
bis über beide Ohren in Schulden
   stecken, 162
bis über beide Ohren rot werden,
   162
bis über beide Ohren verliebt sein,
   162
bis zum Abwinken, 6
bis zum Letzten, 137
bis zum Sankt-Nimmerleins-Tag
   warten, 187
bis zur Neige auskosten, 157
bis zur Neige leeren, 157
blasen, 32
Blatt, 33
Blatt hat sich endlich gewendet, 33
blau, 33
blauäugig, 33
Blaue, 33
blauer Brief, 38
blauer Dunst, 33
Blaue von Himmel herunterlügen,
   33
blau machen, 33
blau sein, 33
Blech, 34
Blech reden, 34
bleiben, 34
blind, 34
blinden Alarm schlagen, 34
blinder Passagier, 34
Blümchen, 34

Blümchenkaffee, 34
Blume, 34
Bock, 35
Bock/Lust haben auf, 35
Boden, 35
Bogen, 35
Bohne, 35
Bohnen in den Ohren haben, 35
bombensicher, 36
Boot, 36
Braten, 36
braun, 36
braungebrannt, 36
Brei, 37
breit, 37
brennen, 37
Bresche, 37
Brett, 37
Brett/Holz bohren, wo es am
   dünnsten ist, 37
Brief, 38
bringen, 38
Brot, 38
Brötchen, 38
brotlos machen, 38
Brotzeit, 38
Bruch, 39
bruchlanden, 39
Brücke, 39
Brücken schlagen, 39, 192
Brüderschaft trinken, 215
bügeln, 39
Buhmann, 39
Bühne, 40
bunt, 40
bunter Abend, 40
Busch, 40
Butter, 40

C

Chaot, 41

D

dabei bleiben, 34
Dach, 41
Da hilft kein Jammer und kein
    Klagen., 98
Damm, 41
Dämpfer, 41
Dampfer, 41
darauf brennen, etwas zu tun, 37
dass die Fetzen fliegen, 65
dass die Wände wackeln, 225
dasselbe in Grün sein, 86
dass sich die Balken biegen, 23
dastehen wie Piksieben, 169
Dauerbrenner, 42
dauern, 42
Daumenchem, 42
Daumen drehen/Däumchen drehen,
    42
Da wird der Hund in der Pfanne
    verrückt!, 105
Decke, 42
dem Fass den Boden ausschlagen,
    62
dem lieben Gott den Tag stehlen,
    84
den Amtsschimmel reiten, 10
den Anfang machen, 11
den Anfang nehmen, 11
den Bach heruntergehen, 22
den Ball wieder rund machen, 24
den Bauch voll schlagen, 25
den Beruf verfehlt haben, 29
den Boden unter den Füßen
    wegziehen, 35
den Bogen heraushaben, 35

den Bogen überspannen, 35
den Braten riechen, 36
den Daumen aufs Auge halten, 42
den (die) Daumen drücken, 42
den Führerschein machen, 71
den ganzen Betrieb aufhalten, 30
den Grund legen, 86
den Hals nicht voll genug kriegen,
    89
den Hof machen, 103
den Hut nehmen müssen, 106
den Kanal voll haben, 111
den Karren aus dem Dreck ziehen,
    46
denken, 42
denken an, 43
denken über, 43
den Kinderschuhen entwachsen
    sein, 116
den Kreis (schon) eckig kriegen,
    126
den Laden schmeißen, 129
den letzten Nerv rauben, 158
den lieben Gott einen guten Mann
    sein lassen, 84
den Mund voll nehmen, 151
den Nacken steifen/stärken, 154
den Nacken steifhalten, 154
den Nagel auf den Kopf treffen,
    155
den Prozess machen, 172
den Rang ablaufen, 176
den richtigen Riecher (einen guten
    Riecher) haben, 181
den Riemen enger schnallen, 181
den Sack schlagen, und den Esel
    meinen, 59
den Salat haben, 186
den Schein wahren, 190

den schwarzen Peter zuschieben,
240
den Sprung schaffen, 204
den Tag vor dem Abend loben, 209
den Teufel an die Wand malen, 211
den Ton angeben, 213
den toten Punkt überwinden, 172
den Weg des geringsten
Widerstandes gehen, 228
deutsch, 43
deutsche Michel, 43
Diät, 43
diät essen/kochen/leben, 43
Diät machen, 43
dicht, 43
dichten, 44
dichtmachen, 43
dick, 44
dicke Ende, 56
dicke Luft, 44
dick machen, 44
dick werden, 44
dienen, 44
Dienst, 44
dieser Tage, 209
Ding, 45
dingfest machen, 45
donnern, 45
doppelt, 45
doppelter Boden, 45
doppelt gemoppelt, 45
Dornröschen, 46
Draht, 46
Drahtesel, 46
Dreck, 46
Dreck am Stecken haben, 46
drehen, 46
dreizehn, 47
dreschen, 47
dritte Zähne, 237

drücken, 47
drum, 48
drunter, 48
drunter und drüber, 48
du, 48
dumm, 48
dumm aus der Wäsche gucken, 226
Dünkel, 48
Dunkel, 48
Dunkelmann, 49
Dunkelziffer, 49
dünn gesät, 185
durch, 49
durch Abwesenheit glänzen, 6
durchbeißen, 49
durch den Kakao ziehen, 110
durch dick und dünn gehen, 44
durch die Bank, 24
durch die Blume sagen, 34
durch die Lappen gehen, 131
durchdrehen, 49
durchgehen, 49
durchgreifen, 49
durchnehmen, 49
Durch Schaden wird man klug.,
188
durchschneiden, 50
durchs Examen sausen, 188
durch Vitamin B (Beziehungen)
kriegen, 222
Durst, 50
Durst haben, 50
Durst haben auf, 50

E
Ebbe, 50
Ebbe in der Kasse/im
Geldbeutel/im Portemonnaie, 50
Ecke, 50
Ecken und Kanten haben, 50

Index

edel, 51
Edelschnulze, 51
Edelstahl, 51
Edelstein, 51
Effeff (aus dem Effeff verstehen), 51
Ehe, 51
Ehre, 51
ehrenamtlich, 52
Ei, 52
Ei des Kolumbus, 52
Eile, 52
Eile haben, 52
eilen, 52
Eimer, 52
ein, 53
ein abgekartetes Spiel, 203
ein alter Hase, 94
ein anderes Gesicht bekommen, 80
ein Arbeiterdenkmal machen, 16
ein As auf der Bassgeige sein, 18
ein aufgeblasenes Nachthemd sein, 154
ein Begriff sein, 26
ein Bein stellen, 27
Einbildung ist auch eine Bildung!, 32
ein Brett vor dem Kopf haben, 38
ein Chaot sein, 41
ein dicker/großer Fisch, 67
ein dicker Hammer, 90
ein dicker Hund, 105
ein dickes Brett bohren, 38
eine Alibifunktion haben, 8
eine alte Jacke, 108
eine andere Platte auflegen, 170
eine Anzeige aufgeben, 19
eine Bärenruhe haben, 24
eine Biege fahren, 31
eine dicke Nummer haben, 161

eine donnern, 45
eine Ecke sein, 50
eine Fahne haben, 60
eine Frage stellen, 70
eine grüne Hand haben, 91
eine gute Partie sein, 165
eine Hungerkur machen, 106
Eine Krähe hackt der anderen kein Auge aus., 126
eine Kuh/Kröte schlucken müssen, 193
eine lange Leitung haben, 137
eine Lanze brechen für, 130
eine Leiche im Keller haben, 134
einem das Wasser reichen, 227
eine Meise unterm Pony haben, 147
Einem geschenkten Gaul schaut man nicht ins Maul., 74
eine Mine legen, 148
einem übel werden, 217
einen Abschluss haben, 4
eine Nadel im Heuschober/Heuhaufen suchen, 154
einen Affen gefressen haben, 7
einen an der Waffel haben, 225
einen auf die Lampe giessen, 130
einen Bärendienst erweisen, 24
einen Beitrag leisten, 136
einen Besen fressen, 29
einen Beweis liefern, 138
einen Bock schießen, 35
einen Dämpfer aufsetzen, 41
einen dicken Kopf haben, 124
einen Draht haben, 46
einen Eid leisten, 136
einen Gang nach Kanossa machen/einen Kanossagang machen, 73
einen Gang zurückschlaten, 73

einen großen Bahnhof bereiten, 23

einen großen Bogen machen, 35

einen großen/glücklichen Wurf tun, 235

einen großen Zauber ausüben, 237

einen Haken haben, 89

einen Hammer haben, 90

einen heben, 96

eine Niederlage einstecken, 55

eine Niederlage in einen Sieg ummünzen, 219

einen Kater haben, 114

einen Klaps haben, 117

einen Kloss im Hals haben, 121

einen Korb geben, 124

einen langen Arm haben, 17

einen langen Hals (lange Hälse) machen, 89

einen lichten Moment (lichte Momente), 150

einen mächtigen Hunger haben, 143

einen Narren gefressen haben, 156

einen Pferdefuß haben, 168

einen schmettern, 194

einen sonnigen Nerv haben, 158

einen Sparren (zu viel/zu wenig) haben, 202

einen Sprung in der Schüssel haben, 204

einen Streit vom Zaun brechen, 237

einen Strich durch die Rechnung machen, 178

einen Strich unter etwas machen/ziehen, 207

einen trinken gehen, 215

einen über den Durst trinken, 50

einen ungeheuren Dünkel haben, 48

einen Vogel haben, 222

einen vom Pferd erzählen, 168

einen vom Wald erzählen, 225

einen Weg einschlagen, 54

einen weichen Keks haben, 115

einen Zahn zulegen, 237

einen zwitschern, 241

eine pfeffern, 167

eine Rede halten, 90

eine Reise machen, 180

eine Rolle spielen, 182

einer Sache auf den Grund gehen, 86

einer Sache Herr werden, 99

einer Sprache mächtig sein, 143

eine runde Kugel schieben, 184

eine Runde schmeißen, 184

eine Sause machen, 188

eine scharfe Klinge führen, 120

eine Scheibe abschneiden, 190

eine steile Karriere machen, 205

eine weiche Birne haben, 32

einfallen, 53

ein falscher Fünfziger (Fuffziger) sein, 61

ein Fass ohne Boden, 62

ein für alle Mal, 144

ein für allemal, 53

Eingang, 53

Eingang finden, 53

eingängig, 53

eingängig erklären, 53

ein ganzes/gutes Stück, 207

ein Garn spinnen, 74

ein gefundenes Fressen, 71

eingehakt, 54

eingehen, 53–54

ein gerüttelt (und geschüttelt) Maß, 145

ein Gespräch führen, 71

ein Glück sein, 82

ein Haar in der Suppe finden, 87

einhaken, 54

ein halbes Hemd, 89

ein Hammer sein, 90

ein heißes Eisen, 55

ein heißes Pflaster, 168

einhergehen, 54

ein Herz und eine Seele sein, 100

ein hohes/großes Tier, 212

ein Hühnchen zu rupfen haben, 105

ein Katzensprung sein, 114

ein Klotz am Bein sein, 121

ein Kreuz mit etwas haben, 126

ein Licht aufstecken, 138

ein Lied/Liedchen singen können, 138

Ein Lob dem Küchenchef., 140

ein Loblied anstimmen, 140

ein Loch in den Bauch fragen, 140

ein Loch in den Bauch reden, 140

ein Loch in den Tag schlafen, 140

ein lockeres Handgelenk haben, 92

ein Machtwort sprechen, 144

einmal, 54

einmal ist keinmal, 54

Ein Mann, ein Wort., 145

ein Nickerchen halten/machen, 160

ein Opernnarr sein, 164

ein Quirl sein, 174

ein Rädchen zuviel haben, 175

eins auf den Hut kriegen, 106

eins auf den Pelz geben, 166

ein Schattendasein fristen, 189

ein schiefes Maul ziehen, 146

einschlagen, 54

ein Schlag ins Kontor, 124

ein Schlag ins Wasser, 191

ein Schnäppchen machen, 195

ein Schuss in den Ofen, 197

eins/einen drauf setzen, 200

einsetzen, 55

einsitzen, 55

eins jagt das andere, 108

ein sonderbarer Heiliger, 97

Einstand geben, 74

einstecken, 55

ein Sturm im Wasserglas, 208

ein teures Pflaster, 169

ein toller Hecht, 97

ein Tropfen auf den heißen Stein, 216

ein Übriges tun, 218

ein unbeschriebenes Blatt sein, 33

ein von und zu sein, 222

ein warmer Regen, 178

Einwegflasche, 67

ein weißer Rabe, 175

ein Wink mit dem Zaunpfahl, 233

ein X für ein U vormachen, 235

einzig Senkrechte, 200

ein Zimmer frei haben, 70

Eisen, 55

Eisen Bahn, 23

Eisenbahn, 55

Elefant, 55

Ellbogen, 56

Eltern, 56

Empfang, 56

Ende, 56

Ende gut, alles gut., 57

Ende machen, 57

Ende vom Lied, 57

Entwicklung, 57

Entwicklungsland, 57

Erfolg, 57

Erfolg haben, 57

Erfolg hat viele Väter., 57

ernähren, 58

Ernst, 58

Ernst des Lebens, 58

erst, 58

Erstaunen, 58

Erste/große Geige spielen, 77

ersten Ranges, 176

Erstens kommt es anders, und zweitens als man denkt., 123

es abgesehen haben, 4

es/alles beim Alten lassen, 10

es angetan haben, 15

es auf etwas ankommen lassen, 13

es auf etwas bringen, 38

es dick haben, 44

es drehen und wenden, wie man will, 46

es eilig haben, 52

Esel, 59

Eselei, 59

Eselsbrücke, 59

es faustdick hinter den Ohren haben, 62

es gibt, 74

es gut sein lassen, 87

es in sich haben, 88

Es ist nichts so fein gesponnen, es kommt doch ans Licht der Sonnen., 203

Es ist noch nicht aller Tage Abend., 2

Eskimo, 59

es kleiner haben, 119

es leid sein, 135

es mit beiden Parteien halten, 165

es mit etwas haben, 88

es nicht übers Herz bringen, 101

essen, 59

es über sich bekommen, 28

es weit bringen, 38

es wird (höchste/allerhöchste) Zeit, 238

Es wird nie so heiß gegessen wie gekocht., 98

Es zieht wie Hechtsuppe hier!, 239

es zu bunt treiben, 40

etwas an die große Glocke hängen, 82

etwas auf dem Herzen haben, 101

etwas aufs Korn nehmen, 124

etwas aus dem Boden stampfen, 204

etwas auslöffeln, 22

etwas gewachsen sein, 224

etwas hinter die Ohren schreiben, 162

etwas im Alleingang tun, 9

etwas im Schilde führen, 191

etwas in die Wege leiten, 228

etwas lassen, 131

etwas links liegenlassen, 140

etwas madig machen, 144

etwas nicht riechen können, 181

etwas spinnen, 203

etwas übers Knie brechen, 121

etwas um die Wette tun, 231

etwas zu Protokoll geben, 171

etwsa hinter den Ohren haben, 162

Eule, 59

Eulen nach Athen tragen, 59

Eulenspiegelei, 59

F

Fach, 60

Fachchinesisch, 60

fachsimpeln, 60

Faden, 60

Fäden spinnen, 60

Fahne, 60

fahnenflüchtig werden, 61

fahren, 61

fallen, 61

falsch, 61

Farbe, 61

Index

Farbe bekennen, 61
Fass, 62
Fass zum überlaufen bringen, 62
faule Fische, 67
fauler Zauber, 237
Faust, 62
faustdick, 62
Feder, 62
Feier, 63
Feierabend, 63
Feierabendbeschäftigung, 63
Feierabend machen, 63
fein, 62
Feinste vom Feinen, 62
Feld, 63
ferner, 63
ferner liefen, 63
fernsehen, 64
Fernweh, 229
fertig, 64
fertig machen, 64
fertig werden, 64
fest, 64
fest befreundet sein, 64
Festbeleuchtung, 64
festfahren, 64
festsitzen, 64
Fett, 64
Fett abschöpfen, 64
fetten Jahre, 65
fettgedruckt, 65
Fetzen, 65
Feuer, 65
Feuer geben/haben, 65
Feuer haben, 65
Feuerprobe, 66
Feuer und Flamme sein, 65
Feuer vom Himmel holen, 65
Filme drehen, 47
finden, 66

Finger, 66
fingerfertig, 66
Finger lassen, 66
Fingerspitzengefühl, 66
Fingersprache, 66
Fisch, 66
Flachs, 67
Flagge, 67
Flagge zeigen, 67
Flasche, 67
Fleiß, 68
Fleisch, 67
Fleischergang/Metzgergang/
    Schneidergang, 73
Fliege, 68
fliegen, 68
fliegender Händler, 93
Fliege/'ne Fliege machen, 68
Flinte, 68
Flinte ins Korn werfen, 68
Floh, 68
Flöhe husten (niesen) hören, 68
flöten, 69
flöten gehen, 69
Flötentöne beibringen, 69
Flucht, 69
Flucht noch vorne greifen/antreten,
    69
Fluss, 69
Föhn, 69
Folge, 69
Folge leisten, 69
fönen, 69
Frage, 69–70
frei, 70
Freiberufler, 70
freie Bahn, 23
frei von der Leber weg reden, 133
Fressen, 71
fressen, 71

Freude bereiten, 28
Friedrich Wilhelm, 71
frisch, 71
Fuß, 72
Fuchs, 71
Fuß fassen, 72
führen, 71
Führerschein, 71
fünf, 72
fünf gerade sein lassen, 72
fünf Minuten vor zwölf, 72
fünfte Rad am Wagen sein, 175
funkeln, 72
funkelnagelneu, 72
für bare Münze nehmen, 152
Fürchten, 72
Fürchten lernen, 72
für die Katz sein, 114
für dumm verkaufen, 48
für einen Apfel und ein Ei, 16
für einen Pappenstiel, 165
für etwas zu haben sein, 88
für nichts und wieder nichts, 159
fürs Erste, 58
für sich, 72

G

Gang, 73
Gänge machen, 73
gang und gäbe sein, 73
ganz, 73
ganz Ohr sein, 163
ganz schön kassieren, 113
ganz und gar, 73
Garn, 74
Gasse, 74
Gast ist wie der Fisch, er bleibt nicht lange frisch., 67
Gaul, 74
geben, 74

Gebet, 75
Geburtstag, 75
Geburtstag haben, 75
Gedacht, getan!, 43
Geduld, 75
Geduld bringt Rosen., 75
Geduld reißen, 75
das Gefallen, 75
Gefallen finden, 75
Gefallen finden an, 75
gefragt sein, 70
gegen eine Wand reden, 225
gegen etwas nicht ankommen, 13
Gegenwind, 232
geheim, 76
Geheimtipp, 76
gehen, 76
gehen um, 77
gehüpft wie gesprungen sein, 106
Geige, 77
Geist, 77
Geisterfahrer, 77
geistern, 77
Geld, 78
Geld regiert die Welt., 78
Gelegenheit, 78
Gelegenheit macht Diebe., 78
geliefert sein, 138
gelingen, 78
gelten, 78
geltend machen, 78
genießbar, 79
gepfeffert, 167
gerade, 79
geradeaus, 79
gerade dabei sein, 79
gerade recht kommen, 79
geraten, 79
Gerede, 79
Gericht, 80

gern, 80

gern/gut leiden können/mögen, 135

gern haben, 80

geschniegelt und gebügelt, 39

gesellschaftlich absteigen, 5

Gesicht, 80

Gesicht wahren, 80

Gespräch, 80

gesund, 81

gesundbeten, 81

gesund und munter, 81

getrennte Kasse machen, 113

Getretener Quark wird breit, nicht stark., 173

Gewalt, 81

gewinnen, 81

gießen, 81

Gift, 81

Gift und Galle spucken, 81

Glas, 81

Glashaus, 82

gleiche Lied singen, 138

Glocke, 82

Glück, 82

glücken, 82

Glück haben, 82

glücklich, 83

Gnade, 83

Gnadenbrot geben, 83

Gnadenstoß, 83

Gold, 83

goldene Berge versprechen, 28

Goldgräberstimmung, 83

Gold in der Kehle haben, 83

Goldkind, 83

goldrichtig, 83

Goldwaage, 84

Gott, 84

Gras, 84

Gras wachsen hören, 84

Gras wachsen lassen, 84

grau, 85

greifen, 85

Grenze, 85

grenzüberschreitend, 85

Griff, 85

groß, 86

große/dicke Töne reden/spucken, 213

große Los ziehen, 141

große Teich, 211

große Welt, 230

Groschen, 85

Groschen fällt pfenningweise, 85

groß Stücke halten auf, 208

Groß und Klein, 86

grün, 86

Grund, 86

gut, 87

gutachten, 87

gut aufgehoben sein, 20

gute Miene zum bösen Spiel machen, 148

gute/schlechte Laune haben, 132

gutheißen, 87

gut/schlecht andgeschrieben sein, 14

gut/schlecht rechnen können, 177

gut/schlecht um etwas stehen, 205

gut sein, 87

gut sein lassen, 131

H

Haar, 87

Haare auf den Zähnen haben, 87

Haare vom Kopf fressen, 87

haben, 88

Hahn, 88

Hahn im Korb sein, 88

Haken, 89

Haken schlagen, 89
halb, 89
halbe Miete sein, 148
Halbstarke, 89
halbwegs, 89
Hals, 89
halten, 90
halten auf, 90
halten mit, 90
halten von, 90
Hammer, 90
Hand, 91
Handel, 92
handeln, 92
handeln mit, 92
handeln über; handeln von, 92
Handel und Wandel, 92
Handgelenk, 92
Handkuss, 92
Händler, 92
Handtuch werfen, 216
Hand und Fuß haben, 91
Handwerk, 93
Handwerk hat einen goldenen
    Boden., 93
Handwerk legen, 93
hängen, 93
Hans, 93
Hansdampf in allen Gassen sein, 93
Hans Guckindieluft, 93
Hans im Glück sein, 93
Harnisch, 94
hart, 94
hart auf hart kommen/gehen, 94
hart im Nehmen sein, 94
Hase, 94
(nicht ganz) hasenrein sein, 94
Haube, 94
hauen, 94
Haufen, 95

Hauruck-Verfahren, 95
Haus, 95
Haus an Haus wohnen, 95
haushoch, 96
haushoch gewinnen, 96
haushoch überlegen sein, 96
Haut, 96
Das haut den stärksten Eskimo vom
    Schlitten!, 59
hautnah, 96
Hebel, 96
heben, 96
Hecht, 97
Hecht im Karpfenteich sein, 97
Hehler, 97
Hehlerei, 97
Der Hehler ist sodium schlimm wie
    der Stehler., 97
heiß, 98
Heide, 97
Heidengeld, 97
Heidenrespekt, 97
heile Welt, 231
Heilige, 97
Heiligenschein, 98
heiligsprechen, 98
Heimchen, 97
Heimchen am Herd, 97
Heimspiel, 98
Heimweh, 229
Held, 98
helfen, 98
hell, 98
Hemd, 99
Das Hemd ist näher als der Rock.,
    99
Hengst, 99
Herr, 99
herrschen, 99
herum, 100

herumlungern, 100
herunterfahren, 100
Herz, 100
Herz auf dem rechten Fleck haben, 100
heute, 101
heute Morgen, 101
heute Nacht, 101
heute oder morgen, 101
Heute rot, morgen tot., 183
Hickhack, 101
Hieb, 101
hieb- und stichfest, 101
Hier trennen sich unsere Wege., 228
Hilf dir selbst, so hilft dir Gott., 98
Himmel hängt voller Geigen, 77
hingehen, wo der Pfeffer wächst, 167
hinter, 102
hinter her sein, 102
hinter Schloss und Riegel, 193
hinters Licht führen, 137
hobeln, 102
hoch, 102
Hochhaus, 102
hoch hinaus wollen, 102
hoch im Kurs stehen, 128
hochnäsig, 102
Hochrechnungen, 102
höchst, 102
höchste Eisenbahn sein, 55
höchste Zeit sein, 102
hoch und heilig versprechen, 102
Hocker, 103
Hof, 103
Höhe, 103
höher, 102
höhere Gewalt, 81
hohes Alter, 102

hohe Wellen schlagen, 230
Holz, 103
Holzhammermethode, 103
Holz in den Wald tragen, 103
Honig, 104
Honig um den Bart (Mund) schmieren, 104
Hopfen, 104
Horn, 104
Huhn, 104
Huhn, das goldene Eier legt, schlachten, 104
Hühnerauge, 105
Hund, 105
hundert, 105
Hunger, 106
Hunger haben, 106
Hunger ist der best Koch., 106
hüpfen, 106
Hut, 106–107
Hut ab!, 106

I

Idee, 107
Ihm tut kein Zahn mehr weh., 236
im Ab-/Aufwind sein, 232
im Anmarsch sein, 14
im Anschluss an, 14
im Argen liegen, 17
im Ärmel haben, 18
im Begriff sein etwas zu tun, 26
im Busch sein, 40
im Dunkeln liegen, 48
im eigenen Saft schmoren lassen, 185
im Eimer sein, 52–53
im Fluss sein, 69
im Gang sein, 73
im Ganzen/im großen Ganzen/im Großen und Ganzen, 73

im Geheimen, 76
im Gespräch sein, 80
im Griff haben, 85
im Grunde seines Herzens, 101
im grünen Bereich sein, 86
im Handumdrehen, 93
Im In-und Ausland verkauft sich
    die Maschine gut., 107
im Keller sein, 115
im Kommen sein, 123
im Lot sein, 141
im Magen haben, 144
Immer mit ser Ruhe!, 184
im Nachhinein, 153
im Rampenlicht stehen, 176
im Regen stehen lassen, 178
im Sack haben, 185
im selben Boot/in einem Boot
    sitzen, 36
im Stillen, 206
im Trüben fischen, 216
im Voraus, 223
im Westentaschenformat, 231
im Zaum halten, 237
im Zeichen eines Tierkreises
    geboren sein, 238
im Zeichen von etwas stehen, 238
Im Zug von etwas sein, 240
in aller Herrgottsfrühe, 99
in aller Munde sein, 151
in aller Ruhe, 184
in Anspruch genommen sein, 14
in Auge fallen, 20
in (bester) Butter sein, 40
in Betrieb nehmen, 30
in den April schicken, 16
in den besten Jahren sein, 30
in den Griff bekommen, 85
in den Keller fallen/gehen, 115
in den Kinderschuhen stecken, 116

in den Knochen sitzen/stecken, 122
in den Ruhestand treten, 184
in den sauren Apfel beißen, 16
in den Sellen hängen, 199
in den Sternen stehen, 206
in den Tag hineinleben/von Tag zu
    Tag leben, 210
in den Wind schlagen, 232
in den Wind schreiben, 232
in der Entwicklung sein, 57
in der Fachwelt, 60
in der Hinterhand haben, 91
in der Klemme sitzen, 120
in der Kreide stehen, 126
in der Lage sein, 130
in der letzten Zeit, 137
in der Schwebe liegen, 198
in der Tinte sitzen, 212
in die Arme laufen, 17
in die Binsen gehen, 32
in die Breite gehen, 37
in die Breite wirken, 37
in die Brüche gehen, 39
in die Geschichte eingehen, 54
in die Höhe gehen, 103
in die Jahre kommen, 109
in die Knie gehen, 122
in die Krone steigen, 127
in die Luft sprengen, 142
in die Parade fahren, 165
in die Pfanne hauen, 166
in die Quere kommen, 174
In die Wiege legen, 232
in einem weg, 228
In einem Zug leern, 239
in einer Tour, 214
in Empfang nehman, 56
in Erstaunen setzen, 58–59
in erster/zweiter Linie, 139
in Fetzen gehen, 65

in Fluss bringen, 69
in Frage kommen, 70
in Frage stellen, 70
in Gang bringen, 73
in Grund und Boden, 87
in guter Hut sein, 107
in Harnisch bringen, 94
in jungen Jahren, 109
in Kauf nehmen, 114
Inland, 107
in Lohn und Brot sein, 141
in/mit gleicher Münze heimzahlen, 152
in/mit Massen, 146
in nichts nachstehen, 153
in Null Komma nichts, 161
in rauhen Mengen, 147
in Rente gehen, 180
in Ruhe lassen, 131
in Saus und Braus leben, 188
ins Blaue hineinreden, 33
ins Blaue schießen, 33
ins Bockshorn jagen, 108
in Schuss, 197
ins Fettnäpfchen treten, 65
ins Garn gehen, 74
ins Gebet nehmen, 75
ins Geld gehen, 78
ins Gerede kommen, 79
ins Gericht gehen, 80
ins gleiche Horn stoßen, 104
ins Gras beißen, 84
ins Handwerk pfuschen, 93
ins Haus schneien, 195
ins Haus stehen, 95
ins Leben rufen, 133
ins Leere gehen, 133
ins Lot bringen, 142
ins offene Messer laufen, 148
ins Reine kommen, 179

ins Schwimmen kommen, 198
ins Stocken geraten, 79
in Strömen gießen, 81
ins Uferlose gehen, 218
ins Vertrauen ziehen, 221
ins Wasser fallen, 227
ins Zwielicht geraten, 241
in Teufels Küche kommen, 211
in trockene Tücher bringen, 216
in- und auswendig kennen, 108
in Verlegenheit bringen, 221
inwendig, 108
in wilder Ehe leben, 51
I-Punkt, 107
Das ist ein Hammer!, 90
Das ist keine Kunst!, 128
I-Tüpfelchen, 107
I-Tüpfel-Reiter, 107

J

Ja, 108
Jacke, 108
Jacke wie Hose sein, 108
jagen, 108
Jahr, 109
Jahr und Tag, 109
Jakob, 109
Jede Bohn' hat ihren Ton, 36, 213
jede Menge, 147
Jedem Tierchen sein Pläsierchen., 212
jeden Moment, 150
Jeder ist seines Glückes Schmied, 194
Jeder ist sich selbst der Nächste., 153
Jeder Topf findet seinen Deckel., 213
jeder Zoll, 239

Jedes Böhnchen gibt sein Tönchen, 36

Jedes Böhnchen hat sein Tönchen, 36

jemandem auf die Hühneraugen treten, 105

jemandem das Wasser abgraben, 227

jemandem den Marsch blasen, 32

jemandem die Ohren langziehen, 163

jemandem die Suppe versalzen, 208

jemandem dreht sich alles im Kreis, 126

jemandem einen Bären aufbinden, 24

jemandem im Nacken sitzen, 154

jemandem in den Ohren liegen/jemandem mit etwas auf den Ohren liegen, 163

jemandem sitzt der Schalk im Naken, 189

jemandem recht geben, 178

jemands Bier sein, 31

jemands Kragenweite sein, 125

Jetzt geht die Post ab!, 170

Jetzt schlägt's (aber) dreizehn!, 47

jmdm. an die Angel gehen, 12

jmdm. auf den Senkel gehen, 200

jmdm. hinter die Stirn sehen, 207

jmdm. in den Senkel stellen, 200

jmdm/ einen Floh ins Ohr setzen, 68

jmdm./etwas Beine machen, 27

jmdn. auf den Arm nehmen, 17

jmdn. das Fürchten lehren, 72

jmdn. herunterputzen, 173

jmdn. mit ins Boot holen, 36

jobben, 109

jung, 109

junge Hunde regnen, 110

Jung getan, alt gewohnt., 109

Jüngste Gericht, 80

Jux, 110

K

Kaffee, 110

Kaiser, 110

Kaiserwetter, 110

Kakao, 110

kalt, 110

kalter Kaffee, 110

Kalter Kaffee macht schön., 110

kalt erwischen, 111

kaltmachen, 111

Kamm, 111

Kanal, 111

Kandare, 111

Das kannst du dir an den Hut stecken!, 106

Kanone, 111

Kante, 112

kapern, 112

Kapitel, 112

kaputt, 112

kaputtmachen, 112

kaputtreden, 112

Karte, 112

kartenlegen, 113

Kartoffel, 113

Kasse, 113

Kasse machen, 113

Kassenschlager, 113

kassieren, 113

Kater, 114

Katerstimmung, 114

Katze, 114

Katze aus dem Sack lassen, 114

Katze im Sack kaufen, 114

Index

Die Katze lässt das Mausen nicht., 114

Katzenwäsche machen, 114

Kauf, 114

Kauf dir 'nen Keks!, 115

Kavalier, 115

Kavaliersdelikt, 115

keine Antwort Schuldig bleiben, 15

keine Ellbogen haben, 56

keine großen Sprünge machen können, 204

keine Miene verziehen, 148

keinen (blassen) Schimmer haben, 191

kein Ende nehmen, 57

keinen Pfifferling wert sein, 168

keinen Rat wissen, 176

keinen Spaß verstehen, 202

keinen trockenen Faden mehr am Leib haben, 60

keine Umstände machen, 219

keine zehn Pferde, 168

kein großes Kirchenlicht sein, 117

kein großes Licht sein, 138

kein gutes Haar lassen, 87

kein Haar krümmen, 87

kein Held in etwas sein, 98

kein Honig(sch)lecken sein, 104

Keks, 115

Keller, 115

Kind, 115

Kind beim rechten Namen nennen, 115

Kinderschuh, 116

Kinderschuhe ausziehen, 116

Kind mit dem Bad ausschütten, 115

Kind schon schaukeln, 116

Kippe, 116

Kirche, 116

Kirche im Dorf lassen, 116

Kirchturmpolitik, 117

Kirsche, 117

Klacks, 117

klappen, 117

Klaps, 117

klar, 117

klarkommen, 118

Klartext reden, 118

klar wie Klärchen sein, 118

Klasse, 118

klasse sein, 118

klatschen, 118

klauen wie ein Rabe, 175

kleckern, 118

Klee, 119

Kleider, 119

klein, 119

klein, aber fein, 63, 119

klein, aber mein, 119

klein beigeben, 119

kleine Brötchen backen, 38

Die Kleinen hängt man; die Großen lässt man laufen., 119

kleinere Brötchen backen, 39

Kleinkleckersdorf, 119

kleinkriegen, 119

kleinschreiben, 120

Klemme, 120

Klinge, 120

klingende Münze, 152

Klingen kreuzen mit, 120

Klinke, 120

Klinkenputzer, 120

klipp und klar sagen, 118

Kloss, 121

Klotz, 121

klug, 121

Der Klügere gibt nach., 121

knapp bei Kasse sein, 113

Kneifzange, 121
Knie, 121
Knochen, 122
Knochenarbeit, 122
Koch, 122
kochen, 122
Köchin, 122
Komfort, 122
kommen, 123
kommen zu, 123
Das kommt mir spanisch vor, 201
Kommt Zeit, kommt Rat., 238
Kompromisse eingehen, 54
können, 123
Konto, 124
Kontor, 124
Kopf, 124
Kopf an Kopf, 124
Kopf stehen, 124
Korb, 124
Korn, 124
koste es, was es wolle, 125
kosten, 125
Kraft, 125
Kragen, 125
Kragen platzen, 125
Krähe, 126
Kreide, 126
Kreis, 126
Kreise ziehen, 126
Kreuz, 126
Kriegsbeil, 126
Krimi, 127
Krippe, 127
Krone, 127
Kuckuck, 127
Kuh, 127
Kuh fliegen lassen, 127
Kuhhandel, 128
Kuh vom Eis bringen, 127

Kulturbeutel, 128
Kunst, 128
Kurs, 128
kurz, 128
kurz angebunden, 11
kurzen Prozess machen, 172
Kürzeren ziehen, 128
kurz und gut, 128
kurz vor Torschluss, 214
Kurzweil treiben, 214

L

lachen, 129
Lack, 129
Der Lack ist ab., 129
Laden, 129
laden, 129
Ladenhüter, 130
Lage, 130
Lampe, 130
lang, 130
Länge, 130
lange Finger machen, 66
lang und breit, 130
Lanze, 130
Lappen, 131
Lärm, 131
lassen, 131
lassen + infinitive, 131
lassen müssen, 131
Last, 132
Latein, 132
laufen, 132
Laune, 132
Leben, 132
leben, 132
Leben in die Bude bringen, 133
leben wie die Made im Speck, 202
Leber, 133
Leberwurst, 133

Index

leer, 133

Leere Töpfe klappern und leere Köpfe plappern am meisten., 213

Leib, 134

Leibgericht, 134

leiblich, 134

leibliche Wohl, 134

Leib- und Magenspeise, 134

Leiche, 134

Leichenschmaus, 135

leichte Muse, 152

leicht von der Hand gehen, 91

leid, 135

leiden, 135

leidtun, 135

Leim, 135

Leine, 136

Leine ziehen, 136

leise, 136

leiser stellen, 136

Leisten, 136

leisten, 136

Leitung, 137

letzt, 137

Letzten Dinge, 137

Letzten Endes, 137

letzten Endes, 57

Der letzte Rock hat keine Taschen., 182

letzte Schliff, 192

letzte Schrei, 196

Leute von Besitz und Bildung, 32

Licht, 137

Licht der Welt erblicken, 137

lichten, 138

Liebe, 138

Die Liebe geht durch den Magen., 138

Lied, 138

liefern, 138

liegen, 139

liegen bleiben, 139

Lieschen Müller, 139

Linie, 139

links, 140

Lippe, 140

Lob, 140

loben, 140

Das lob ich mir!, 140

Loch, 141

Löcher in die Luft gucken, 141

locker vom Hocker, 103

Lohn, 141

Los, 141

Lot, 141

Luft, 142

Luft anhalten, 142

Lüge, 142

lügen, 142

Lügen haben kurze Beine., 142

Lügen strafen, 142

(sich nicht) lumpen lassen, 142

Lupe, 142

Lust, 143

Lust haben, 143

lustig, 143

M

Maß, 145

Mach, dass du fortkommst, 143

machen, 143

mächtig, 143

Das macht nichts., 143

Machtwort, 144

Mädchen, 144

Mädchen für alles, 144

madig, 144

Magen, 144

maßhalten, 146

Das Maß ist voll., 145
Makulatur, 144
Makulatur reden, 144
Mal, 144
Mann, 145
Manschette, 145
Manschetten haben, 145
Mark aus den Knochen saugen, 145
Maul, 146
Maul aufreißen, 146
Maul halten, 146
Maulsperre kriegen, 146
Maus, 146
mehr schlecht als recht, 192
Mehrwegflasche, 67
mein, 147
Meine Daman und Herren!, 147
mein und dein verwechseln, 147
Meise, 147
Meister, 147
Menge, 147
merken, 147
Messer, 147
Miene, 148
Miene machen, 148
Miete, 148
Mine, 148
mir, 149
mir nichts, dir nichts, 149
mit Abstand, 5
mit Ach und Krach, 6
mit Ach und Weh, 6
mit allem Komfort und zurück, 122
mit allen Drum und Dran, 48
mit allen Hunden gehetzt sein, 105
mit allen Wassern gewaschen sein, 227
Mit dem/der/denen ist nicht gut Kirschen essen., 117
mit dem Geld aasen, 1

mit dem Hund Gassi gehen, 74
mit dem Schrecken davonkommen, 196
mit der Faust auf den Tisch dreschen, 47
mit der heissen Nadel genäht, 155
mit der Kneifzange anfassen, 121
mit der Lupe suchen müssen, 142
mit der Tür ins Haus fallen, 216
mit einem Affenzahn, 8
mit einem blauen Auge davonkommen, 21
mit einem Heiligenschein umgeben, 98
mit einem lachenden und einem weinenden Auge, 21
mit einem Mal, 144
mit einem Schlag, 191
mit einer/einem von verheiratet sein, 222
mit etwas auf den Bauch fallen, 25
mit etwas jagen, 109
mit etwas klappen, 117
mit etwas nicht umgehen können, 219
Mit Geduld und Spucke fängt man eine Mucke., 75
mit Haken und ösen, 89
mithalten, 149
mit Hand anlegen, 91
mit Handkuss, 92
mit harten Bandagen kämpfen, 24
mit jemandem Pferde stehlen können, 168
mit jmdm. über Kreuz sein/stehen, 126
mit Kanonen auf Spatzen schiessen, 111
mit Kind und Kegel, 116
mit Leib und Seele, 134

mit links, 140
mitmachen, 149
mit Mann und Maus untergehen, 145
mit Rat und Tat, 177
mit Sack und Pack, 185
mit seinem Latein am Ende sein, 132
mit seiner Gesundheit aasen, 1
mit sich zu Rate gehen, 177
Mit Speck fängt man Mäuse., 202
Mittag, 149
Mittag machen, 149
mit Verachtung strafen, 220
mit von der Partie sein, 165
mit Vorsicht zu genießen sein, 223
mit Zittern und Zagen, 239
mit zweierlei Maß messen, 146
mogeln, 149
Mogelpackung, 149
Das Moment, 150
Der Moment, 150
Moos, 150
Moos ansetzen, 150
Morgenluft, 150
Morgenluft wittern, 150
Morgenstunde, 150
Mücke, 150
Muckefuck, 151
Mücke machen, 150
Mucken, 151
Mund, 151
Mündel, 152
mündelsicher, 152
mundtot machen, 151
Münze, 152
Muse, 152
musisch veranlagt, 152
Muskelkater, 114
Muskeln spielen lassen, 203

N
Nabel, 152
Nabel der Welt, 152
Nabelschau, 153
nach, 153
nach Adam Riese, 153
nach dem Mund reden, 151
nach den Sternen greifen, 206
nach gar nichts schmecken, 194
nach Geld stinken, 78
nach Hause gehen/fahren, 95
nach jemands Geige tanzen, 77
nach Kanossa gehen, 76
nach mehr schmecken, 194
nachsehen, 153
Nachsehen bleiben, 153
nach seiner Fasson selig werden, 199
nächst, 153
nachstehen, 153
Nächstenliebe, 153
Nacht, 154
Nachthemd, 154
Nachtigal, ich hör dir trapsen!, 154
Nachtigall, 154
Nacht um die Ohren schlagen, 154
nach und nach, 153
nach wie vor, 153
Nacken, 154
Nadel, 154
Nagel, 155
Nägel mit Köpfen machen, 155
nagen, 155
nah, 155
nahe treten, 156
Nähkästchen, 156
Nahrung, 156
Nahrung geben, 156
Name, 156

Name ist Schall und Rauch., 156
Narr, 156
Närrin, 156
Nase, 156
Nase in die Bücher stecken, 156
Nase rümpfen, 156
Nase voll haben, 157
Nase vorn haben, 157
Nase zu tief ins Glas stecken, 157
nehmen, 157
Neige, 157
neppen, 158
Nepplokal, 158
Nerv, 158
nerven, 158
Nessel, 158
neu, 158
Neue Besen kehren gut., 29
neuen Antrieb geben, 15
neun(e), 159
nicht abreißen, 3
nicht alle in der Reihe haben, 179
nicht alle Nieten an der Hose
    haben, 160
nicht auf den Mund gefallen sein,
    151
nicht aus Holz sein, 103
nicht bei der Sache sein, 185
nicht bei Trost sein, 216
nicht das Salz in der Suppe gönnen,
    186
nicht die Bohne, 36
nicht einmal, 54
nicht für voll nehmen, 157
nicht ganz auf der Höhe sein, 103
nicht (ganz) bei Groschen sein, 86
nicht ganz dicht sein, 43
nicht gelingen wollen, 78
nicht grün sein, 86
nicht hinter dem Berg halten, 28

nicht im Traum an etwas denken,
    43
nicht in Frage kommen, 70
nicht in jemands Haut stecken
    mögen, 96
nicht kleckern, sondern klotzen,
    118
nicht leiden können, 135
nicht mit Gold aufzuwiegen sein,
    83
nicht nach ihm und nicht nach ihr
    schmecken, 194
nicht riechen können, 181
Nichts, 159
nichts, 159
nichts am Hut haben, 106
nichts dafür können, 123
nichts übrig haben für, 218
nichts zu sagen haben, 186
nicht über die Lippen bringen
    können, 140
nicht umsonst, 219
nicht umzubringen sein, 218
nicht von schlechten Eltern sein, 56
nicht von ungefähr sein, 219
nicht wahr, 225
nicht wegzudenken sein, 229
nicht wohl in seiner Haut sein, 96
nicht zu genießen sein, 79
Nickerchen, 160
Niere, 159
Niete, 159
Niveau, 160
Niveau haben, 160
noch an den Weihnachtsmann
    glauben, 229
noch zu haben sein, 88
Not, 160
Not bricht Eisen, 160
Notnagel, 160

nottun, 160
Null, 161
nullachtfünfzehn, 161
Null-Bock-Generation, 161
Nulldiät, 161
Null Komma nichts erreichen, 161
Nummer, 161
nur ein Klacks sein, 117
nur ein Rädchen im Getriebe sein, 176
Nur über meine Leiche!, 134
nur zum Spaß machen, 202

O

oben, 161
obenhinaus wollen, 162
oben nicht ganz richtig sein, 161
ober, 162
oberen Zehntausend, 162
offen, 162
offene Türen einrennen, 162
offen gesagt, 162
Ohne Fleiß, keinen Preis., 68
ohne Punkt und Komma reden, 173
ohne Saft und Kraft, 185
Ohr, 162
Ohren steif halten, 162
Olympiade, 164
olympiaverdächtig, 164
Olympionike, die Olympionikin, 164
Oper, 164
Opern quatschen, 164
Oppositionsbank drücken, 47
Otto Normalverbraucher, 164

Ö

Öl, 163
Öl auf die Wogen gießen, 163

ölen, 163
Öl ins Feuer gießen, 163

P

pachten, 164
Päckchen, 164
Palme, 164
Pantoffel, 165
Pantoffelheld, 165
Pappenstiel, 165
Parade, 165
Paragraphenreiter, 180
Partei, 165
Partei ergreifen, 165
Partie, 165
Pauke, 166
Pech, 166
Pechvogel, 166
Pelle, 166
Pelz, 166
perfekt, 166
Perlen vor die Säue werfen, 187
Pfanne, 166
Pfeffer, 167
pfeffern, 167
pfeifen, 167
Pfeil, 167
Pferd, 168
Pferd am Schwanz aufzäumen, 168
Pferde durchgehen, 168
Pferdefuß, 168
Pffennig, 167
Pfifferling, 168
Pflaster, 168
Phrasen dreschen, 47
piepen, 169
Pike, 169
Piksieben, 169
Pistole, 169
Pistole auf die Brust setzen, 169

Platte, 169
Platte kennen, 169
Platte putzen, 170
Platz, 170
Platzhirsch, 170
Porzellan, 170
Porzellan zerschlagen, 170
Post, 170
Posten, 170
Pott, 171
Pranger, 171
Probe, 171
Probe aufs Exempel machen, 171
Profil, 171
Profil haben, 171
Protokoll, 171
Protokoll führen, 171
Prozess, 172
Pudel, 172
Pulver, 172
Pulver nicht erfunden haben, 172
Punkt, 172
Puppe, 173
Puppen tanzen lassen, 173
putzen, 173

Q

Qual, 173
Quark, 173
quasseln, 174
Quasselwasser getrunken haben, 174
Quecksilber, 174
Quecksilber im Leib haben, 174
quer, 174
Querdenker, 174
quer durch, 174
quer schießen, 174
Quertreiber, 174
Quirl, 174

R

Rabe, 175
Rabenmutter, 175
Rache, 175
Rad, 175
Rädchen, 175
Radieschen, 176
Radieschen von unten betrachten, 176
Rampenlicht, 176
Ran an den Speck!, 202
Rang, 176
rasten, 176
Rat, 176
Raubbau, 177
Raubbau mit seiner Gesundheit treiben, 177
Raupe, 177
Raupen im Kopf haben, 177
rechnen, 177
Rechnung, 177
recht, 178
recht behalten, 178
recht haben, 178
reden, 178
reden wie einem der Schnabel gewachsen ist, 178
Regen, 178
Regenbogen, 178
Regenbogenpresse, 178
Register, 179
reibungslos über die Bühne gehen, 40
reichen, 179
Reihe, 179
rein, 179
reinen Wein einschenken, 179
reinsten Wassers, 180
Reise, 180
Reiter, 180

Rennen, 180
Das Rennen ist gelaufen., 180
Rennen machen, 180
Rente, 180
Rest, 180
Rest geben, 181
riechen, 181
Riecher, 181
Riemen, 181
Risiko eingehen, 53
Ritt, 182
Rock, 182
Rolle, 182
röntgen, 182
Ross, 182
Rosskur, 182
Ross und Reiter nennen, 182
rot, 182
rote Laterne tragen, 183
rote/schwarze Zahlen schreiben, 236
Rubel, 183
Der Rubel rollt., 183
Rückenwind, 233
Ruder, 183
Ruder (he)rumreißen, 183
Ruder in der Hand haben, 183
Ruf, 183
rufen, 183
Rufmord, 183
Ruhe, 184
Ruhestand, 184
rund, 184
Runde, 184
Runde machen, 184
rund um die Uhr, 184

S

Sache, 185
Sack, 185

säen, 185
Saft, 185
sagen, 186
Sagen haben, 186
sage und schreibe, 186
Salat, 186
Salon, 186
salonfähig, 186
Salonkommunist/Salonanarchist, 186
Salontiroler, 186
Salz, 186
Salz auf die Wunde streuen, 187
Sankt-Nimmerleins-Tag, 187
Sau, 187
sauer, 187
saufen, 187
saufen wie ein Loch/Schlauch, 187
saugen, 187
Sau rauslassen, 187
Sause, 188
sausen, 188
sausenlassen, 188
Schaden, 188
Schadenfreude, 188
Schadenfreude heißt, sich über das Unglück anderer freuen., 188
schadenfroh, 188
Schäfchen, 188
Schalk, 189
Schall, 189
Schall und Rauch, 189
scharf, 189
scharf auf, 189
scharf schießen, 189
Schatten, 189
Schattendasein, 189
Schau, 190
Schaum, 190
Schaum schlagen, 190

Scheibe, 190
Schein, 190
Der Schein trügt., 190
Schickimicki, 190
schießen, 190
schief geladen haben, 129
Schild, 191
Schildbürger, 191
Schimmer, 191
Schlag, 191
Schlag auf Schlag, 191
schlagen, 192
Schlange, 192
Die Schlange beißt sich in den
    Schwanz., 192
Schlangenmensch, 192
Schlange stehen, 192
schlecht, 192
schlechthin, 192
Schliff, 193
Schliff backen, 193
Schloss, 193
Schlot, 193
Schlotbaron, 193
schlucken, 193
Schluss, 193
Schlüssel, 193
schlüsselfertig, 193
schlüssig, 194
Schlusslicht, 194
Schlusslicht sein, 194
Schluss machen, 193
schmecken, 194
schmettern, 194
Schmied, 194
Schmock, 194
Schmöker, 194
schmökern, 194
schmutzige Wäsche waschen, 226
Schnäppchen, 195

Schnapsfahne, 195
Schnapsidee, 195
Schnapszahl, 195
Schneider, 195
schneien, 195
Schock, 195
Schönheitsfehler, 196
Schrecken, 196
Schrei, 196
Schreibtischhengst/
    Verwaltungshengst, 99
Schritt, 196
Schritt halten, 196
Schulbank drücken, 47
Schuld, 196
Schulden machen, 196
Schule, 196
Schule machen, 196
schulmeistern, 196
Schulter, 196
Schulterschluss, 197
Schuss, 197
Schwamm, 197
schwarz, 197
schwarzarbeiten, 197
schwarzbrennen, 197
schwarzfahren, 197
schwarzsehen, 198
schwarz wie ein Rabe, 175
Schwebe, 198
Schwein, 198
Schwein haben, 198
schwer, 198
schweres Geld kosten, 198
schwer fallen, 198
Schwerpunkt, 198
Schwerverbrecher, 198
schwer von Begriff sein, 26
schwimmen, 198
See, 199

Seele, 199
Seele baumeln lassen, 199
sehen, 199
sehenden Auges, 20
Seil, 199
Seilschaft, 199
sein blaues Wunder erleben, 33
sein Dichten und Trachten, 44
seine eigene Suppe/sein eigenes
    Süppchen kochen, 209
seine Ellbogen gebrauchen, 56
seinem Affen Zucker geben, 7
seinem Herzen Luft machen, 101
seine Mucken haben, 151
seine Nase in jeden Quark stecken,
    173
seinen Mann ernähren, 58
seinen Mann stehen, 145
seiner selbst nicht mächtig sein, 143
seinesgleichen, 199
seinesgleichen suchen, 199
seine Stimme abgeben, 206
sein Fett kriegen, 64
sein Gebet verrichten, 75
sein Glück machen, 82
sein Päckchen (zu tragen) haben,
    164
sein Pulver verschossen haben, 172
sein Schäfchen ins Trockene
    bringen, 188, 215
sein wahres Gesicht zeigen, 80
seit Kurzem, 128
seit Urzeiten, 220
selig, 199
Senkel, 200
senkrecht, 200
Serie, 200
serienreif, 200
serienweise, 200
setzen, 200

sich abspielen, 5
sich als Kuckucksei erweisen, 127
sich am Riemen reißen, 181
sich an die Krippe drängen, 127
sich ärgern, 17
sich auf den Hals laden, 89
sich auf den Weg machen, 228
sich auf die Fahnen schreiben, 60
sich auf die Lappen machen, 131
sich auf die Reise machen, 180
sich auf die Socken machen, 201
sich auf die Suche machen, 208
sich aufs Ohr legen/hauen, 163
sich auf Talfahrt befinden, 210
sich aus dem Staub machen, 205
sich Bahn brechen, 23
sich bedienen, 26
sich bewahrheiten, 31
sich breit machen, 37
sich das Jawort/das Jawort fürs
    Leben geben, 108
sich das Maul zerreißen, 146
sich dicke tun, 44
sich die Beine in die Hand nehmen,
    28
sich die Ehre geben, 52
sich die Hände wund arbeiten, 234
sich die Hörner ablaufen, 104
sich die Jacke anziehen, 108
sich die Klinke in die Hand geben,
    120
sich die Nase begießen, 157
sich die Waage halten, 224
sich drücken, 47
sich durchbeißen, 49
sich durchschlagen, 50
sich ein Armutszeugnis ausstellen,
    18
sich ein Bild machen, 31
sich eine Abfuhr holen, 2

sich eine goldene Nase verdienen, 157

sich einen Affen kaufen, 8

sich einen Ast lachen, 129

sich einen hinter die Binde gießen, 81

sich einen Jux machen, 110

sich einsetzen, 55

sich erfreuen, 58

sich ernähren, 58

sich etwas angelegen sein lassen, 13

sich etwas aus den Fingern saugen, 187

sich etwas gefallen lassen, 76

sich etwas kosten lassen, 125

sich etwas leisten können, 137

sich etwas unter den Nagel reißen, 155

sich finden, 66

sich fragen, 70

sich geben, 74

sich gleichen wie ein Ei dem anderen, 52

sich großer Beliebtheit erfreuen, 58

sich Hals über Kopf verlieben, 90

sich handeln um, 92

sich herumsprechen, 100

sich hervortun, 100

sich in den Haaren liegen, 88

sich in die Bresche schlagen für, 37

sich in die Büsche schlagen, 40

sich in die Länge ziehen, 130

sich in die Nesseln setzen, 158

sich in die Wolle geraten, 234

sich in neuen Bahnen bewegen, 23

sich ins eigene Fleisch schneiden, 67

sich ins Fäustchen lachen, 62

sich in Szene setzen, 209

sich ins Zeug legen, 238

sich in Unkosten stürzen, 208

sich Kämpfe liefern, 139

sich keinen abbrechen, 1

sich kleinkriegen lassen, 119

sich kräftig in die Riemen legen, 181

sich lassen + infinitive, 131

sich leisten, 136

sich lieb Kind machen, 116

sich lohnen, 141

sich lustig machen, 143

sich mit der Absicht tragen, 4

sich mit fremden Federn schmücken, 62

sich nach der Decke strecken, 42

sich neppen lassen, 158

sich profilieren, 171

sich pudelwohl fühlen, 172

sich rechnen, 177

sich rentieren, 180

sich schlüssig werden, 194

sich schwertun mit, 198

sich sehen lassen, 199

sich selbst im Weg stehen, 229

sich totlachen, 214

sich um ungelegte Eier kümmern, 52

sich vom Acker machen, 7

sich vor Lachen den Bauch halten, 25

sich wichtig machen/tun, 232

sich wie ein Elefant im Porzellanladen benehmen, 55

sich wie reife Kirschen verkaufen, 117

sich wund laufen, 234

sich zu fein sein, 63

sich zur Ruhe setzen, 184

sieben, 201

Siebensachen, 201

Signale, 201

sitzen, 201
sitzenbleiben, 201
sitzenlassen, 201
Socke, 201
Spaß, 202
Spaß machen, 202
spanisch, 201
spanische Reiter, 201
Sparren, 202
Spaßverderber, 202
Speck, 202
spendieren, 202
Spendierhosen anhaben, 202
Spesen, 203
Spiel, 203
spielen, 203
spinnen, 203
Spitze, 203
Spitzenreiter, 180
Sprechstunde, 204
springende Punkt, 172
Sprung, 204
Spucke, 204
Spucke bleibt weg, 204
stampfen, 204
Stange, 204
Stange halten, 204
Staub, 205
staubsaugen, 205
Stegreif, 205
Stehaufmännchen, 205
stehen, 205
stehen auf, 205
steil, 205
Stein, 205
Stein des Anstoßes, 206
Stein ins Rollen bringen, 206
Stern, 206
Sternstunde, 206
Steter Tropfen höhlt den Stein, 216

still, 206
Stimme, 206
stimmen, 206
Stirn, 206
Stirn bieten, 206
stoßen, 207
strahlen wie ein Honigkuchenpferd, 104
streng geheim, 76
Strich, 207
Stück, 207
Stunde, 208
Sturm, 208
Sturm laufen, 208
stürzen, 208
Suche, 208
suchen, 208
Suppe, 22, 208
Szene, 209

T

Tacheles reden, 209
Tag, 209
Talfahrt, 210
Tamtam, 210
Tante-Emma-Laden, 130
Tapete, 210
Tapeten wechseln, 210
Tastenhengst, 99
Taufe, 210
tausend, 210
Tausende und Abertausende, 210
Techtelmechtel, 211
Teich, 211
Teufel, 211
Teufelskreis, 211
ticken, 211
Tier, 212
tierischer Ernst, 58, 212
Tierkreiszeichen, 212

Tinte, 212
Tinte gesoffen haben, 212
Tisch, 212
Toi, toi, toi, 212
Ton, 213
Der Ton macht die Musik., 213
Topf, 213
Topfgucker, 213
Tor, 214
Torschlusspanik, 214
tot, 214
totschlagen, 214
Tour, 214
Trab, 214
treiben, 214
trinken, 215
trinkfest, 215
trocken, 215
Tropf, 215
Tropfen, 216
Trost, 216
Trostpflaster, 216
Trost spenden, 216
trüb, 216
Trübsal blasen, 32
Tuch, 216
Tür, 216
Tür und Tor öffnen, 217

U

übel, 217
über, 217
über alle Berge sein, 28
über alles Lob erhaben, 140
über den Berg sein, 28
über den Daumen peilen, 42
über den grünen Klee loben, 119
über den Haufen werden, 95
über den Kopf wachsen, 224
über den Mund fahren, 61

über den Tisch ziehen, 212
über die Achsel ansehen, 7
über die (alle) Maßen, 146
über die grüne Grenze gehen, 85
über die Klinge springen lassen, 120
über die Lippen kommen, 140
über die Runden kommen, 184
über einen Kamm scheren, 111
über etwas weg sein, 228
überfragt sein, 70
über Gott und die Welt reden, 84
Über Kurz oder lang, 129
über Leichen gehen, 135
über sein, 217
Über seinen eigenen Schatten kann man nicht springen., 189
über seinen eigenen Schatten springen, 189
übers Ohr hauen, 163
über Tage, 210
übertrumpfen, 218
über und über, 217
übrig, 218
übrigbleiben, 218
übrigens, 218
Ufer, 218
umbringen, 218
um den heißen Brei herumreden, 37
um des Kaisers Bart streiten, 25
um die Ecke bringen, 51
um die Wurst gehen, 235
um ein Haar, 88
Umgang, 218
Umgangssprache, 218
umgehen, 219
ummünzen, 219
um sich greifen, 85
umsonst, 219
Umstand, 219

Index

Umständen entsprechend, 219
unberufen, toi, toi, toi, 212
ungefähr, 219
ungefähr können, 219
Unrat, 220
Unrat wittern, 220
unte aller Sau, 187
unter aller Kanone, 111
unter Beweis stellen, 31
unter Dach und Fach bringen, 41
unter dem Pantoffel stehen, 165
unter der Hand, 91
unter der Haube sein, 94
unter die Arme greifen, 17
unter die Lupe nehmen, 143
unter die Räder kommen, 175
unter einen Hut bringen, 107
unterm Strich, 207
unterm Strich sein, 207
unter Schock stehen, 195
unter Tags, 210
unter Umständen, 219
unter uns gesagt, 186
unter vier Augen, 21
Urknall, 220
Urne, 220
Urnengang, 220
Urzeit, 220

V

Verachtung, 220
verboten, 221
verboten aussehen, 221
Verdacht, 221
verhexen, 221
verlängerte Arm, 17
Verlegenheit, 221
Vernunft, 221
Vernunft annehmen, 221
Verrückt und fünf ist neune!, 159

Versuch nicht, alles auf einmal zu tun., 54
Vertrauen, 221
verwechseln, 222
viel Aufheben(s) machen, 19
viel auf Reisen sein, 180
Viele Köche verderben den Brei., 122
Viel Lärm um nichts., 131
viel um die Ohren haben, 163
Vitamin, 222
Vogel, 222
Vögelchen, 222
voll, 222
völlig fertig sein, 64
voll und ganz, 222
vom Blatt abspielen, 5
vom Dienst, 45
vom Fach sein, 60
vom Fass, 62
vom Feinsten sein, 63
vom Hocker hauen, 103
vom Hocker locken, 103
vom Hundertsten ins Tausendste kommen, 105
vom Leibe bleiben, 34
vom Regen in die Traufe kommen, 178
vom Tisch sein, 212
vom Wegsehen kennen, 229
vom wilden Affen gebissen sein, 8
von, 222
von allen guten Geistern verlassen, 77
von Amts wegen, 10
von Beruf sein, 29
von der Hand weisen, 91
von der Muse geküsst werden, 152
von der Pelle gehen, 166
von der Pike auf dienen/lernen, 169

von etwas ausgehen, 21
von Haus(e) aus, 95
von Haus zu Haus, 95
von heute auf morgen, 101
von höherer Warte aus, 226
von Kindesbeinen an, 116
von klein auf, 119
von langer Hand vorbereiten, 91
von Neuem, 159
von oben herab, 162
von sich geben, 75
von vorherein, 222
von wegen, 223
vor, 223
vor allem, 223
vor allen Dingen, 45
vor Anker gehen, 13
vorbei, 223
vorbestraft, 223
vor dem Nichts stehen, 159
vor den Kopf stoßen, 124, 207
Vordermann, 223
vor die Flinte kommen, 68
vor die Hunde gehen, 105
vor die Tür gehen, 76
vor die Tür setzen, 217
vor Gericht stellen, 80
vor Kurzem, 129
vor leeren Bänken spielen, 24
vorn und hinten bedienen, 26
Vorreiter, 180
Vorsatz, 223
Vorsätze fassen, 223
vor seiner eigenen Tür kehren, 217
Vorsicht, 223
Vorsorge, 223
Vorsorge treffen, 223
Vorteil schlagen, 192
Vorwurf, 223

W

Waage, 224
wachsen, 224
Waffel, 225
wagen, 225
wahr, 225
wahre Jakob, 109
Wahrheit die Ehre geben, 51
Wald, 225
Wald vor lauter Bäuman nicht
    sehen, 225
Wand, 225
Das war also des Pudels Kern!, 172
War die Köchin verliebt?, 122
Das waren noch Zeiten!, 238
warm, 226
warm ums Herz werden, 226
Warte, 226
warten, 226
warten auf, 226
warten bis man schwarz wird, 226
Wartung, 226
wartungsfreundlich, 226
was, 226
Wäsche, 226
waschecht, 227
waschen, 227
Wasch mir den Pelz, aber mach
    mich nicht nass., 227
was das Zeug hält, 238
Was dem einen recht ist, ist dem
    anderen billig., 178
Was ist das schon groß?, 86
Was ist in dich gefahren? Fahr zum
    Teufel!, 61
Was macht die Arbeit?, 143
Was macht die Kunst?, 128
Was man nicht weiß, macht man
    nicht heiß., 226

Index

Wasser, 227

Wasser auf die Mühle, 227

Was Sie nicht sagen!, 226

Wecker, 227

weder ein noch aus wissen, 233

weder Fisch noch Fleisch/weder
    Fisch noch Vogel, 67

weder Maß noch Ziel kennen, 146

weder Salz noch Schmalz haben,
    187

Weg, 228

weg, 228

wegdenken, 229

wegsehen, 229

weg sein, 228

Der Weg zur Hölle ist mit guten
    Vorsätzen gepflastert., 223

Weh, 229

wehtun, 229

Weiche, 229

Weichen stellen, 229

weiche Welle, 230

weiße Mäuse sehen, 146

Weihnachtsmann, 229

weinen, 230

weit, 230

weit entfernt sein, 230

Welle, 230

Welt, 230

Weltanschauung, 231

Die Welt ist ein Dorf., 230

Wem die Jacke passt, der zieht sie
    an., 108

Wenn die Katze aus dem Haus ist,
    tanzen die Mäuse auf dem
    Tisch., 114

Wer das Kleine nicht ehrt, ist des
    Großen nicht wert., 119

Wer den Pfennig nicht ehrt, ist des
    Talers nicht wert., 167

Wer den Schaden hat, braucht nicht
    für Spott zu sorgen., 188

Wer im Glashaus sitzt, nicht mit
    Steinen werfen., 82

Wermut, 231

Wermutstropfen (im Becher der
    Freude), 231

Wer rastet, der rostet., 176

Wert, 231

Wert auf etwas legen, 231

Wer Wind sät, wird Sturm ernten,
    232

Wer zuletzt lacht, lacht am besten.,
    129

Westentasche, 231

Wette, 231

Wettergott, 232

wichtig, 232

wie, 232

wie am Schnürchen laufen, 132

wie angewurzelt stehenbleiben, 16

wie aus dem Ei gepellt, 52

wie aus der Pistole geschossen, 169

wie aus einem Munde, 151

wieder auf dem Damm sein, 41

wieder auf den Beinen sein, 28

wieder auf die Beine kommen, 28

wieder in die Reihe kommen, 179

wieder zu Kräften kommen, 125

wie die Made im Speck leben, 133

Wie du mir, so ich dir, 232

wie du mir, so ich dir, 149

wie durch den Wolf gedreht, 233

wie ein begossener Pudel, 172

wie ein Schlot qualmen, 193

wie Espenlaub zittern, 239

Wiege, 232

wie gedruckt lügen, 142

wie gehabt, 88

wie geölt, 163

wie gerufen kommen, 183
wie gesät, 185
wie geschmiert laufen, 132
wie Gott in Frankreich leben, 84
wie Luft behandeln, 142
Wie man in den Wald hineinruft, so
    schallt es heraus., 225
wie seinesgleichen behandeln, 199
wie seine Westentasche kennen, 231
wie verhext, 221
wie von/durch Geisterhand, 77
wie von ungefähr, 220
Wind, 232
Windei, 233
Wind machen, 232
Wink, 233
Winterschlaf, 233
Winterschlaf halten, 233
wissen, 233
wissen, was die Glocke geschlagen
    hat, 82
wissen, wie der Hase läuft, 94
wissen, wo der Hund begraben
    liegt, 105
Woge, 233
Woge glätten, 233
Wo gehobelt wird, da fallen Späne.,
    102
Woher nehmen und nicht stehlen?,
    157
wohnen, wo sich die Füchse gute
    Nacht sagen, 71
Wolf, 233
Wolke, 233
Wolkenfelder, 233
Wolkenfelder schieben, 233
Wolkenkuckucksheim, 233
Wolle, 233
wollen, 234
Wort, 234

wund, 234
Wurf, 235
Würfel, 235
Würfel sind gefallen, 235
Wurm, 235
Würmer aus der Nase ziehen, 235
Wurst, 235
wursteln, 235
Wurst sein, 235
Wurzeln schlagen, 192

X

X-Beine, 236
X-Beine haben, 236
x-beliebig, 236
das x-temal, 236

Z

Zahl, 236
zahlen, 236
Zahn, 236
Zähne zusammenbeißen, 236
zappeln, 237
zappeln lassen, 237
zart, 237
zartbesaitet, 237
Zauber, 237
Zaum, 237
Zaun, 237
Zeichen, 238
Zeichen setzen, 201
Zeit, 238
Zeug, 238
Zicke, 238
Zicken machen, 238
ziehen, 239
zittern, 239
Zitterpartie, 239
Zoll, 239
Zoll für Zoll, 239

Index

zu Abend essen/Abendbrot essen, 59
zu allem übel, 217
zu allem überfluss, 217
zu Brei schlagen, 37
Zubrot, 239
zu bunt werden, 40
Zucker, 239
Zuckerbrot und Peitsche, 239
zu denken geben, 43
zu Ende führen, 57
zu Felde ziehen, 63
Zug, 239
zu Geld kommen, 123
zugrunde gehen, 240
zu haben sein, 88
zu Händen von, 91
zu Hause, 95
zu hoch sein, 102
zu Kreuze kriechen, 126
zu kurz kommen, 129
zu Lasten gehen, 132
zu Leib gehen/rücken, 134
zum Abschluss bringen, 4
zum Affen halten, 8
zum alten Eisen zählen, 55
zum Anbeißen sein, 11
zum Besten haben/halten, 30
zum einen...zum ander(e)n, 240
zum Ersten, zum Zweiten, zum
    Dritten., 58
zum ersten Mal, 144
zum Glück, 82
zum Halse heraushängen, 90
zu Mittag essen, 59, 149
zum Junge-Hunde-Kriegen, 110
zum Kuckuck schicken, 127
zum Narren halten, 90, 156
zum Nulltarif, 161
zum Schein, 190
zum Schießen sein, 191

zumuten, 240
zumute sein, 240
zum Verwechseln ähnlich sehen, 222
zum Vorwurf machen, 223
zum Weinen bringen, 230
zum x-tenmal, 236
Zünglein an der Waage sein, 224
zu Pott(e) kommen, 171
zu Rate zienen, 177
zur Hand haben, 91
zur Kasse bitten, 113
zur Last fallen, 132
zur Neige gehen, 157–158
zur Sache kommen, 185
zur Schau stellen, 190
zur Schau tragen, 190
zur See fahren, 199
zur Urne gehen, 220
zur Vernunft bringen, 222
zur Vernunft kommen, 222
zur vollen Stunde, 208
zu Schaden kommen, 188
zuschieben, 240
zu suchen haben, 208
zu tief ins Glas schauen, 81
zu Wort kommen lassen, 234
zwei Fliegen mit einer Klappe
    schlagen, 68
Zweig, 240
zwicken, 240
zwicken und zwacken, 240
Zwielicht, 241
zwielichtig, 241
zwischen, 241
zwischen Baum und Borke sitzen, 26
zwischen Tod un Teufel/zwischen
    Baum und Borke sein, 241
zwischen Tür und Angel, 241
zwischen zwei Feuer geraten, 65
zwitschern, 241